ALBERT V. EASON

Albert V. Eason

5-12-1994

" Saint Crispin's Men "

a history of Northamptonshire's shoemakers

Park Lane Publishing

15 Park Lane, Duston, Northamptonshire

0604 753745

1994

"Saint Crispin's Men"
a history of Northamptonshire's shoemakers

Published by
PARK LANE PUBLISHING
15 Park Lane, Duston, Northamptonshire NN5 6QD

Copyright ©Park Lane Publishing 1994
and Albert V Eason 1994

ISBN 0 9523188 0 6

Designed and edited by Malcolm Deacon. Cover design and major photography by Charles Ward Photography (Earls Barton) 01604 812465, and printed by The Book Factory, 35/37 Queensland Road, London N7 7AH.

CONTENTS

List Of Illustrations

The Crispin Trade

The Crispin Trade! What better trade can be?
Ancient and famous, independent free!
No other trade a brighter claim can find,
No other trade displays more wealth of mind!
No other calling prouder names can boast,
In arms in arts - themselves a perfect host!
All honour, zeal, and patriotic pride;
To dare heroic and in suffering tried!

Joe Devlin. Craftsman, Poet, Journalist

"If God gives us work to do, and fits us for it, and strengthens us in it, that is enough".

William Carey. Shoemaker, Scholar and Pioneer Missionary.

DEDICATION

To the many former Boot and Shoe Makers of Northamptonshire whose craftsmanship, determination, organisation and skills built the industry for which Northampton and the County are world famous. In particular, this book is dedicated to my brother George who was for fifty years a Boot and Shoe Operative in one of Northampton's largest factories.

FOREWORD
by Councillor Frank Tero

Vice President Northampton Branch NUFLAT 1972-1982
Mayor of Northampton 1992-1993

Northamptonshire has been for more than a century famous the world over for its fine quality boots and shoes. It is sad that massive import penetration during the past twenty years has seen the number of factories decline, although there are still many famous firms still making fine footwear. In this record of history, completed mainly during the year of my Mayoralty, the author traces the beginnings of some of the factories whose founding fathers, by their enterprise, contributed to the greatness of our once "staple industry". It is a tribute to the many manufacturers and operatives who contributed so much to public life.

I was proud to have been a Boot and Shoe Operative, starting work in the Making Room of the Manfield factory at the age of 14. I spent my whole working life, except for war service from 1939-45, in the industry. After the war I became involved in the Boot and Shoe Union NUFLAT as an executive member, serving on its Board of Conciliation and Arbitration. I became very aware of the achievements of all operatives in the trade. I am therefore honoured and pleased to commend this book not only to past and present employees in the industry but to all who are interested in the history of our County of Northamptonshire, "the Rose of the Shires".

Councillor Frank Tero.

AUTHOR'S PREFACE

As a Northamptonian born and bred and the son of a shoemaker, I am conscious that those who were born in the town and those who have made our ancient Borough their home have inherited much of which we have a right to be proud. Once the great "Metropolis of Boots and Shoes" Northampton is sadly no longer so. The footwear industry which long dominated the whole of the county has declined in its importance over the past forty years due to foreign competition, modern techniques and the consequent decline in the tasks needed in shoe production, and new technology creating as many problems amongst the operatives as did the introduction of shoe machinery in the nineteenth century. The era of the micro-chip has thus had its effect upon the staple industry of the town.

Part of my early working life of some seventeen years was spent as an operative in one of the larger Northampton factories. There is a great story to be told of this and other factories; their origins, progress and success, and their decline and closure.There must be older citizens, former boot and shoe operatives, who can look back on many years of service in the industry reflecting that the names once known as leaders of our boot and shoe heritage are ,alas, no more. Few of the old factories have survived, most being demolished for new building projects or road improvements.

Albert V. Eason. St Crispin's Day 1994.

Saint Crispin

Saint Crispin was formerly a Roman citizen who became a saint and martyr. He was believed to have been martyred for his faith in Soissons, Northern France, after he had fled from Rome and taken up shoemaking with his brother Crispian. He became the Patron Saint of shoemakers and Saint Crispin's Day, 25th October, was noted for its lavish processions led by the Shoemaker's Guilds. Every shoemaker who took part in the procession was given one shilling and sixpence on Saint Crispin's Day. As most of them avoided working on Mondays it was a common saying: "Sir, the anniversary of Saint Crispin is the first Monday in every week."

Memorials to Saint Crispin are to be found throughout Northampton; in the stained glass of the Roman Catholic Cathedral in Barrack Road, at Christchurch in Wellingborough Road, Saint Peter's Weston Favell and in the Central Museum in Guildhall Road. An electoral district in the town is called Saint Crispin Ward whilst the former shoe factory of Allinsons at the corner of Earl Street and Clare Street was known as Saint Crispin's Factory. At the corner of Great Russell Street the public house, the Jolly Crispin (now the Dick Turpin) recalls the nickname for shoemakers.

In 1946 the Rev Edwin White, minister of Primrose Hill Congregational Church, endeavoured to revive the celebration of Saint Crispin's Day amongst local shoemakers. Representatives of the trade, the Boot and Shoe Union and civic dignitaries attended a special service to mark the occasion. It was repeated the following year but interest gradually declined and once again Saint Crispin's Day faded into obscurity.

Saint Crispin (sketch by Stephanie Deacon).

Prologue

The mark of the master craftsman.

"Saint Crispin's Men" has long been an apt appelation for those shoemakers, both men and women, who have been the "salt" of the industry from earliest times. Before the days of mechanisation the shoemaker, working from his home, would soak his sole leather, put it over a lapstone between his knees and hammer it to make it smooth and durable. Shoemakers were familiar figures in the Northampton streets with their aprons flying full mast as they and their apprentices scurried between the warehouses, as the early factories were called, delivering leather and finished shoes.

The old-time cordwainer was filled with a sense of independence, as tough as the leather he manipulated. It stemmed from a long tradition going back into the 17th century, a consciousness of being part of a community of craftsmen. The Cordwainers Company received its Royal charter in 1272 and scrupulously upheld the dignity of the craft and the character of its members. Fines were imposed on anyone making boots or shoes from inferior leather, and an act of Parliament fixed a penalty of twenty shillings on "every cordwainer that shod any man or woman on the Sunday" or made shoes "after a preposterous manner".

By 1831 a third of Northampton men were shoemakers and this rose to two thirds by 1871. The chapters that follow outline the immense changes brought about by mechanisation; the shift of work from the home into the factories and the resulting specialisation of operations in shoe production. It amounted to a deskilling of the craft with fewer and fewer able to make a shoe from start to finish. Old-time craftsmanship became marginalised into a hobby for some rather than a full-time occupation.

Such a craftsman was my father who actually learned his craft from my mother. He was proud to be able to make complete boots and shoes, a skill which he was unable to use in his job of working a pounding machine in Roland Fisher's factory in Bearward Street. As a child I was fascinated by him as he worked away in the cellar, making and repairing shoes for family and friends. When setting out to make a new shoe leather was soaked in the kitchen, lasts would be sorted out and my mother or aunt would "close" the uppers using a shoe sewing machine. My father would pull the leather over the last, making sure both lining and uppers were smooth. With a mouthful of tacks, the traditional way in which shoemakers worked, he would spit out just one tack at a time with uncanny accuracy right where it was needed; this tacking operation was performed with a tool called a driver. He would then round off (trim) the sole by hand after it was attached to the last. He then would make a channel near to the edge of the sole for the welt sewer or stitcher to sew the sole to the upper, that is if the shoes were not to be handsewn by himself and were to be machine sewn by someone else.

As I grew older I was able to take the shoes to the premises of George Bishop in Broad Street or to Harry Shaw in Military Road; they were recognised stitchers and sewers in the trade. There were always plenty of men there bringing footwear of all shapes and sizes from "the smaller workshops that did not possess the machinery for this specialised work".

Sometimes I went to the shoe mercers A. J. Letts in Grafton Street and E. R. Bush at the corner of the Mounts and Lady's Lane for leather and grindery. As I returned home I often peered over the railings of the Mounts factory of Parker & Teale to watch the men operating the machines in the basement. I could see the belts from the overhead shafts whirling around and hear the distinctive whine of the pounding machines; the strong smell of leather pervaded the entire neighbourhood. Lunchtimes would see men, still wearing their aprons, taking a break but soon to be finished by the 1.30pm buzzer which, as it did every weekday at 7.30am, summoned them to attend to their machines.

Thus I write from my own memories, as well as those of my father, brother and uncle who all worked in the same factory. When Edward, Prince of Wales, visited the town in 1927 he commented that "ever since the days when men left off going barefooted Northampton has been known for the excellence of its footwear. Our forefathers came to Northampton to get their feet shod, and we today know that Northampton boots and shoes are second to none". It was a justifiable tribute to the craftsmen that have made the town and county the acknowledged home of the world's finest footwear.

Mr Fred Coe handsewing boots 1915.

Chapter 1

Settlers on the Banks of the Nene

Man's use of footwear probably dates back at least 30,000 years; during primitive times his ingenuity led him to seek some form of protection for his feet against the intense cold. As the forestlands of Great Britain were inhabited by an abundance of animal life he was able to hunt the animals and use the hides and skins for making warm clothing. Some parts of these skins would provide him with wrappings for his feet. Sandals may have been developed as a protection against grit and sand for they certainly existed in Egypt in 3,000 B.C. Later Greeks and Romans were known to have worn highly decorated sandals. Moccasins and boots made from soft skins are still the footwear used by the North American Indians and Eskimos who also wear boots made from hard skins. The sabot, a wooden type of shoe is still worn by workers in France, and some parts of Europe. The Dutch have always had their distinctive clogs and similar footwear was worn by the old mill workers of Lancashire. Some centuries-old styles are still with us. Specimens of Roman sandals and other early footwear can be seen in the Northampton Museum.

Long before the days when boots and shoes were made here Northampton had made history. Ancient Britons established a tribal home along the banks of the River Nene. Animals were killed, not only for food but for the skins which provided both clothing and footwear. Without knowing it man had found the basic materials for the production of leather. Oak bark was used in tanning the raw hides and skins, and even today it is still recognised as one of the finest tanning agents. Evidences of shoemaking in Britain have been traced to the time of Roman occupation. Relics of this era are to be seen in the Northampton Museum such as various archaeological finds, around parts of the County. Legend has it that when the Danes and Saxons struggled for the mastery of "Hamtune" in 890, King Alfred the Great was helping his brother King Ethelred to defeat the Danes. He set them to work making army boots in Northamptonshire. King Alfred divided the country into shires of which our beloved County is one.

In the days of our Saxon forefathers Northampton or Northamtun(e) appears to have been a place of little importance. In the year 917 it was occupied by the Danes. The town was twice burned down and at the time of the Domesday Survey in 1066, when it was recorded as both Hantone and Northantone, many of the houses were still in ruins. It owed most of its restorations to the first Norman Earl Simon-de-Senlis, who during the reign of William Rufus, rebuilt the town, surrounded it with a wall, and erected a strong castle at its West gate. He also founded a House of Cluniac monks nearby. For the following three centuries Northampton was one of the most important towns in England. During the time of the Plantagenet Kings, Parliament met here more frequently than any other place in England, London only excepted. In 1675 Northampton was practically destroyed by a disastrous fire, but the although the medieval town has gone a number of its features still remain. When the Normans rebuilt the town it became the principle town in the Midland shires. Northamptonshire, with its contrasting colours of the countryside, was a wide area of pleasant green grasslands, rich brown soil, with some forestlands. There was the ancient Royal Salcey Forest, Rockingham Forest and Whittlebury Forest, which were so characteristic of the extensive forestlands, which at one time blanketed the county. The countryside has really altered little with the passing of the centuries, yet all the features of our historic county (pasturelands, oak forests and animals) remain the principal reasons why the shoe industry commenced in and around Northampton.

The first reference to Northampton shoemakers is recorded c1200. In the 14th century shoemaking had become a significant part of the town's industries. A document dated 1361 in the Public Record Office mentions the existence of shops in "Shoemakers Street" Northampton. There is evidence that royal patronage began in 1213,
and the first trade organisation in 1401. In the Liber Custumarum (Book of Customs) of the town, compiled about 1450, is a record of an ordinance for the craft of shoemakers; this set the amount to be paid by every man "commencing a shop in the said craft". There were also notable statutes protecting the quality of leather tanned in Northampton and the County; leather had to be remain in the tanning pits being steeped in liqueur extracted from oak bark for a year and a day. Specimens of leather which have survived in good condition for over four hundred years testify to the conscientiousness of these early tanners. Thus Northamptonshire had become the natural centre of the footwear trade and the home of the boot and shoe craftsman.

"Is it not a matter of pride that we ought therefore to preserve the reputation of the Town, which claims to still make the world's finest shoes; and always acknowledge the debt to Northampton whose craft was so deeply rooted in the past, and can be traced back to the year 890 A.D."   Anon.

Chapter 2

Craft and Fashions of the Early Shoemaker

Primeval man began binding up his feet with raw cowhide, the hairy side outwards and so fashioned the first kind of footwear. Since those early days fashions in boots and shoes have fluctuated fearfully and wonderfully over the centuries. In the 14th Century, during the reign of Richard the Second (1377-1399) ordinary men as well as eminent persons and aristocrat wore shoes with pointed toes as long as six inches. Some of these so-called fashion shoes were the most ridiculous specimens of footwear ever seen. When men became tired of the pointed Poulaines they changed to Duckbills, so named because they had a beak or bill of four or five inches in length.Pointed toes eventually gave way to a broader type of footwear, especially slippers. Fashions continued to alternate between broad shoes and pointed toes; for example, in the reign of Edward the Fourth (1461-1470) pointed toes were fashionable for a while. Eventually a petition was presented to the king asking him to pass a law enforcing shoemakers to keep the points of shoes within reasonable bounds. An act was accordingly passed in 1463 when all persons of high or low degree were prohibited from wearing pointed shoes more than two inches in length. Shoemakers who disobeyed the order were ordered to be fined and cursed by the Clergy. The act remained in force until the reign of Henry the Eighth when it was repealed.

Fashions changed over the centuries. Most medieval footwear could be exquisitely stitched. The long pointed shoes of the 14th Century or the horned toed shoes of the 16th Century also had sturdy soles and were shaped right or left. High leather boots made of soft leather were fashioned as a protection to the leg after men-at-arms ceased to wear full armour. Proper heels were not known before the time of Elizabeth the First, though 'wedge' heels were known earlier. The modern type of footwear that we know today is a development which started in the early 16th Century as the Vamp and Quarters pattern. As the fashions in footwear changed craftsmen achieved a considerable degree of perfection in producing footwear for every occasion.

Roman footwear was made in pairs, but the "Duckbill" or "Horn-Toed" shoes of the 16th century were made for either right of left feet. Until the 17th century, most footwear had no soles of the type that shoes have today. Uppers and bottoms were made of soft leather which were sewn together then turned as 'inner soles' were then added. Thick soled boots and shoes developed from the campaigns of the English Civil War. It is believed that the demands of Cromwell's armies needing strong footwear may have played a considerable part in the development of the modern boot and shoe.

Little attention was paid to foot comfort until the turn of the present century. Many elderly people suffered deformities of the toe and foot, caused by wearing ill-fitting shoes in childhood, and even in early adult life. Today chiropodists say that practically all foot deformities, callouses and corns, are the result of wearing bad footwear. Shoe designers all consider the suitability of every shoe they design in accordance with the structure of a particular foot and grade them in sizes with careful attention to fitting. Some retailers even began to use X-ray apparatus to ensure a correct fitting. This method was particularly used in high class shops selling children's footwear. However, X-ray machines in shoe shops were banned in 1971.

Northampton has for several centuries been the metropolis of boots and shoes and yet it was not until the middle of the 17th Century that there is any record of the town specialising in the trade. Historical records show that in 1642 an order for 4000 pairs of shoes and 600 pairs of boots were made during the Irish rebellion for a Thomas Pendleton who was later Mayor of Northampton. They were to be sent t
o the English Army in Ireland. Though they were promptly delivered it appears that the account for £208 was never fully settled. A further large order for boots was manufactured for the victorious Roundhead army of Cromwell which overthrew King Charles the First at Naseby. Cromwell wanted his men shod with Northampton-made boots and it is stated that 1500 pairs were forwarded to Leicester where Puritan forces marched after the Battle. Northampton supplied boots for William the Third's army at the battle of the Boyne. On 23rd October 1689 the paymaster of the forces wrote to the king: "Four thousand pairs of shoes have been distributed which i caused to be made at northampton. At first Lieut. General Douglas said they were the best and cheapest he had ever met with; but now he does not like them, though all the English colonels do". Apparently the manufacturers had not given any "palm oil"(bribe) to the officer concerned.

The town also came to the rescue of the Duke of Cumberland's men who were supplied with a thousand pairs of boots for their march to Scotland in 1745. Northampton supplied boots for the American Civil War in 1775-6, and in 1855 eleven thousand pairs were delivered in twelve weeks for soldiers in the Crimea. Even Napoleon had to turn to Northampton for boots; flushed with triumph after Austerlitz he had tried to ruin England's trade with a continental boycott. Yet, due to the effects of smuggling, when he marched against Russia at Eylen his army was shod with boots from Northampton and wore tunics made in Leeds. In the early years of the nineteenth century Northamptonshire made boots for the Duke of Wellington but they never reached their destination. Whilst the soldiers were fighting barefoot some thirty thousand pairs of boots every week were being wrongly shipped to every port in Spain and Portugal in the hope of catching up with the army. Later in the century during the Boer War the county supplied boots but, as in the case of Thomas Pendleton in the seventeenth century, the manufacturers made financial losses.

The modern growth of the shoe industry dates from the beginning of the 19th century and is in a large measure due to the then member of parliament for the town, Spencer Perceval who later succeeded William Pitt the Younger as leader of the House of Commons and then in 1809 became Prime Minister. He influenced government orders for boots in a period when wars and rumours of wars stimulated demand until practically all the people in the town were engaged in the industry. The work was then entirely done by hand. Sadly, after only three years in the premiership, Spencer Perceval was assassinated by a crazy bankrupt named Bellingham on May 11th 1812.

"Hope is like the sun, which as we travel towards it casts the shadows behind us."

Chapter Three

From Man to Machine

With the introduction of machinery into industry tremendous changes were brought about creating every possible hardship for all the working people were caught up with them. Until the reign of George III from 1760-1820 most Englishmen lived in the country and worked for a living in their own homes. Although the advent of machinery meant that in the long term, it would be a benefit to all classes, the haphazard and unorganised way in which it was introduced into industry destroyed the very standard of living for people in most trades at the very beginning. It was the textile industry that first came under the influence of machinery. Workers were divided into the two groups the spinners and weavers. In the days before machinery was used spinning was very badly paid although there was not often enough yarn to supply the needs of the weavers.

The weavers were the first to encounter machine methods for the introduction of the flying shuttle more than doubled the speed at which cloth could be woven. The result was that thousands of handweavers found themselves faced with cruel competition. Not only that the hand spinners could not produce anything like enough yarn. In 1764 the introduction of the Spinning Jenny helped the spinner against the weavers but once more subjected the spinners to cruel competition, because they could not afford to buy the equipment. However, worse was to come. The earlier inventions did not destroy the 'home' industry. Early machines were simple and so the majority of workers were able to buy and use them. But as the complicated an more efficient and expensive inventions came, they required larger space to operate them. Eventually special buildings had to be built to accommodate them and their motive power.

Mechanisation in the shoe trade did not take place until about 1857. A change however did occur in one hand process, that of closing (the stitching together of the sections of leather forming the upper) The process was largely taken over by women and children. Young children worked up to 14 hours a day, often in small over crowded rooms, ill ventilated, houses belonging to their masters, who paid them pitifully low wages 1/- (5p) being paid for a weeks work after a wageless apprenticeship of six months. In this period female and child workers were introduced on a huge scale and family homes were turned into sweatshops where men women and children turned out shoes for a pittance.

In 1852 the Howe sewing machine was invented by Elias Howe. It was adapted by shoe manufacturers for stitching the leather used for the uppers, in 1856-57. Alarm spread amongst shoemakers for fear of unemployment and the greater use of female labour. In February 1859 the towns principal manufacturers used the Howe machine for the stitching of all uppers. By 1865 some 1500 machines were being used in the district and so hand closing gradually disappeared except for very high quality work. The age of mechanisation had begun. In 1869 there were numerous machine closing premises in Northampton, young women operating treadle drive sewing machines earned between 9 shillings and 18 shillings a week. Young girls of 14 years of age were employed as fitters to fit together all sections of the upper ready for the machinists. These girls earned between 7 shillings and 12 shillings a week, whilst much smaller children were employed as knot tiers whose job it was to pick out and knot the end of the machines threads. Their small wage was one shilling and sixpence and three shillings a week.

As the changeover to a mechanised industry increased it was no longer possible for the weaver spinner or shoemaker to own the tools of their trade. He could no longer live as his own master. With results which no one could forecast textile workers and shoemakers alike were forced to give up selling the products of their labours and merely sell their working power to the people who possessed the capital to buy the expensive new machinery to make the product, which hitherto had been their specialist craft. These new factories created a new industrial working class. The machinery in the factories gradually increased human comfort by making the necessities of life cheaper. The art of the old craftsmen who had used their hand in their own homes was destroyed. The new working class grew up in economic slavery from which individuals could escape only by very exceptional luck or eventual starvation.

The working hours in those days were from 7 a.m. in the morning until 6 p.m. at night with an hour midday for lunch. Towards the end of the 18th century the hours of work and conditions under which employees worked were so bad that in 1802 Sir Robert Peel introduced the first of the Factory Acts. It was for the protection of apprentices. It forbade work for more than 12 hours in one day. By the time of the Factory Act of 1833 was introduced employees were forbidden to employ children under nine years of age.

The hours of work for children under 13 years of age was limited to nine hours and for young people from 13 to 18 years of age to twelve hours. There was, however, evidence of children having to work much longer hours. Some government reports gave instances that children of only five years old, being sent to work for 13 hours a day and frequently of children of 9, 10, and 11 were expected to labour for 14 and 15 hours a day in factories. The result of the Act of 1833 was that children too young for employment in factories were sent to the coal mines. Some went down the pits with men at 4 a.m. in the morning and remaining in the pit for 11 and 12 hours. In 1847 the hours of work for young people was further reduced by the passing of the 10 Hours Bill in 1853. The normal working day of 10.5 hours was established by Law for factory workers, other than adult males, but it soon became law for them as well. The Factory and Workshops Consolidation Act of 1878 fixed the number of hours in textile factories at 56.5 hours a week but in other factories the limit was 60 hours.

The number of hours worked in the shoe trade prior to the First World War was 53.5 hours a week, but after the war it was reduced to 48 hours. These hours were still being worked in the 1930's. In most factories this represented an 8.75 hour day (with 1.25 hours for lunch) with 4.25 hours on Saturday morning; starting time was usually 7.30 a.m. There were, however, men at work at that time who could say they started work at the age of nine and worked from 6 a.m. to 8p.m. every day and until 5pm on Saturdays for one shilling a week. (Shoe and Leather Records, March 1922). What a long way industry has come from those days. No longer are men and women required to work all hours of the day, with little leisure time for them and their families but the five day week and shorter hours and longer holidays have given every worker in every trade much more leisure. The modern phenomenon of unemployment, partly brought about by technology, has reversed the situation.

The change from the domestic to the factory system was virtually complete by 1894 in that year the Men's Union demanded that no work should be done "outside". The local branch of the National Union of Boot and Shoe operatives reported in September 1895, "They (the manufacturers) always try to rush the men working on the machines, notice being given to discharge men not doing sufficient work. When we know that the men are doing their duty and doing an honest days work".

Again in June 1898 the Union persisted that "the introduction of machinery has so divided the workers that the good all round man hardly knows what to do with such a system." Machinery virtually destroyed craftsmanship, save for a few handworkers; craftsmen were not needed and unskilled workers only were needed to train as machine minders. They were taught to operate a machine which did only a single operation to a shoe.

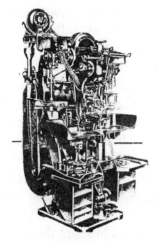

No. II HEEL ATTACHING MACHINE

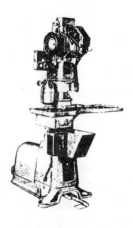

GOODYEAR WELT
SEWING MACHINE
MODEL L

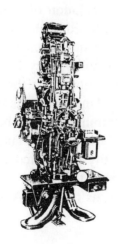

No. 9
TOE LASTING
MACHINE

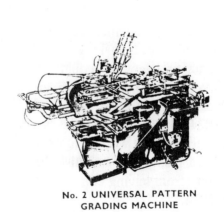

No. 2 UNIVERSAL PATTERN
GRADING MACHINE

Illustrations of shoe making machinery.

"Be Humble or you stumble".

Chapter Four

A New Environment

One could almost say that the commencement of the new factory system began an era of three dimensions - 3D - desperation, despair and deceit. During the final stage of hand production some large manufacturers had employed certain men or women to do special work like cutting out uppers, or soles, fixing soles and heels to the shoes and so on. Little did they realise it at the time but it was really the beginning of the factory system; preparing the way for machines to take over from men.

The Industrial Revolution brought appalling changes, creating despair and desperate revolt on the part of the suffering masses. Employees distrusted the manufacturers thinking them full of deceit. The machine in the eyes of the worker was a revolutionary innovation and enemy within which had driven them from their homes to the factories. There was also little sympathy with disposed handworkers, and that eventually brought a sharp conflict between he people who owned the factories and the workers. They felt something like the infuriated weavers who smashed the Spinning Jenny and made the inventor Hargreaves fly for his life. As the Industrial Revolution continued the worker felt oppressed and deprived of his livelihood. He had but one weapon to use against any who exploited him - his Trade Union. The hard facts of factory life taught all workers a discipline which benefited only employers at first but later, with the coming of the Trade Union, workers began to benefit. Whilst it seemed that the machinery had created a new class of people in whose working lives there was no liberty or equality the coming of the Trade Unions brought them into a new fraternity with their fellows.

No trade unions operated in the 19th century for the regulation of hours and wages. Men worked just as hard or as leisurely as they liked. Compared with their fathers' generation textile all workers including shoemakers possessed two new things: firstly, thanks to the factory system, they had a training in a discipline; secondly, they had an emerging union structure, which sooner or later they could turn to advantage. At the beginning of Queen Victoria's reign workers had no political power. Trade Unionism was in its infancy and the early struggle both difficult and cruel. In 1799 all combinations had been made illegal and remained so until 1824. In 1834 the Grand National Consolidated Trades Union came into being "to raise the wages of the workmen, or prevent any further reduction therein" and to " diminish the hours of labour - to establish the paramount rights of industry by preventing the idle parts of society from having control over the fruits of toil". A union for shoemakers was established in 1874.

The rapid development of Northampton in the 19th Century owed everything to the major industry - Boots and Shoes. Its expansion totally changed the town's character and made the name of Northampton synonymous with the Boot and Shoe trade throughout the world. In 1801 there were about 7000 people in Northampton. That figure had more than doubled to 15,000 by 1831 and by 1871 the population had rocketed to 40,000. The Boot and Shoe industry dominated Northamptonshire between 1870-1890. Many firms started in two storey factories and workshops, later moving into the typical three and a half storey factory with its semi-basement and hoist; clickers worked on the top floor as there was no machinery involved, and the rough stuff men worked with their heavy machinery in the basement. There is still some evidence of these old buildings in Northampton and also the highly ornamented shoeworkers' houses. In 1879 footwear factories were small but played an important role as a link between the hand-made shoeworkers who worked in their homes. The leather was cut in the factories and the necessary components were collected by the manufacturers who completed the shoes. The average price per pair - even in 1900 was only six shillings.

The reason for the dramatic growth in the boot and shoe trade came as the handworker transferred to the factory and became an integral part of the machine age. In that first revolution in industry businesses wanted to move out of London to the provinces. Although the Northampton shoe industry had established itself in the late 18th century it wasn't until 1812 that the boom really began. Following labour troubles in London the wholesalers began to push more business Northampton's way. The link was strengthened in 1815 when a consortium of local manufacturers established a warehouse in the capital. The opening of the Grand Union Canal in the same year eased transport problems and over the next sixty years Northampton became what Stoke was to pottery, Lancashire to cotton. London wholesalers were attracted to the town by the cheapness of labour compared with the capital.

The development of the sewing machine cut down the number of workers needed. The industry still employed two out of every five men in the town in 1871. Handworkers had vigorously opposed the introduction of sewing machines for sewing the uppers and, but for their hostility, the neighbouring city of Leicester might never have become a rival shoe centre. The idea of making shoes by machinery had occupied the minds of inventors for almost a century. A machine for rivetting shoes was in use in England in 1810 invented by Brunel. The first American sole fixing machine of which there is any record, was a pegging machine, patented by Samuel Preston of Danvers U.S.A. in 1833. His patent was signed by Andrew Jackson, the President of the U.S.A. A machine for making pegs was perfected in 1820. Previous to that the shoemakers split their own pegs. Another pegging machine was invented by Charles D. Bigelow in 1851. Metallic fastenings began to supersede pegs about 1880.

The machine which revolutionised the shoe trade was the Blake Sewer; it was the invention of an Englishman, Lyman R Blake, of Massachussets. In 1865 it was brought into active operation by the war between the Northern and Southern States (Confederates and Yankees). It was found that boots could not be made fast enough for the army by the old methods. The Blake machine which had been invented a few years before the war supplied their exceptional demand. In time the Blake machine was installed in the Northampton factories. Much improved over the years it is still in constant use and has never been superseded for the work it was intended to perform. In turn this was to lead to a great increase in the export trade.

1859 **LYMAN BLAKE'S** Sole Sewing Machine was first used in Leicester and machine-sewn footwear soon outrivalled the hand rivetted method which Thomas Crick had patented. The Blake Sewer was a revolutionary achievement leading to the eventual mechanisation of the industry.

The wood model made by Blake of his original sole sewing machine

Lyman Blake's Sole Sewing Machine.

Sewing machines were first adapted for sewing the seams in the uppers and linings. The uppers being cut from light cattlehides, calfskins, sheepskins, goatskins, and even lizard skins and snake skins; the last being quite expensive fashions in footwear, mainly used in the production of ladies shoes. For both soles and uppers it was found that the most satisfactory material was leather unlike rubber which is also widely used, or some of the modern "man made" materials such as plastics and vinyls. Leather is said to "breathe" giving good ventilation to the shoe making it healthy and comfortable to wear. Leather soled shoes are mostly made from heavy cowhide and today are most expensive. One of the first machines to be introduced into the factory was a leather press for cutting soles; nowadays the great presses known as Revolution Presses turn out hundreds of soles a day.

Traditionally, boot and shoemaking was divided between five departments. The Clickers who became known as the elite, or gentlemen of shoemakers, cut up the sections of upper leather, originally using moon shaped knives. The Closers using the Howe sewing machines sewed leather pieces together making the shoe upper. The Rough Stuff Men cut and matched the heavier bottom stock leather, needed for the insoles and soles. Workers in the making and lasting room joined the sole and upper using a foot-shaped last and attached a heel. The Finishers then trimmed smoothed and finally coloured and polished the heels, edges and bottoms of the boots and shoes. The last department known as the Shoe Room gave the shoes a final polish, and prepared them for packing.

It is not known when "lasts" were introduced but it is not a modern invention. It is the shell on which a shoe is built, and sometimes the shoemaker would build up the last with strips of leather to suit a particular shape of foot. The last is the primary essential in shoe manufacture, and a separate and highly mechanised industry of lastmakers supplies the shoe industry with the lasts, which are specially designed for a given purpose and graded into sizes to provide for all varieties of feet. Using the last as a basis, the shoe designer produces patterns, after taking into account the needs of the many mechanised operations in shoemaking. Like the lasts the patterns are graded, (proportionally enlarged or reduced) into the required patterns for the style of shoes being manufactured.

It was not conceived within the bounds of possibility that a machine would be constructed that would do lasting. The shock was succeeded by the extensive development of the invention and the introduction of "indoor" labour; workers were drafted wholesale into the factories to work in teams with the new machines which were known as consol lasters. The upheaval led to a lockout in 1895 but it was the last labour dispute connected with mechanisation that was of any consequence. The new indoor labour changes led to more factory buildings or extensions to premises on a great scale. The effect of transferring work from home to factory was dramatic. One notable feature that was recorded at the time was that this change had been effective in reforming the habits of workers, and promoting the moral and physical welfare of the people. This new-found prosperity gave Northampton the proud distinction of having the largest number of working people owning their own houses, as well as the highest percentage attending places of worship.

New processes continued to be discovered and other new machines quickly followed bringing a whole new concept in the boot and shoe making. The closing room operatives had skiving machines to trim the edges of the uppers as well as the sewing machines to sew them. Lacing machines laced the uppers together to hold the sides in proper relationship to one another. The closer (as the operative became known) then sewed up the seams. There were also eyeletting machines to insert eyelets and beading machines for putting fancy trim on the uppers. Rolling and stripping machines were introduced for the thickness cutting of soles and in the making room a large machine known as a pulling over machine, pulled the upper over the last, and held it fast whilst the bedlaster machine smoothed out the wrinkles in the upper and tacked it in place. A stitching machine or a blake sewer attached the sole to the bottom of the last, with its edges reaching round to the edges of the insoles. A narrow strip of leather called the welt was fastened below these and the outer sole then sown to the welt. Heeling machines were introduced that attached the heels which were usually built up from sections of leather. These were generally cemented together and pressed.

The Finishing Department had heel and edge trimming machines, heel and bottom scouring machines and edge setting machines to wax the edges of the soles. Heel and bottom padding machines which were waxed and finished the heels and soles giving them the "shop window look". It was beginning to be difficult to find an operation to a show for which a machine could not be made to do the work. so much so, that in October 1905, the following report appeared in the Northampton Independent: "The process of invention has of late years revolutionised Northampton's staple industry, and large numbers of workmen have been displaced by inventions which perform delicate operations which at one time were exclusively done by hand. These changes have not only displaced handwork but they have enormously increased output for it is a fact that so far the output of boots and shoes for Northampton this year has beaten all previous records. The report then went on to tell of another invention, which if successful, will displace a considerable number of workmen. There are machines in general use for edge-setting in polishing and brightening the edges of the soles of boots. These machines are non automatic and a skilled operator has to hold the boot or shoe to the machine which does the work. this is described as one of the hardest and most trying operations in the industry and the vibration is extremely exhausting. To meet this difficulty a new machine has been invented by Mr William J Spiers of Leicester which will do the work automatically. The boots have only to be placed on a jack by an ordinary attendant and the machine does the rest. It is claimed that a youth could attend to several machines but probably a skilled workman would be required to adjust the machine for varying thickness and substance of the soles, this machine makes another great advance in the industry".

The machine became known as the auto-setter, and was adopted by many firms as part of their finishing process. Nevertheless, there were some manufacturers who continued to use the non automatic type of setting machine. In fact the factory in which the writer was employed were using non auto machines at the outbreak of the Second World War. The ingenuity of the inventor continued to flourish and furnish the industry with capable machinery and mechanism soon become complete. Machine had taken over from man and over the year many processes were added, until in the Shoe factory of the 1950's there were known to be 150 types of machinery and 460 operations in a factory-made boot or shoe. Today there are new processes which can produce some types of shoes in practically one operation. Much property and business came to the town as a result of the expansion and a new thoroughfare of attractive shopping streets sprang up around the ancient Market Square dominated by its ornate fountains. This was the new 19th Century town of Northampton.

"Mans inhumanity to man, makes countless thousands mourn". Burns.

Chapter Five

Personalities of the 19th and Early 20th Century

"Altogether St Crispin's favourite shrine in England is a quantily piquant place to wander in", this is the very title given to Northampton in an old manuscript *How our working people live*. Published in 1869, and to be found in the Northampton library. The writer describes therein its old churches and houses of mottled brown and cream coloured stone; so oddly blended with two, three and four floored new brick shoe factories with trim villakilns and new streets running - bramble blocked into cornfields or up to scarped banks of meadows. "Pallid men stubbly chinned, and smudged as to the cheeks, and with aprons looking like lodging house slave blackleading a grate are loafing in every corner. Ditto men and boys, untidy women and girls are going to shop with bagfuls of faggots of boots and shoes and soleless uppers. The women seem to toil under the heaviest loads. The Northampton shoemaker I am told too often makes his wife a beast of burden".

William Hickson.

Henry Wooding.

One of the very early manufacturers was a man named Williams Hickson who came to Northampton from London in 1801 to make shoes for the home market and the export trade. Hickson established his family business about 1808 and was later joined by his son. It was one of the oldest established firms in the town having a factory in St Giles Street. He was one of the first shoe manufacturers to cultivate an export trade. History dictates that there was talk of exports from Northampton as early as 1689. Hickson manufactured the "Ubigue" boots and was said to be the first person in Northampton to use machinery. As early as 1812 he set up a warehouse in Smithfield, London so that Northampton manufacturers could use it to exhibit their footwear. The venture was successful for a time and was probably the very first idea of a shoe and leather fair as we know it today. The ownership of the firm eventually passed to a grandson, also named William Hickson who became managing director and was supported by Tom A Hickson and G Hickson. This William Hickson became president of the town's Boot Manufacturers Association from 1893-1904. The Hickson enterprise made a significant contribution to the early history of shoe manufacturing in the town ultimately giving way to those who had greater resources to expand into even larger companies.

Another of Northampton's oldest shoe manufacturers was Henry Wooding who was born in Northampton in 1837, the year of Queen Victoria's coronation. He went to work as a handstabber at the early age of eight and after becoming a manufacturer remained active in business until the age of 75. Wooding's first venture into business was in 1861 as a manufacturer of uppers ("closing") in St Peter's Street. In those days there was no machinery of any kind. After the introduction of machinery and with his business succeeding he took to manufacturing high class footwear and built up a large and prosperous business. Although little is known of the size to which the business expanded or the number of workers employed records show that the factory was ultimately housed in a building which Henry Wooding had erected in St Edmunds Road and Pytchley Street. He remained the owner of the factory until he retired in 1905 when he was succeeded by Gladstone Wooding and Henry Wooding junior. It was said that Henry Wooding cherished memories of the early shoe trade, which were both interesting and extensive. He used to relate to his friends of the time when all the shoework was done by hand and the operative families had to work long hours in squalid surroundings at home. One of the most pitiful sights of the era was that children of a tender age seated round a table on which stood their only illumination, a lighted candle. Here they were engaged in shoework until nine o'clock at night, or even later. Even in 1878 finishing a shoe was done almost entirely in the homes of the workers. Frequently the whole family worked at it by sharing operations. There were many women finishers, some working on their own account, but the majority working with their husbands. It was a usual thing to see them with a dozen pairs of shoes or more on each arm, bare to the elbow, their dresses open necked and chests black with shoemaker's ink taking the finished work to the factory. Also around 1880 the demand for rivetters was so heavy that hundred of agricultural workers came into Northampton to train as rivetters and gave their services to the trade, for two or three weeks, under regular craftsmen employed by manufacturers like Henry Wooding. These temporary rivetters earned twenty five shilling a week when they became fully qualified operatives. Many stayed in the trade as the work was not at all difficult to master; chiefly it required activity and vigour.

Although he became a busy shoe manufacturer Wooding found time to take a prominent part in civic government and was created a justice of the peace in 1908. He was largely responsible as a councillor for the old East Ward in 1891 for introducing electric trams to the Borough and was chairman of the Tramways Committee when the system was electrified in 1904. He took an active part in founding the Northampton Boot and Shoe Manufacturers Association with Moses P Manfield who was its first president. Wooding served as a vice-president to Manfield for seven years, and succeeded him as president for six years. He was a founder of the Arbitration Board and National Federation of Shoe Manufacturers. A pillar of Nonconformity he first joined King Street Congregational Church at its formation in 1874. He was a Sunday School teacher for fifty years, a life Deacon and a president of the Sunday School Union.

Not all of Northampton's earliest manufacturers were like Henry Wooding, Northamptonian born and bred. Some came to Northampton as young men to seek their fortunes in business. One such was Moses Philip Manfield, a young man of twenty-four and another was Frederick Bostock. The honour of being the oldest shoe manufacturer operating in Northampton goes to the Bostock family whose successors, Lotus Ltd, are still manufacturing high class footwear today. Their story actually begins in Staffordshire an area which, like Northamptonshire and Leicestershire, is rich in pasturage for cattle and forests for oak bark used in tanning leather. Thomas Bostock, a native of Heage in Derbyshire moved to Stafford in 1814 to set up a small business as a boot and shoe maker. He prospered in the new business and later with his three sons Frederick, Edwin and Henry founded businesses at Stafford and Stone. In 1836 they acquired premises in Freeschool Street, Northampton. Thomas Bostock retired in 1840 and his eldest son Edwin took over the Stafford factory which specialised in the production of women's shoes; Frederick managed the Northampton factory which was then in College Street and manufactured fine quality men's shoes.

It was not until 1890, however, that Frederick Bostock acquired a new factory in Victoria Street where he lived at the time. The premises were extended several times on the site between Victoria Street, Newland and Lady's Lane in 1916, and in 1921 when it became a three storey building. Finally a fourth storey was added becoming the clicking room. These premises of the Eversley Commercial Hotel in Newland were also acquired for the employees canteen and staff shop. At the time most of the adjacent terraced houses in both Newland, Greyfriars Street and Lady's Lane were the homes of shoemakers. The firm became a private company in 1912 with Frederick Bostock as managing director. The firm traded as Frederick Bostock Ltd and was familiarly know in the shoe trade for many years as Bostocks. In 1913 another factory was opened in Countess Road, Northampton with E S Perry as factory manager. This factory began to produce the famous "Veldtschoen" shoe. The idea for producing this shoe came from South Africa where they were originally worn to keep out ticks. The shoe was extremely waterproof and was one reason for their popularity. This type of shoe, which is still produced by Lotus Ltd, helped to make the company's name famous.

Lotus Ltd was created by the amalgamation in 1919 of the company in Northampton and Edwin Bostock of Stafford and Stone. Henry Bostock of Stafford became chairman, Frederick Bostock of Northampton became vice-chairman and the managing directors were Henry John Bostock and Frederick Marson Bostock of Stafford. Lotus Ltd became manufacturers and distributors of boots and shoes sold under the "Lotus" and "Delta" trade names which related to Egypt, the land of the lotus and the Nile Delta - trademarks for which they are widely known. Both factories continued to be run separately with the Stafford and Stone factories making ladies shoes and the Northampton factory making mens shoes. The Countess Road factory was closed in 1921, and in 1940 the various factories of Lotus Ltd were integrated with the largest factory at Stafford becoming also a warehouse for the shoes made at the other factories.

When Frederick Bostock died his son Neville became the managing director of the Victoria

Street factory in Northampton. James Bostock became the managing director of the Stafford factory, and in 1946 James Bostock,managing director of Lotus, retired and a reconstruction of the board took place to include younger executives. Karel Kucek was appointed group managing director, Dennis Taylor, finance director and Miss Annabel Bostock, fashion director. Peter Goffe joined the board as group production director and Brian Blundellm, general manager also became a director. James Bostock continued as non executive chairman with James Spooner (a senior partner in Dixon, Wilson Tubbs and Gillett and a man of wide city experience) was elected deputy chairman. On the 1st January 1971, shortly after his 68th birthday, James Bostock resigned as chairman and a director of the company with James spooner as chairman. A new office of honourary president was conferred on James Bostock who continued as chairman of the staff pension scheme.

Like so many other family concerns in Northampton, Lotus Ltd. became the victim of the big financiers. Control had already passed from the remaining members of the Bostock family in 1969 when the company was taken over by a financial group controlled by Isaac Wolfson who in turn sold the business to the Argo Caribbean Group, an overseas company associated with David Rowland early in 1972. In July of the following year the company became a subsidiary of Debenham Ltd owners of over 70 department stores throughout the country. In the early 1970's the employees of the Victoria Street premises were gradually moved to a new all-purposes built single storey factory on the Holloways Industrial Estate, Weedon Road, Northampton with Mr Marris as the general manager. The old factory was eventually demolished with other properties in the area to partly make way for the Greyfriars Bus Station. The successors of the Bostock enterprise begun in Northampton and Stafford still produce high quality men's and ladies' shoes and sold through some four thousand agents, mail order firms and in High Street stores.

Chapter Six

Dynamism of a New Industry

In medieval days the shoemakers, or cordwainers as they were called, became an important craft guild. At that time one man was responsible for making the whole shoe and carried out all the work in his own cottage. Wars were often the cause of the introduction of new methods and the Napoleonic Wars were no exception. They promoted Marc Isambard Brunel the famous engineer to seek a quicker method of making army boots. In 1810 he invented the first machine for rivetting the sole to the upper, but the process fell into disuse after the wars, and it was nearly fifty years before rivetting machinery was again introduced to the trade.

The first shoe machine to arrive in Northampton was known as the Thomas Sewing Machine, and one was exhibited in the Old Milton Hall in Newland in 1859. The innovation of this machine staggered the shoe operatives. The Number Two Thomas Machine was specially adapted for binding the edges of leggings and gaiters. There was immediately aroused such alarming visions of the workers being deceived and deprived of employment that they promptly rioted. It was,however,the improved sewing machine of Elias Howe and Isaac Singer,invented in 1853,that was finally introduced for stitching together the upper parts of footwear that caused widespread strikes and disputes in the trade. Singer had invented his sewing machine in 1851 and he spent a lifetime perfecting it; in the following year he made the first machine capable of sewing leather. No efforts were spared to make it thorough in its workings and the result was that eventually almost every shoe factory equipped their closing rooms with Singer machines. The first machines used, however, were inclined to be clumsy. The work was held in one hand and the crank was turned by the other; women found it difficult to operate them. Despite the workers' opposition to the introduction of the machines they were finally accepted and they became a major influence in the development of footwear.

In 1859 the Blake Sole-sewing Machine was introduced having been first patented in 1858 and in 1865 the Welt-Sewer. The 1870's saw a series of machines designed to copy the evolving handsewn method of construction. These were basic inventions and although the industry is now highly mechanised most of the machines now used are refinements of the originals. As far as Northampton was concerned the building of the familiar red brick factories and the innovation of the sewing machines,the Blake Sewer and the other machinery which was to follow, placed the shoe industry on the threshold of a revolutionary period in industry which the enthusiastic new manufacturers were quick to exploit.One Northamptonshire author writing of this Victorian era in which he lived in *The Northampton Shoemaker* described an area of the Town Centre of that period: "Bearward Street, thereabouts bears used to be baited and adjoining Narrow Lane - (Narrow Toe Lane still stands near the Moat House Hotel in Silver Street) - tells of proclivities which the present race of Northampton leatherworkers have doubtless inherited from their far off ancestors, who made the town famous for its leather bottles".

Northampton was principally a market and county town and the seat of the shoe industry. Between 1841 and 1861 the number of people employed in shoemaking in the town was more than doubled to over six thousand workers. Around half of the households in the town were absolutely dependent upon shoemaking and its ancillary trades. The industry was predominantly a hand made craft, with new machinery gradually making an impact during the second half of the nineteenth century. Amidst such conditions in the seventh year of Queen Victoria's reign in 1844 the firm of Manfield and Sons was founded by Moses Philip Manfield.Born in Bristol on the 26th July 1819 Manfield was perhaps Northampton's greatest shoe entrepreneur, and he was only 25 years of age when he founded the business. Philip Manfield,as he liked to be known, had no formal education. His mother took upon herself the task of teaching him to read and write until he was seven years old when he went out to work. From that time he became practically self educated and derived a lot of his knowledge from his great interest in books. At the age of sixteen he became a skilled craftsman having been apprenticed to a boot closer at twelve years of age. With four years apprenticeship as a cordwainer he obtained a position with a Mr Brightman, a retailer of boots in the Drawbridge at Bristol, until 1843 when he left for Northampton.

His first task in Northampton was to manage a shoe factory for a Mr Swann who was related by marriage to Brightman. At 24 years of age he had managed to save £150 which was a considerable achievement for a working lad in those days. From his earliest years he had attended the Bristol Unitarian Sunday School under a Miss Carpenter who gave him a letter of introduction to the Minister of the Unitarian Church in Northampton. Here he was able to continue his religious interest in the denomination to which his mother and family had worshipped. No sooner had he settled in Northampton when he realised that Mr Swann's business would have to be discontinued. The wife of his employer became very attached to Philip and his family. When the factory was due to close she urged him to join her brother, another shoe manufacturer in the town, but he decided to return to his native Bristol. However, just before he was due to return home Mrs Swann decided to make another appeal to him to stay in Northampton and as a last resort when she saw he was determined to return home said, "Philip why don't you start for yourself?" He decided to sleep on the advice. After giving much thought to the possibility and with the £150 he had saved in 1844 he launched himself as a shoe manufacturer.

Moses Philip Manfield.

The Manfield Factory.

Manfield rose to be a leading manufacturer in the town and his firm soon sprang into prominence largely due to the enthusiastic talents of the founder who was possessed of exceptional abilities. These enabled him to pioneer his way in his own business and to a large extent the whole of the Northampton trade, right through those transformations of hand labour to the multitude of machinery processes which still exist in the boot and shoe factories today. The first factory was in Silver Street on the present site of the Moat House Hotel. By 1849 the firm moved to nearby Regent Street, where the business flourished for 20 years. From here a move was made in 1857 to a new factory at Campbell Square. This building survived until 1984 when it was demolished to make way for new developments; thus Northampton's first automated shoe factory was removed. Philip Manfield ("Moey" to those who worked for him) was a born organiser being quick to adapt to the latest methods. It was said of him that he kept a working man's point of view all his life and was a natural leader of industry. His two sons Harry and James inherited many of the gifts of their father and contributed many of their own talents to the business learning the trade alongside the workers in various departments of the factory. In 1878 Philip took his two sons into partnership and the firm became known as Philip Manfield & Sons. As the factory on Campbell Square expanded a warehouse in nearby Inkerman Terrace was rented for lasters and houses in Newland acquired for workshops. Presses for sole cutting were introduced into the basement of the main building and other machines such as Blake Sewers and Keats and Good Year Stitchers were added later.

The reputation of Philip Manfield in the Borough steadily grew, not only as a founder father of the Boot and Shoe industry but as a distinguished politician. His friends agreed that there was no greater philanthropist nor any one man more active in social reforms and religious matters. He remained all his life a consistent Liberal. He was elected Mayor of Northampton in 1883 and was honoured with a knighthood from Queen Victoria in 1894 for his services to industry. In January 1891 on the death of the towns M.P. Charles Bradlaugh he was unanimously chosen to represent the Liberal Party and Northampton in Parliament. He was elected by an unprecedented majority and re-elected at the dissolution of Parliament in 1892. As Liberal M.P. from 1891-1895 his services to the town were acknowledged when he was awarded the Freedom of the Borough. Sir Philip became a very fluent speaker and few would have suspected that he was an entirely self-made man and had never been to school. He had accumulated a library of some 5,000 volumes. He was described as a man of changing personality with fine voice, strong sense of humour and with warmest sympathy for all working men. He was a strong supporter of the Mens' Union knowing that without union protection the men were at the mercy of unscrupulous manufacturers. He felt the need to create a system of what might be called a combination of collective bargaining and on the 19th December 1878 called a meeting of nineteen manufacturers which resulted in the formation of the Association of Boot Manufacturers; but in 1887 celebrations of Queen Victoria's first jubilee were marred, because they coincided with the great shoe trade lockout arising out of the introduction of machinery into factories.

A strike had begun at Mr Padmore's factory in the town and soon spread to other factories. The manufacturers in self defence locked out all men at all federated factories five weeks before Christmas. Hostility at first was against the firm where the strike had started but was soon directed against Manfield as Chairman of the Association. However, his position was firm and just and the arbitration which followed was conducted with masterly patience. The men, too, came to recognise that Sir Philip was indeed their best friend, for it was stated some years later that through a private channel he had at his own expense fed many thousands made destitute through the lockout and his popularity abounded. The life of this dedicated man and the esteem in which he was held closely resembled the career of that distinguished politician of later years, Ernest Bevin. When Manfield died in 1899 at the age of 80 after a lifetime of service to the shoe industry and the Borough more than 15,000 people attended his funeral procession; they formed a column of mourners over a mile long paying their last tributes to the man who had become one of the pillars of industrial Northampton.

During this progressive period of the industry the material rewards of the shoemaker was only in the finished product, for his earnings from his labours were far below other groups of workers. Yet C.J. Battle wrote in *Workshops Old and New (Shoe and Leather Record* 25th Jan 1895): "Many of the workshops were so small and stifling in the extreme but the shop was the Liberty Hall. The men were free and independent and consequently happy." It is true that there was much poverty and squalor but there had also been gigantic efforts on the part of enlightened people like Sir Philip Manfield to alleviate conditions amongst the poorest. There was a class distinction of a kind that is unknown today.

Sadly there were those folk who had been under the delusion that Northampton was a grimy town of shoe factories. This statement appeared in one of the early Manfield brochures and was rejected by the following statement: "If anything were needed to convince our customers that their boots and shoes are produced under the best conditions a visit to the factory would give them assurance abundantly, the first impression is rather that of a Sanatorium than of a factory". This was a statement which was true and referred to the new factory built for Manfield on Wellingborough Road which had opened in 1892. Standing on a four acre site it was the first shoe factory to be built entirely on one floor; it was an impressive building heralding a new concept in design and with its production methods became the envy of its many rivals. When first erected the factory was on the outskirts of the town in the open countryside. Prior to the beginning of the development in 1890 it was a spinney facing Abington Park with is historic "Abbey". The Manfield factory with its modern machinery and up-to-date methods obviously encouraged the owners to publicise the Company and so answer in full the many critics who had hitherto looked upon the town as a conglomeration of ill-equipped dirty factories.

The task of taking Manfields into the 20th Century fell to Philip Manfield's two sons Harry and James. By 1885 most of the business control had been delegated to them. Philip Manfield retired in 1890 due to political and public work but remained senior partner. Harry Manfield married later in life and had no children, but James Manfield married Louisa Bostock in 1881 and this brought together two well-known boot and shoe families. They had two sons and six daughters. The new factory burst into production by only making six varieties of boots and shoes until between the First and Second World Wars the company was making many hundreds of pairs a week, and the seal of public favour upon Manfield's boots and shoes became emphatically endorsed at many international exhibitions where they won the highest awards. The work of many of their earliest craftsmen became renowned and a specimen of the unique work of an early handsewn worker, Mr A Lightwood, is still preserved in the local museum. Another employee Thomas Barry, who worked continually at Manfields for 50 years had a remarkable career in the boot and shoe trade. He won medals at the Franco Exhibition of 1900 and the Brussels Exhibition in 1910. Barry also visited King George VI at Windsor and Sandringham and three times at Buckingham Palace; in 1937 had the honour of designing the shoes worn by King George at his coronation. The Wellingborough Road factory played a vital role in furthering the fortunes of the Manfield family and of the boot and shoe trade in general. It was the vital catalyst in bringing prosperity and development to the district. Until 1905 when horse-drawn trams appeared in the town the only possible way for workers to reach the factory was either on foot or by using a bicycle. Most operatives walked to and from work but after 1892 many new houses began to spring up in the area, namely Wantage and Roseholme Roads. Some of these were rented by workers of the factory. This was the beginning of the continuity of Abington. When the horse-drawn trams travelled from the Town Centre to Abington Park, transport for employees who did not live close-by became easier.

From their early years Manfields had a largely export trade. In 1900 it could boast 36 retail branches including six continental shops. The first Paris branch was at 3 Boulevard Montmartre, which opened in 1889; the branch at 97, Rue St Lazare opened in 1898. Manfields entered the American retail market in 1922 by opening a shop in the exclusive city of Philadelphia. Manfield and Sons not only pioneered the way of the modern shoe factory but of making their own retail outlets as well. The Company also had a large handsewn department at the Wellingborough Road factory with some operations done by hand and some by machine. The Manfield Hotspur football boot emerged in 1904 and became a sensation. This famous boot was adopted by Tottenham Hotspur Football Club and because of its popularity more and more clubs became wearers. Eventually 80% of British teams and one hundred thousand other players in other parts of the world were wearers of the boot.

James Manfield.

Harry Manfield.

Under the leadership of the Manfield brothers the firm gathered momentum and became world famous. James Manfield was the continuing driving force whilst his brother Harry was chairman of the company. James became a popular Liberal councillor and was Mayor of the Borough in 1905. Harry became a Liberal M.P. in 1906 and was thrice elected M.P. for Mid-Northants. Both brothers had succeeded to two of the roles in public life occupied by their father. James' flair for business was inherited by his elder son Harold who joined the company in 1903 but who later left to study for the medical profession. Neville Manfield the youngest son of James and Louisa had hoped to join his father in business, but was tragically killed in the Great War in 1917. In 1901 Harry Manfield had purchased the country estate of Moulton Grange with its well laid out gardens and ornamental lake and James in the same year built a house on a piece of land just outside Northampton in what was then part of the Weston Favell Parish. This was also beautifully landscaped with a lake. He named it Weston Favell House and was destined to become a well known building in the town. The former Manfield home at Moulton Grange also became the home of yet another well known local shoe manufacturer, Dennis George Webb, in later years.

Manfield and Sons was not only the earliest of the larger shoe factories but it was also the training ground of many craftsmen, some of which later became shoe manufacturers in their own right. An offshoot of Manfields called Saxone Shoes started in 1908 in St James by a few personnel from the Manfield factory. Two employees, Jack Sears and George Plowright, between 1907 and 1909 left to found their own firm which later became known as Trueform.

C.E. Gubbins who was a foreman under Philip Manfield at the Campbell Square Factory joined his grown-up sons to establish a business which eventually specialised in surgical boots a firm still existing. G T. Hawkins opened a factory in Overstone Road, George Swan in Brockton Street, Kingsthorpe Hollow, (later became Webbs, Mentone) The Arnold brothers did work at home taking it to the factory. It was also thought that J H Crockett (Later Sir James, Chairman Crockett & Jones) once worked as a pattern cutter at the Manfield factory. William Barratt (later Barratts Footshape) was also thought to be employed at Manfields Shoe Shop 28, The Poultry, London, whilst Clarks of Kilmarnock and F and G Abbot can claim their origins from the Manfield factory.

The welfare of Manfield employees was ever uppermost in the minds of the owners and everything possible was done to achieve a close relationship between worker and management. It was a legacy that became adopted in certain other factories and created a kind of industrial society that was not known in many other industries. Many other firms held social events for the workers at various times, but none will be remembered with more affection locally than the Musical Society which emerged at the Manfield factory, almost by accident. This was the famous Manfield Choir which was first formed in 1908 as a male voice choir under W. F. Marshman. The first choir was one of thirty male voices but after a short while it became a mixed choir with ladies participating. The choir sometimes operated as both a mixed and a male choir and became quite renowned under Marshman's leadership. The choir was also coached for Northants and national musical competitions by C. J. King a local musical celebrity. On 13th September 1913 the choir appeared by Royal Command before King George V at Althorp House the home of Earl Spencer (grandfather of the present Earl). During the 1914-18 war the choir gave many charitable performances visiting many parts of the British Isles, and after the cessation of hostilities toured many parts of the continent. The choir attained widespread fame and functioned for many years giving lots of pleasure not only to those employees who were members but also those sections of the public who were privileged to hear it. This ensemble was however just a small part of the welfare and social system which Manfields had built up.

The death of Harry Manfield on February 9th 1923 robbed Manfields of its Chairman at the age of 67. Just two years later the premature death of James Manfield in 1925 ended yet another era of the Manfield family. James was only 68 and his passing was a great shock to all his employees. It was his wisdom that had brought the company to such great heights . One of the great tributes paid to him was this: "His coat of arms a spotless life and honest heart his crest". With no sons to succeed him in the business his daughter Ellen (Mrs Pigott) took over the Chairmanship of the Company and remained its head for some twenty years. Ellen shared all the ambitions and aspirations of her father and one of her first tasks was to inaugurate in 1926 a workers council. Employees were elected representing all departments to run concurrently with and subject to the Board of Directors creating a new relationship between employer and workers. This had long been an idea in the mind of James Manfield whose radical approach to many of the problems faced by worker and management alike had ensured a happy partnership in striving for the general prosperity of the business and the welfare of all employees.

Mrs Piggott was a member of the Council of Industrial Welfare Society in London. Under her leadership those who pioneered the welfare system at Manfields might well have set many other firms on the same road. In 1930 a complete welfare department was established consisting of an organiser and a workers' council. An assembly hall and other meeting rooms were provided for employees recreational pursuits. There was a canteen for providing cups of tea to workers during factory hours. It has always been a well known fact that the British habit of tea drinking was no less habitual in the shoe factories and those employees who did not take advantage of bringing a thermos flask to work would boil water for tea on adjacent gas rings. At that time the canteen provided facilities for workers staying to lunch who wanted pre-heated food. Later staff were employed to cook and serve meals. The cost of these was subsidised by the company. In addition to all these things a First Aid room was available and there were facilities for getting or giving confidential advice. There was also a monthly magazine which was circulated to all employees in factory and shops.

Nowadays most large factories have their Personnel Departments which administer to the needs of all employees with a qualified personnel manager in control; the value of having such departments have proved to be essential in the running of a very modern factory. The welfare department of Manfield & Sons was a pioneer of distinction in personnel management, and the continued prosperity of Manfields remained a lasting tribute to Sir Philip, his sons and their families. Later it became a part of the giant British Shoe Corporation and subsequently was controlled by Burlington International. The factory remained in full production until 13th March 1992 when it closed down. The firm which Manfield and his sons built up had survived for 144 years.

"The way to have friends, is to be one".

Chapter Seven

Reform, Progress and Endeavour

Before 1850, there were more than sixty master shoemakers in the Town of Northampton. Some of them started measures of reform against much opposition and in the face of much difficulty. Possibly they would not have been successful had there not have occurred the disastrous "machine" strike which, although not realised at that time, changed the history of the shoe trade in Northampton and also in the County. When the sewing machine for closing uppers was introduced in Northampton factories in 1857 it was the first serious use of machinery in the industry since 1814. All shoemakers resolutely opposed it; they implied that it would displace labour, and starve the workers. Resolutions were passed almost everywhere, refusing to make footwear with machine closed uppers. Operatives insisted that the machines be destroyed and for nearly two years there was 'guerilla warfare'. Whilst some manufacturers succumbed in February 1859 the remainder decided at all hazards to install the new machines and to use them. Women workers were trained to operate them for it was either that or going out of business. The men then refused to work and hundreds, even thousands, of craftsmen left the town to seek work elsewhere where there were no sewing machines. The machine was everywhere, for footwear could not be made by hand to compete with it in price. Many men returned to Northampton beaten and dispirited. The strike collapsed in July 1859 and Northampton was busy making footwear again. Factories soon surged ahead as new methods were accepted.

The next decade brought other firms and one such company who owed its progress to its founder is the story of H. E. Randall Ltd. This firm's founder, Henry Randall, began his business in 1869. This story is also one of a great commercial achievement inextricably woven with the personality of one great man. In his youth Henry had come to Northampton with his parents his father owning a drapers shop at the top of Bridge Street. With no special qualifications he eventually attended the Northampton Grammar School. At the age of 14, Henry went to work at the shoe factory of his uncle, William Jones, whose business was in Newland. He received half a crown (12.5p) a week, and after a period of six months obtained a rise of sixpence (2.5p). On attaining the age of 21 along with a friend, Thomas Wicks, he started manufacturing on his own account. This was just a few years earlier than Philip Manfield who had started his business at the age of 25. Henry was full of youthful enthusiasm. He fashioned and guided the business for more than half a century. Even when mature in years he still brought to bear upon his many-sided activities a brain unimpaired by the passage of time and a shrewd and seasoned judgement which were invaluable assets to a firm caught up in times of evolution and change.

Like so many other rival firms H. E. Randall's grew from small beginnings. It never stood still built up by a sound industrial and commercial policy. In 1896 it became a limited liability company with its head office and works in Lady's Lane at the Wood Street junction. About 300 were employed in this factory turning out thousands of pairs of high-grade footwear, renowned the world over for its quality productions. A staff of over three hundred managers and assistants manned the company's retail shops. The watchword of their trading system was always quality and a first class article at a reasonable price. H. E. Randall produced shoes for both sexes which not only testified to the capability of their designers but also to the versatility of the operatives. Their many departments turned out every style of delicate turn-shoes to sporting boots and during the first World War did a large share of army business.

Henry Randall rose to become a public figure. He was well respected in local government as a member of Northampton Town Council, a Justice of the Peace for twenty five years a task he carried out with dignity and wise counselling. His devotion to his public duties led to his appointment as Chief Magistrate and Mayor of the Borough in 1894, and again in 1897 the year of Queen Victoria's Diamond Jubilee. During this second term of office as Mayor he was instrumental in the opening of Abington Park, the gift of Lady Wantage, for the benefit of the citizens of the town. Randall was knighted by Queen Victoria in 1905 and in 1909 was appointed a High Sheriff of the County, the first citizen of the town to be so honoured.

Sir Henry Randall.

Sir Henry was a devoted churchman one of the earliest church wardens of St Paul's Church Semilong Northampton. When he removed his home to Monks' Park Hall he transferred his interest to the new church of Christchurch. He was a founder of the Queen Victoria Nursing Institution known for so many years as the 'Queen's Nurses.'He was a member of the Northampton Musical Society and its treasurer for many years, and also held a number of other charitable offices. It was said that anyone who was in need of help or assistance could approach him for in his private and public benefactions his name figured in all the charitable lists. His enthusiasm outside his business interests included a devotion to healthy sport and recreation and an almost passionate love of his native town. He became an owner of racehorses and in this field he achieved success winning over 150 events during his association with the turf. During the earliest days of the first World War 1914-18 through Sir Henry Randall's prompt and persevering efforts, Northampton factories received an order for half a million pairs of boots for the French Army to be produced in about six weeks. His efforts in this direction was entirely voluntary, as he could not cope with any of the orders at his own factory, but it earned the hearty thanks of the local manufacturers association for his efforts.

He was always known for being a kind and considerate employer who had the welfare of his people at heart, and for this he was in turn regarded with respect and affection.

This token of esteem was revealed when the firm celebrated its jubilee in December 1919, together with the Sir Henry's fifty years continuous management. On this occasion he received from his employees a solid silver -gold plated tea and coffee service with salver being inscribed: "Presented to Sir Henry Randall and Lady Randall, by staff and employees of H. E. Randall Ltd; on the occasion of the 50th Anniversary of the commencement of the firm, as a token of their sincere appreciation and esteem". From his co-directors he received a cheque for £5,000 and a silver-gilt casket containing a copy of the resolution authorising the gift, beautifully inscribed on vellum. The address was highly ornate and worked on burnished gold. In addition he was presented with a magnificent portrait of himself in oils by Arthur Harker R.A. The gift of £5,000 was immediately handed over to the Mayor to be used for the benefit of his fellow townsmen, a gesture that is fully told in a later chapter of this book. This magnificence was aptly described by a shareholder of the Company who in paying tribute said: "Many Hundreds of years ago a great Emperor had said that his idea of a perfect man was that he lived rightly, hurt no one, and gave every one his due. It was felt," he said, "that in Sir Henry, they had a living representation of the Emperor Justinian's views".

"Unclaimed promises are like uncashed cheques. They will keep you from bankruptcy, but not from want".

Chapter Eight

Further Great Names

Since 1935 the name of Norvic was known as one of the principal and most successful shoe manufacturing companies in Northampton. Yet the history of the two Northampton firms which became part of this well known Group of Companies goes back many decades. The firm of John Marlow & Sons was founded by John Marlow in 1866 and rapidly secured a high reputation as makers of mens shoes. Their extensive factory in St George's Street, known as Phoenix Works, was built in 1879, enlarged in 1896 and 1912 and remained a shoe factory until well into the 1980's the building being occupied by the Leicester firm of Brevitts. After being left empty for some years the building was devastated by a fire in 1994.

The Phoenix Factory of John Marlow & Sons.

In 1910 the John Marlow Company purchased the business of Henry W. Wooding and in 1913 acquired the goodwill and trade marks of Aurora and Lastwells which were the trade marks of P.W. Panther for high class ladies footwear. The goodwill being acquired after the Panther factory was taken over by Trueform. The factory was the first to introduce a complete plant for welted work. They were awarded a Silver Medal at Melbourne in 1888 a Gold medal and Diploma in Milan in 1906 the Grand Prix at Brussells in 1910 and the Grand Prix at Turin in 1911. They were also the first firm to export footwear to America. John Marlow was later joined as a Director by his sons John H Marlow and Albert E. Marlow who together greatly expanded the business and added the making of womens footwear. John H Marlow became a Managing Director and was a very well known figure in the trade. He was president of the Manufacturers Association in 1909, and founded and was associated with the Northampton Mens Own until his death in 1945.

John Marlow.

A E Marlow.

J H Marlow.

The Northamptonshire journal *Footwear* published the following tribute in its pages which told of this world wide reputation. The report stated that "Messrs John Marlow and Sons, who although they have something like forty years connection with the shoe trade in Northampton are full of energy and spirit as ever, they have been exporting boots and shoes to the various markets in the world for upwards of thirty years. At the present time they have resident agents in Australia, New Zealand, India, West Africa and various Eastern markets; the manufacture of its men's boots is only in best and medium qualities and the aim is to maintain the sterling character of British made footwear".

It was, however, the firm of Oakshott and Finnemore who became the first Northampton shoe firm to become part of Norvic in 1935. This Company was started at a later date than that of John Marlow being founded in 1902. The founders were Henry Oakeshott and Walter Finnemore and it was founded with the express desire to make and sell shoes in overseas markets. Both men had spent many years of service with the firm of Turner Bros. and Hyde. Henry Oakeshott was the elder partner and he remained at the helm until his retirement in 1931. Henry was a man of very high principle just in all his dealings and with an intimate and practical knowledge of the making of mens shoes. He died in 1936 and was described by a friend as "a benevolent and generous soul, with more than a touch of autocrat in him". Walter Finnemore was some years his junior and had been responsible for the selling side of the business. He eventually became a Director of Norvic. His knowledge and experience of the shipping trade and his untiring energy were responsible for the high regard and wide distribution of the Company's products in many overseas markets.

No attempt was made to sell shoes in Great Britain and the company's trade marks, although well known in Africa, India, China, Japan and the Isles of the South Sea were unknown in England. After the 1914-1918 war, South Africa (which was by far the largest customer) began to make shoes in a new industry. Like other firms who exported to South Africa the Company found it became increasingly difficult to sell shoes to the Cape. It was then that an association was formed with the Norwich firm of Howlett and White. This close association was made through Cecil Coleman in 1922, and the Norwich firm were engaged in making shoes for women and children. As they wished to add mens shoes to their ranges, the mens "Norvic" and "Mascot" the new export names of Oakeshott and Finnemore were added. Thus the foundations of good shoemaking in mens shoes laid by Henry Oakeshott and Walter Finnemore and the marketing of goods under these brand names in the home markets brought the firms new and greater business and prosperity. Oakeshott & Finnemore became an integral part of the Howlett & white Group and Henry Oakeshott and Walter Finnemore were joined on the board by Sir Ernest White and Cecil Coleman on January 1st 1929. Frank Haynes a friend of Cecil Coleman joined the Company and this relieved Cecil Coleman of his weekly visits to Northampton made since the merger. He further developed the sale of Norvic and Mascot shoes for men on Henry Oakeshotts retirement. He was made a Director and in 1935 when the group became known as Norvic he became a Director of the Group. Four years later, Frank Haynes, through a friend met Sir Herbert A Barker, K.T. Sir Herbert was a specialist in the art of manipulative surgery. He specialised in the cure and alleviation of derangements of knee cartilages, the correction of flat feet, metatarsalgia and other kinds of abnormalities of the joints by manipulation and without surgical interference. Haynes first discussed with Sir Herbert the making of special shoes for his own wear. After much experimenting and not a little discussion and instruction, there was made in the Talbot Road Factory of Oakeshott & Finnemore what Sir Henry Barker characterised as "the most perfect shoe ever seen and worn". This shoe was such a success that Frank persuaded Sir Herbert to sponsor the shoe; it became known as the Sir Herbert Barker Shoe and became widely available. Sir Herbert in his unique position as the greatest of all artists in manipulative surgery had very fixed and definite beliefs as to what should or should not be worn on the feet. His authority on the subject and his marvellous cures, demonstrated his art in practice. The birth of the "Sir Herbert Barker Shoe" was duly celebrated and became one of Norvic's most famous brand names. Sir Herbert Barker became manipulative surgeon to the Nobles Hospital in the Isle of Man in 1941. He died on 21st July 1956 and will be remembered not only for his knowledge of manipulative surgery but that he gave his name to one of Northampton's finest brands of footwear, Thus the Northampton factory built up a special character and standing which was due to the genius of Frank Haynes.

The Norvic Group continued to expand and other factories were taken over. These were the Manfield Shoe Company founded by John Gascoigne and George Nice about 1868. Kiltie Ltd (S.L. Witton Ltd) founded by Sydney L Witton (a former draper) began by buying childrens shoes from small makers, and going out to sell them in 1926 S L Witton built a modern factory facing Howlett & Whites' factory in Muspole Street on St Georges Plain, Norwich with the idea of making childrens shoes under the brand name of "Kiltie". This factory was purchased by Howlett & White in 1934 and Kiltie shoes also became part of the Norvic Footwear Group. When eleven years later John Marlow joined the Group two of Northamptons finest shoemaking firms who both specialised in shoes for the export market were brought together and the name of Norvic became an established trade name in Northampton. Sadly, the former factory of Oakeshott and Finnemore in Talbot Road and the Phoenix factory of John Marlow in St George's Street are no longer shoe factories.

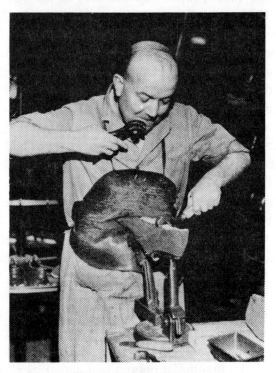

Hand Lasting Sides.

"Pride is at the bottom of all great mistakes".

Chapter Nine

"Church's of Duke Street"

"Northampton made shoes are a supreme instance of intimate co-operation of craftsmanship and machinery which has unique dignity and a classic reality which cannot be matched elsewhere. Furthermore it is known that an expert on shoes would distinguish a Northampton shoe in any part of the world; with this kind of craftsmanship the supremacy of Northampton shoes can never be challenged". These words written by Arthur Adcock F.J.J. in his book entitled "The Northampton Shoe" are no less evident today. Craftsmanship is still the hallmark of the Northampton and County leading shoemakers of the twentieth century.

One such firm of Northampton shoemakers which can claim to be making shoes of classic beauty with a supremacy which cannot be challenged is the factory of Church & Company Ltd. This well known company was founded in 1873 in the early days of shoemaking when craftsmen worked at home in the small outbuildings at the bottom of their back gardens, the beginning of the boot and shoe trade. This firm was first established by Alfred Church in partnership with his father Thomas and his brother William. Later he was joined by another brother Thomas Dudley Church who began his working life in the clicking room of the first factory in Duke Street, and worked his way through all the departments. So began another Northampton family partnership in the shoe trade. Alfred Church was the father of L.H. Church who was later to become Chairman of the Company in 1938 and served twenty five years until his retirement in 1963. It is significant that a member of the Church family, J.G. Church F.C.A. is the present (1993) Chairman of the Company.

Former factory of Padmore & Barnes now Church's.

When the firm began in 1873 the cutting and stitching of upper leathers was carried out on their premises; the lasting, making and finishing were done by skilled handworkers in their own homes. They fetched their work from the factory and returned it after completing their tasks. After the advent of the machine age during the latter half of the nineteenth century as shoemakers were gradually taken into factories the brothers Alfred, William and Thomas Church established the company's manufacturing policy. It still remains the production of top quality craftsman-made shoes. During the late nineteenth century, Church & Company built a six storey factory in Duke Street Northampton on the fringe of what has been defined as the centre of the boot and shoe trade. Duke Street is one of the oldest streets in Northampton with a lot of history. The writer has a lasting impression of this famous street, going back to childhood and it is remembered especially for the beautiful Anglican Church of St Lawrence (now the Polish Catholic Church of St Stanislau and St Lawrence) with its significant and imposing crucifix which dominate the street.

Church's well known factory was situated next to the church and there were also one or two smaller factories including a leather merchant. A row of terraced houses faced the factory and a similar row between the Church of St Lawrence and Earl Street which are still there. Below the factory was the Gospel Hall belonging to the Plymouth Brethren, the baby carriage shop of Allens and an ironmonger's shop at the corner with Bailiff Street. The latter business surviving to the seventies. At the upper end of Earl Street a well known fish and chip shop occupied the corner premises and being open until very late hours this was a boon to late night cinema and theatre goers. Nowadays most of the terraced houses, fish shop and smaller factories have gone, to be replaced by modern flats whilst the Gospel Hall is still there and holds its weekly meetings. The old Church's factory is occupied by a number of smaller firms.

When the new factory was built towards the turn of the century, there followed the installation of the appropriate machinery; and this led gradually to the production of all footwear entirely within the factory. Early in the 1900's the market was subject to their adaptability by investing in new mens lasts, and additional machinery which soon enabled them to deal with the competition. Their first venture into the export market came in 1904. When a German-American statesman started selling shoes branded 'Church' in Europe. Considerable business was done in both mens and ladies shoes in Germany the Austro-Hungarian empire, Switzerland, Belgium and a small amount in France. The First World War temporarily put an end to the European trade; but the resilient Church & Company established new markets in South Africa, India and Argentina.

The firm of Church pioneered multiple fitting footwear, in both mens and womens shoes. They developed this theme to such an extent that certain types became available from stock in as many different widths to each half size. Church's craftsmen are still acknowledged to be amongst the finest in the world; and the greatest care is taken in every stage of manufacture, in order to maintain the highest reputation for quality and style; which the Company's shoes now enjoy throughout the world. As early as 1907 a start had been made in selling Church's men's shoes in the United States. Progress was slow until 1910 when a new range of men's lasts was made especially for well known retailers of the trade in New York. Sales improved very quickly and the West Coast and Canada were opened up successfully.

Following the First World War the Duke Street factory in Northampton was overhauled and brought up to date. New machinery was introduced and ladies welted shoes of the remedial type were made; and these had a strongly built-in arch support and were available in four and five width fittings. At that time it was impossible to sell shoes in more than one width to British shoe retailers - they were and still are, Church's principal customers; and Church's arch-moulded shoes, as they were named, soared in volume. In 1921 the Church family opened a store on Oxford Street, London. This new venture was an immediate success and a very large turnover was achieved. This the Church family believed proved to the retail trade that customers wished to be fitted correctly and that greater comfort could be assured only by large ranges of sizes and fittings, correctly fitted by trained assistants.

Church's have their own store in New York - Church's English Shoes. In 1929 the Company opened its first mans shop in fashionable Madison Avenue a very substantial business was soon conducted in the North American market, form 428 Madison Avenue in both mens shoes and slippers. One of their famous ranges of fashion shoes for women "Vedettes", were made available from stock in American fittings AAA-C. These light weight tailored fashion shoes, also enjoyed a very substantial success in this country. In March 1954 Church and Company extended their own retail outlets by opening a number of concession departments (a shop within a shop) in a nationally high class outfitting business with stores in all major cities and town in the U.K. In Northampton the well known outfitters Austin Reed (Formerly Swanns of Gold Street) were until recent times stockists of Church's footwear. A great step was taken in 1955 when Church and Company acquired the existing retail shoes business of A Jones and Sons. This retail firm had shops in London and the South of England which have been extended in subsequent years to most major towns in England, Scotland and Wales. The Church Group now operate 118 shoes shops within Great Britain and a further 62 concession departments in stores throughout the country.

Alfred Church.

After more than fifty years of production in the Duke Street factory, the Company entered into a major development in 1957. This was the purchase of a large building at St James. The factory which had hitherto been the headquarters of the firm of Padmore & Barnes became the new home of Church and Company Ltd. From this factory an upsurge in international operations has been experienced. The year 1963 saw the formations of Church's English Shoes in Belgium when the Company opened its first store in Brussels. They now have two shops in that city and one in Antwerp. In addition to the shops in Belgium, Church's now have two shops in Paris and sixteen in America, plus seven concession departments in stores in European cities. An important visit to the Northampton factory which added distinction and recognition to the Company, was made when Her Majesty the Queen accompanied by His Royal Highness Prince Philip paid a visit to the factory in 1965. Two years later in 1967 the business of Joseph Cheaney and Sons Ltd., of Desborough Northamptonshire and one of the County's oldest established firm of Shoemakers became a subsidiary Company. Further expansion took place in 1971 when the Company acquired the premises formerly occupied by the British United Shoe Machinery Company Ltd at the junction of Earl Street and the Mounts. A start was made to convert these premises into a shoe factory and when completed enabled the project for the manufacture of ladies shoes on separate premises to be realised. This then enabled the production of men's shoes to be concentrated at the main factory in St James.

In 1983 the company won a Queen's Award for Export and in 1993, in spite of the national recession, employed six hundred people in their two Northampton factories and further two hundred in their Desborough factory. Their total national work force numbered 1800. The excellent demand for Church's mens shoes continues, particularly in European markets; their waterproof brand of ladies footwear has had particular success. During 1985 the Scottish retail name of James Allen and Son Ltd was added to the company's chain of stores, and four new stores were opened in the United States, namely Costa Mesa, Seattle, Atlanta and Boston; this made a total of sixteen stores in America and thirty stores in Canada. All of these are heavily orientated to the sale of Church and Cheaney shoes, the latter subsidiary company having attained its century in that year. In 1991 the company had a turnover of £65 - £70 million, with a hundred stores in the United Kingdom and key agencies in France, Italy, Germany and Japan. Church's craftsmen continue to uphold the high standards of quality and service which were the corner stones on which the company was built.

"Of all crafts, to be an honest man is the Mastercraft".

Chapter Ten

The Loan and the Dividend

One of Northampton's most famous firms which is still making footwear well into their second century is the firm of Crockett and Jones of Perry Street Northampton. Launched in 1879 it has also established a world wide reputation for fine shoes. Founded by James Henry Clifden Crockett and his brother-in-law Charles Jones it remains one of Northamptons oldest and largest firms still in business today. As neither of the two partners had sufficient capital to start the business each of them applied for and was granted £100 each by the Thomas White Trust. This was a famous endowment fund founded as far back as the 16th Century, by Sir Thomas White who was later a Lord Mayor of London. The fund was set up to encourage young men to go into business in the City of Coventry and Town of Northampton. A similar fund is still available today and has become familiarly known as the Thomas White Loan.

In the beginning James Crockett took charge of the selling and Charles Jones the manufacturing side of the business; they decided in the early days to concentrate on making mens boots. At that time the manufacture of footwear was only in part a factory business much of the upper closing hand lasting and finishing was done in peoples homes. The parts of the boots were collected a dozen pairs at a time from the factory and were returned as complete boots, to be approved by an inspector passed before payment was made. The price paid for a pair of boots, even as late as 1900, was six shillings (thirty pence) a pair.

Sir James Crockett.

F. M. Jones.

James Crockett was destined to play a very important part in public life. He was born in Northampton on 23rd June 1848 the son of James and Ann Crockett and was educated at All Saints School Northampton. He first started work as an errand boy with a Mr Cordeux a printer, and by diligence and hard work rose to be one of the commanding figures in the town's staple trade, and possibly one of Northampton's greatest and finest gentlemen. Beginning work at such a tender age himself he also saw around him, Children of seven working from six in the morning until seven or eight at night the dark hours relieved by the glimmers of light form globes filled with water. He left the employ of Mr Cordeux to enter the boot and shoe retail trade and gained experience in the trade as far afield as London (where he fitted Princess Louise at Kensington Palace) and at Birmingham, Worcester, Bridport and Kettering. He first started in business as a shoe manufacturer in 1876, when he was only twenty eight years old. Two years later in 1878 he decided to return to his native Northampton and entered into partnership with his brother-in-law Charles Jones to found the business which is still known as Crockett and Jones.

The first factory in Exeter Road (now Exeter Place) was situated between Kettering Road and Wellingborough Road and close to Abington Square. The total number of employees was twenty. The venture duly succeeded and business expanded quite rapidly. In 1884, after five years of experiment, the "Health" waterproof boot was registered and the Swan symbol was first used. Gradually more work was done in the factory and by the 1890's there were rows of handworkers sitting at benches. In those days it was often recognised as a thirsty job, for at the end of each row of workmen stood a barrel of beer! The first really big development of the firm, came in the 1890's when sons of both of the founders had joined the business. It was then largely on the initiative of sons Harry Crockett and Frank Jones that the firm grasped the opportunities being offered by the boot and shoe trade by developing technology. The machinery that was first introduced was the Good Year Welted footwear plant. The problem with this plant as with the many other machines which followed it, was the integration of the machine into the stream of delicate and individual hand operations. This was commonly experienced by all other factories when introducing machinery. There was something like one hundred and seventy operations in all that comprised the making of high class footwear.

The factory which still stands in Maggee Street and Perry Street was built when that part of the town was in open country. By the turn of the century both James Crockett and Charles Jones had felt that business had so increased that larger premises were needed. The new factory provided a new opportunity for further expansion, and between 1900 and 1914 the home market was the mainspring of the firm's trade; this was to continue well into the fifties. There was, however, a remarkably high element of overseas' trading and this characterised the business for well over half a century. The principal consumers abroad were in South America, Egypt, Australia, South Africa, New Zealand, India, China, Belgium, Canada, USA, and South East Asia, including Hong Kong and Malaya. Frank Jones and Harry Crocket along with their fathers needed to exercise great perception and judgement in marrying the immense potentialities of power-driven machinery for factory development whilst maintaining the highest standards of craftsmanship. In the crucial years around the turn of the century the firm succeeded and gained a new reputation for making some of the best shoes in the country. Among the various commissions which the firm received about this time was one in connection with Messrs Jaeger when special footwear and clothing was made for one of the early Shackleton Polar Expeditions. The standard of footwear must have been very high as it was subsequently used by Sir Ernest Shackleton for a further voyage in 1914.

When Crockett and Jones added a larger five storey wing to their Perry Street factory in 1910 it was at the time one of the most advanced industrial buildings in the country. The proportion of glass in its wall surfaces was unusual and because of this, unlike many other industrial buildings in those days, it had superb natural lighting and ventilation. In the early years of the century an alliance was built up between individual retailers and the factory. Crockett & Jones did not have their own retail branches and this gave the "Health" and "Swan" brands of footwear a sound market throughout the world. Under the leadership of Harry Crockett and his father James, and Frank Jones and his father Charles the years before the First World War were the formative years of Crockett & Jones' development. In 1911 Percy Jones, Frank's brother, joined the firm and in 1913 he went to Germany for a year to study certain commercial methods. He returned to England just before the outbreak of the war in 1914 and was commissioned in the Machine Gun Corps. After the war James Crockett became not only a foremost industrialist but a person who came to play an increasingly prominent part in public life. He embodied an almost unique combination of stern business acumen, with a kindly, human and generous nature. He sat for many years on the Northampton Bench as a J.P. and in 1907, 1911 and 1913 was President of the Boot and Shoe Manufacturers' Association. He became a rich man but was in equal proportion rich in good and benevolent works. He was loved and respected by his employees and revered by many with whom he came into contact. He was knighted in 1922 for his public services and was always known by his full name Sir James Henry Clifden Crockett. Sir James was not only a foremost boot and shoe manufacturer but a generous hearted citizen whose qualities won much esteem.

Sir James was largely responsible for setting up one of the benevolent schemes operated by the company for its many employees. Often refered to as the Crockett Bank Book it was a provident fund begun just after the First World War. A donation from the firm was invested in a trust. There were four trustees, two from management and two representing the employees, and the fund was administered by a firm of accountants. It was in fact one of the first schemes of its kind in Northampton. Employees were eligible for non-contributory membership at the age of twenty and after three years service. Crockett and Jones became an admirable example of the "Family Firm" both in its direction and in the loyalties of its workpeople. Not only were the directors' sons and grandson of one or both founders there were instances of generations of the same families following one another into the factory. The partnership spirit between workers and management at Perry Street was exceptionally strong and this was one of the main factors. In the maintaining of quality workmanship the individual responsibility amongst workers at the factory was such that they were conscious not only of the need to do their part but to keep an eye on the job in general. This kind of partnership led to the fact that there were many executives in the shoe trade of later years who owed much to the training they had received at the Crockett and Jones factory.

In 1924 H.R.H. The Duke of York (later King George VI) paid a visit to the factory and this remained a well remembered occasion. Continuing the family tradition in 1927 Mr Gilbert Jones son of Frank and grandson of one of the founders joined the firm. This began the second generation of the Jones family to be associated with the firm. This line of succession was to continue for many years; ten years later Percy Jones was elected Chairman of the Company. During the rise of the Boot and Shoe trade as a manufacturing industry Britain was the largest exporter of footwear in the world. The proportion of Crockett and Jones output in this field was well above average, possibly due to the wide range of shoes manufactured. Part of the Crockett and Jones overseas' trade had hitherto been in hand and bench-made shoes. Before the second World War the firm did big business with South Africa. When in 1948 the South African Government imposed a ban on imported footwear it allowed only a trickle into the country under licence. However, a firm with which Crockett and Jones was associated, the Barker Chiswick Organisation, secured a franchise to make men's shoes under licence in their modern Cape Town factory; and so Crockett and Jones footwear was manufactured in that country.

The major difference to the factory in the period prior to the Second World War was the addition of a second wing to the Perry Street building in 1935. This comprised a new office block and an instock department. Later there came the disappearance of all the old overhead power shafts and driving belts. From that time all machines were driven by individual motors giving a greater degree of safety to all machine operators. Both Sir James and his son Harry died before the Second World War and Frank, son of Charles Jones, who guided the firm throughout its many consolidating years died in 1941. In 1947 the third generation of the Jones' family entered the business in the personage of Richard Jones son of Percy and the grandson of the founder Charles Jones. From Oundle School he went to Cambridge University where he gained a Degree in Engineering. He then joined the Navy in 1944 as an engineering officer. Once in the business, Richard was soon involved in learning the craft of shoemaking and in 1948 he went to the United States where he spent six months working in shoe factories and retail shops. He also visited tanners and component manufacturers. In 1955 he assumed responsibility for the company's export market and in 1957 he became involved in development of the retail side, including the formation of Crockett and Jones (Canada) now one of the Company's flourishing offshoots. In 1948 firm became a Private Limited Company.

During the first seventy seven years of its history up to 1956, the firm made over twenty five million pairs of footwear. This included over a million pairs of footwear for the armed forces in the Second World War. All of this embodied more than three generations of family skill and experience. During the early 1950's after the firm became a limited company, the Board of Directors comprised of Percy Jones (brother of Frank Jones) and Gilbert Jones (son of Frank) who were joint Managing Directors. This team was completed by Percy's son Richard and J. A. Eyton Jones who joined the Company from A. & W. Arnolds in 1950. The former was responsible for design and the latter took charge of production and personnel. The remaining member of the board at that time was Roy A. Barker who had previously founded A. Barker & Sons (Earls Barton) in Capetown, South Africa in the 1930's and was also concerned with the production of Crockett & Jones shoes in that country. Over the years the firm's instock lists have always presented a wide range of styles and the popularity with their retailers has been built on the assurance that what they sell can repeat. Many of their fine styles of shoes can now also be seen in their factory shop in Perry Street. From time to time as fashions changed the firm has used to the full all the new developments in factory technique. This had enabled them to continue to produce shoes, with greater lightness and flexibility than ever before.

The firm has had over the years a very active Sports and Social Club which had a great record between the wars and after on the bowling greens of Northampton. It also boasted a talented cricket team playing in the Leather Trades competitions and town leagues. There were other sections which included angling and cribbage, modern and old time dancing, children's outings and even an annual horticultural show. For a relatively small family controlled business, Crockett & Jones have quite a diverse operation. Besides the factory in Northampton, producing top quality all-leather shoes for men and women, they have interests in retailing at home, manufacturing overseas and both importing and exporting. At home the Company have expanded their retail interest in "shop within a shop" departments specialising in their own shoes. They train the salesmen operating in these departments and undertake to fit them out and put in the stock; this is a procedure which has brought high praise from store owners.

An interesting development on the retail side has been the opening of stores in Canada specialising in men's shoes only; they also own eight high grade shops in the U.K. as well as operating almost twenty five concessions in department stores and in menswear shops. In the factory the Company is always working ahead and keeping abreast of modern trends. Although they still have operatives who are skilled in hand craft operations, they also welcome the latest labour saving equipment and new technology provided that quality standards can be maintained. Much of the company's success has stemmed from the enthusiasm and initiative of Percy Jones. He was appointed Chairman of the Company in 1948 and remained in that office until his death at the age of 85 in 1979. Upon the death of Gilbert Jones in 1977 Richard was appointed Managing Director. His son Jonathan was appointed the first manager of a marketing division set up within the Group, for a gradual streamline of production and some simplification of the product ranges. He spent some time working with the South African Company in Capetown read for a Degree in Classics at Exeter University and also studied law. One of his responsibilities was range building for both the UK and international collections, the instock operations, advertising and promotion. Richard Jones' interest are wide. He was appointed a Justice of the Peace in 1964 and was for three years chairman of Northampton Juvenile Court, and a Deputy Chairman of Northamptonshire Divisional Bench. He is a longstanding member of the South Eastern Branch Committee of the Institute of Directors and was President of the British Footwear Manufacturers Association in 1968-70. In 1980 he was appointed President of the British Footwear Manufacturers Federation on January 1st 1980, and office he occupied for eighteen months.

Since its foundation in 1879 the firm has chosen to steer clear of mass-produced footwear and their craftsmen continue making shoes in the time-honoured traditional way. Emphasis on style has always been paramount but never at the expense of fit or comfort. Painstaking attention is therefore paid to the design and development of the lasts which provide not only the shape but also the essential fitting characteristic of the finished shoe. A uniquely different last is developed for every type of shoe. Hides are chosen from European tanneries where the best leather processing is still carried out. Careful tinting with aniline dyes brings out the rich detail of the leather grain, although such revealing process often means that large areas of the hide have to be discarded because of blemishes or marks. High quality leathers are used for soles, inner-soles and heels. From the clickers bench where the leather is cut to the finishing room where the heels and soles are crease-ironed and hand polished up to thirty individual pieces of leather will undergo two hundred separate operations, lasting as long as eight weeks. Having entered into their second century of manufacture, whether it a classic or light weight shoe that is required all of Crocketts and Jones shoes retain attention to detail, quality,

46

comfort and durability as was the hallmark of their founders, James Crockett and Charles Jones. The company continues to offer quality shoes and specialised craftsmanship in the international footwear industry. Crockett and Jones shoes are the bench mark upon which all others are judged.

Crockett & Jones Factory, Perry Street, Northampton.

Both my mother than the girl I married work here. (at different times) but both in the same office

RETURLAND

Chapter Eleven

Progressive Policy and a Triumph of Dimensions

The story of two of Northamptons' greatest shoe firms which have since sunk into oblivion is the subject of this chapter. Both contributed to the success of the shoe trade in the town and indeed to the prosperity of the Borough in no small measure. Each of them rose to be leading manufacturers in the country, but sadly too few records are available to tell of their achievements in the fullest sense. Both factory buildings were situated in different areas of the town and have long since been demolished. With them had disappeared much of the history of the previous years. What is known however is that both of these companies started as a family partnership of brothers, each company developing its own particular style and clientele. Both businesses commenced within a decade of each other.

The business career of Edward Lewis J.P. was known to be one of the romances of the shoe trade. From a small beginning in Freeschool Street in 1879 he and his brother Charles, launched the factory of C and E Lewis. Later it moved into very extensive works in Marlborough Road, St James and was a factory of five or six floors and contained the most up to date and efficient machinery. Edward Lewis came of Welsh ancestry and was born in Northampton in 1861. His father George was a shoemaker who was said to have founded a factory around 1854. Edward first began work with a farmer but very soon started work in the shoe factory which, with his brother Charles, he was ultimately to own. No one could have made a less auspicious start in business for he was without capital or social influences; but he and his brother by thrift of time and money, plain living and hard work soon began to reap the harvest of their perseverance. Whilst Edward travelled for orders his brother Charles looked after the manufacturing side. The transparent straight forwardness of Edward and his unfailing reliability in supplying goods of high quality soon made the firm of C. and E. Lewis known and respected far and wide. Factory after factory was taken over, until the great "Progressive" works were built, and their younger brother Councillor T.D. Lewis became a partner in the firm.

Edward and his brother by reason of much self sacrifice and shrewdness built up a great shoe manufacturing business which ranked among the largest and most successful in the country. As an employer Edward Lewis, supported by his brothers, looked for good work for a good days pay. The brothers also realised that employers had their responsibilities as well as rights. This led to the establishment of a scheme whereby their employees had a share in the profits of the firm. It was said that wealth never spoiled Edward Lewis. There was always a conspicuous lack of showiness in all his public work and philanthropy. His diffidence in speech was far from connoting any lack of courage but was due to an innate modesty and an entire absence of self seeking. Though he held strong views himself of religious, political and social subjects he was never intolerant or ungenerous in his views concerning those who disagreed with him. Edward became Mayor of the Borough in 1903 and was also chairman of the Watch Committee for many years. He was also President of the Northampton Battalion of the Boys Brigade, the YMCA, the Free Church Federal Council in Northampton and the Northamptonshire Sunday School Union. He became President of the Boot and Shoe Manufacturers Association in 1911 and held office until 1913. He was one time President of Northampton Cymric Society.

Edward Lewis.

Charles Lewis.

The "Progressive" factory produced high grade men's and women's footwear which sold throughout the British Isles. An extensive Export trade was built up, with customers in forty territories overseas. For more than half a century regular employment was maintained through all the fluctuating fortunes in the industry until the closure of the factory in the sixties when vast numbers of personnel were made redundant. Although not among the oldest of the largest established firms C and E Lewis in the "Progressive" works carried out a progressive policy in the firm. At the height of their manufacturing capacity over 800 workpeople operating 300 up-to-date machines, turned out over 11,000 pairs of shoes a week. In their earliest days Charles and Edward Lewis were not only shoe manufacturers but also leather dressers on a large scale. Herein, to some degree, was the secret of their success. Not only were they able to produce boots and shoes at an especially cheap rate but guaranteed the quality of the material used in manufacture; this was because they used their own hides and skins, mostly calves and kids, which amounted annually to approximately five thousand. In addition to this over 300 English bark tanned butts and nearly 500 English bends and American sides which were used for sole leather were produced. There were also 11,000 English bellies and a proportionate number of English shoulders which together were heeling materials; all were required to complete the output. These figures convey some idea of the gigantic business that C and E Lewis built up not only in the United Kingdom but in North Africa, Australia, New Zealand and other foreign markets. Throughout the years of the existence of the firm the welfare of its employees remained a prime consideration. The Company was thought to be the first in the trade to introduce a welfare scheme which benefited employees under special circumstances or on their retirement. In 1900 James and John Lewis (sons of Charles) and George Lewis (son of Edward) joined the business. In 1915 H.G. Lewis (son of T.D. Lewis) also became associated with the Company. Later on

Charles W Lewis, James T Lewis, and Edward Lewis (all grandsons of the original partners) joined the firm. Thus ensured a continuance of the family business until its disbandment in September 1965 when the Company closed.

It was in 1891 (twelve years later than Charles and Edward Lewis) that John George Sears founded a manufacturing business under the name of J Sears and Company. John Sears (known to his colleagues as Jack) was an employee in the Manfield factory when he decided to set up in business on his own account; and in this venture he was first joined by two fellow employees. They commenced work in a small factory in Gray Street making men's shoes and the factory became capable of an output of a few hundred pairs a week. John Sears was eventually joined by his brother William, and together they traded under the name of the True Form Boot Company. John Sears enthusiasm filled the whole of the Boot and Shoe world with amazement. His triumphs reached dimensions which exceeded even the wildest dreams of the Brothers and their early staff; they were achieved by a far seeing judgement and heroic enterprise united with a certain amount of good luck. The Sears Brothers opened their first retail shop in 1897 in Fleet Street, London under the name of Messrs F. Tanner & Company. The shop was an instant success, the takings in the first week being £250. Shortly afterwards when the London County Council wanted to widen the thoroughfare they paid the brothers £1,000 to move a few doors lower down where they took more money than ever before. At the end of the year 1911 the firm owned eighty branches. It was interesting coincidence that when John opened his first shop it was on the ground floor of the premises where Lord Northcliffe was building the basis of his newspaper empire and fortune with the periodical "Answers" which enjoyed much success over several decades. The "Napoleon" of the newspaper world and John George Sears could little have conceived in those early days the heights to which they would both obtain in the business world.

The London shop was to be the forerunner of a vast chain of retail shops and True Form was able to supply its goods from factory to customer. By his personal observations as to where the tide of his customers was thickest J G Sears selected the best sites for his shops and as his business grew developed a genius for choosing the right men to help him. Once he took a man into his confidence he trusted him implicitly and he was rewarded by the loyalty of those around him to an exceptional degree. In 1902 a factory at the corner of Adnitt Road and Stimpson Avenue in Northampton was opened and several extensions to this building were made in 1908, 1910, 1912, and 1914. Eventually the whole block made it one of the largest factories in Northampton employing hundreds of workpeople. John's brother, William Thomas Sears, brought to the firm a practical knowledge and keen business judgement and in 1912 it was decided to form a public company. It was registered as the True Form Boot Company Limited and John became the first Chairman and Managing Director. He engendered the will to work with the assistance of his co-directors and succeeded in making and retailing shoes of quality at prices attractive to everybody. True Form continued to build up a vast chain of retail shops situated in the great thoroughfares of London and all provincial cities and towns throughout the United Kingdom.

In 1913, after the True Form Boot Company became a public company, the firm acquired the factory of F W Panther situated in Barry Road. Frank Panther joined the Board of Directors as Director-Buyer and in 1915 two other experienced business men, John Dickens and Hartley Aspden, strengthened the board of directors. Around the same time Ernest George Elliott, a man with more than twenty years in the trade became company secretary. After the death of the founder in 1916 he was succeeded as chairman by his brother William and as managing director by F.W.Panther.The factory in Barry Road was often known as "Sears Bottom Shop" and was still in operation as part of the British Shoe Corporation in 1990. The whole True Form factory was better known to townsfolk throughout the years of its life as "Sears". The immense impact on the shoe trade made by the True Form Boot Company was a testimony in itself to the thoroughness of its late founder John Sears who could never have ever imagined the extent to which his business was to flourish.

Former office block of J. Sears & Co Ltd (True Form Boot Co.) Adnitt Road, Northampton.

In 1925 the company boasted a workforce of over 3,000 employees. In 1929 the firm acquired the controlling interest in the Leicester firm of Freeman, Hardy and Willis thus becoming the largest group in the industry with nine factories and over eight hundred shops. The firm went on to enjoy great prosperity with retail outlets all over the United Kingdom employing over 2,000 people in their shops. When William T Sears retired in 1947 he was succeeded by D R Church who served as chairman and managing director until 1953. When the renowned financier and creator of monopolies, Sir Charles Clore,took over True Form and created the British Shoe Corporation he commenced the decline of the Northampton shoe industry. In 1968 True Form was merged with the Manfield factory in Wellingborough Road under the title of the British Shoe Corporation.

J. G. Sears.

F. W. Panther.

The former F. W. Panther Factory, now British Shoe Corporation.

"You will never do anything in the world without courage".

Chapter 12

A Romance of Reality

The Reverend Henry J Pickett, one time minister of Grove Road Primitive Methodist Church (now Queensgrove) and a former Principal of Hartley College Manchester, said:- "By Industry, Tact, Perseverance, and beyond all, Character; some of the greatest and most honoured business reputations of this country have been built up". He was referring to one William Arnold Senior an earnest Christian whose religion he said was as the good Shaftesbury wrote in his diary: "one who enters into everything he does (and is) undaunted by adversity and unspoiled by success". His story is of intrinsic value as a testimony to the Christian faith and a guide and inspiration to all young people.

The story of the Arnold family is indeed a rags to riches story which began in the village of Everdon twelve miles south west of Northampton; and led William Arnold to become one of the best known and most revered among the shoe manufacturers of Northampton. William was born on 30th December 1860 at Everdon a village with its own industries: farming, brickmaking, weaving and shoemaking. His father, Matthew, was a poor working man, a typical old-fashioned village shoemaker who was employed by a Mr C Rodhouse in the nearby town of Daventry. He was one of large family of fourteen children and the family were very poor, so William experienced very hard times during his own childhood. There was never sufficient to eat for Williams' father earned about 16 shillings a week except at Harvest time when he obtained extra work alongside the harvesters working in the fields. The work was reaping and lasted for about a month. For the Arnold family it was a continual story of poverty and struggle. During the summertime when the Parish Church at Everdon was open on Sunday evenings young William Arnold would sit with other farm labourers in their working clothes at the back of the church. The family was not a Christian one and never attended any place of worship. William however used to enjoy the service and never really lost his desire to attend some place of worship on Sundays.

At the age of seven William worked as a ploughboy for 2 shillings a week. The job was leading the horses whilst the ploughman guided the plough. When just over the age of seven he went to work in the boot trade as a sprigging boy inserting rivets (sometimes called sprigs) into the sole of the shoe. As a sprigging boy he earned three to four shillings a week. Rivetting was a method that had been developed and used in the manufacture of cheaper kinds of footwear as opposed to handsewn methods. In the time of his youth there were thirty nine shoemakers in Everdon alone; and William had noticed that the old shoemakers were noted for their drinking habits, skittle playing and pitch and toss. This was not peculiar to the village of Everdon as it was widespread in both town and county. Despite receiving low wages shoemakers in general always seemed to be addicted to strong drink and spent much of their time in public houses. Mondays were off days, when no shoemaker of principle would work; and this led to the day being known as 'Saint Monday'. It was an unofficial holiday which Crispin's men always celebrated in a manner most satisfactory to the local brewers, until factory life came and destroyed the custom. Nevertheless, the typical Northampton shoemaker was a hard working thoughtful craftsman with dignity and self esteem.

Working at a young age in this early Victorian era was the sad plight of the children of the nation's poor. William was typical of the youngsters who endured such poverty and appalling conditions of work including long hours of toil. He commenced work at the age of seven and at nine found himself employed as a sprigging boy by George Osborne of Newnham who in turn worked for the firm of Stead and Simpson in Daventry. After a while George Osborne moved from Newnham to Daventry. From then onwards William walked four miles every morning to Daventry leaving before 6 a.m. and then stood at a bench for ten or twelve hours then walked the four miles home to Everdon. At the age of twelve his father, who was a splendid craftsman, taught him how to stitch and sew a boot. He then returned once again to work for Mr Osborne at Daventry. Trade, however, was not good and he was eventually forced to seek work elsewhere. His uncle, Anthony Arnold, lived in Northampton. He was also a shoemaker and he obtained work for him with a shoemaker named Joseph Gibbs who lived in Cyril Street and who specialised in making youths and boys shoes. Trade also became bad in Northampton and when this happened William went back to Daventry. First, he worked for his old employer Mr Osborne but later obtained work direct from Mr Dickens who was George Osborne's employer. In May 1875 he returned to Northampton and became employed at a factory named Laycocks in a cul-de-sac known as Birds' Piece, just off St Edmunds Road. His wage was twenty seven shillings a week, which at that time was remarkably good for a lad of his age. William was popular with the men and very soon found himself following in their wayward ways. He got to like skittles, card playing, and drinking spending a lot of the money he had earned on beer and skittles. Nevertheless he always sent home some of his wages to his family.

It was customary for a fresh man who came to work at a 'factory' to be expected to pay for a gallon of beer. The other men would then add three pence each to the cost of the gallon, which increased the amount, and when that was consumed they would send out for more. Later they would adjourn to the nearest public house. In addition to the evils of drunkenness amongst shoe workers gambling was also popular in workshops. The curate of St. James Church, Dallington reported in 1882 in the Episcopal Visitation Return for St James that "Among the shoemakers this is most universal. The men bet on racing events, pigeon matches and dogs, even political events and Municipal Elections are greatly influenced by the betting men. The masters are some of the betting men and so do not interfere - others are afraid". Another author, G. Battle, in "Workshops Old and New" states that "in many cases earnings were spent on Saturday, Sunday and Monday, with lavish carelessness; and the chief gainer was either the publican or the bookmaker. Others were wise to dissipate their earnings in this way and what was not spent in housekeeping was invested".

At the age of eighteen William had begun to see the evils of wasting money on drink. Resolving to became a teetotaller he joined the Good Templar movement but after two years membership he became bored and returned to drinking. When he reached the age of twenty four he went to work for Philip Manfield in his factory on Campbell Square. In his memoirs he tells of one Friday in June 1884. After being paid for the week he walked to Boughton Green Fair and there, like the Prodigal Son, made merry with his friends which ended with a drinking session. Next day he recalls he found himself on Northampton Market Square and entered into a conversation with a young woman who was later to become his wife. Because of his drinking the previous day and again on the Sunday he was feeling quite ill and taking her advice resolved there and then to stop the habit. He decided to go into All Saints Church where the Reverend Cannon Hull's preaching made a great impression on him. Following the service that Sunday morning after walking to the Racecourse, he vowed that God helping him he would never touch strong drink again. His decision was something more than a determination to become a teetotaller; he put God to the test and felt that he could trust him. Yet another uncle of his was a Rechabite, a member of a very strict teetotal society. He proposed William for membership and this was another turning point in his life.

The lady who became his wife was already a young and earnest Christian. They were married at St Michaels Church and for a time lived with his wife's parents. Eventually they acquired a house to rent in Shakespeare Road with absolutely no means of furnishing it. Later they persuaded a dealer in Gold Street to let them have furniture and pay for it weekly. This, of course, was a matter of trust between shopkeeper and customer as there were no hire purchase or credit facilities in those days. In the early days of his marriage William was working for his uncle Anthony at a small shop in Hunter Street. As business progressed they often talked of becoming a manufacturer of boots but there were nearly three hundred boot and shoe manufacturers in Northampton. Most were quite small businesses but they were regarded as manufacturers. William, his Uncle Anthony and his brother-in-law became partners in a bold step to launch out for themselves. In turn they enlisted the help of Alfred Flint, and together they began their own business under the style of Arnold and Company. Financing the project was difficult. Whilst his uncle and brother-in-law had little money William had none; but he borrowed some from a friend and so contributed a share to the capital. When pooled the money totalled just £94. It was sufficient for them to proceed if only in a small way.

There was a man named Smith who worked at Manfields and he became their pattern cutter and clicker. Anthony cut the sole leathers and William did the rivetting. The finishing of the boots was put out to workpeople working in their own homes. William's wife did the closing and Alfred Flint kept the accounts. As things progressed they rented small premises in nearby Duke Street. Each partner drew only £1 in wages for a week's work whilst other workers were paid what they earned. Out if his £1 wages William paid eight shillings and sixpence rent and rates leaving the remaining eleven shillings and sixpence to keep his wife and three children for the week. From one room in Duke Street the partners moved to a house in adjoining Military Road which became their first factory. After the move they raised their own wages to twenty five shillings a week. To meet demand they worked from seven in the morning until ten or eleven at night. After early struggles which brought with them many disappointments business grew and another move was made to a building in Louise Road. The partners again raised their own wages to thirty shillings a week.

One of their best customers at this time was a large London firm, and trade receipts amounted to £200 a week. However after a year or two of prosperity tragedy struck and the firm failed. They found themselves owing about £1000 and in turn they could not repay what they themselves owed. There was no alternative but to close the factory and a meeting of creditors was arranged. Contrary to all expectations the partners were not condemned by the creditors who saw the collapse as a business tragedy that was unavoidable. At the meeting one of the creditors expressed the feeling that it had been an unwise decision to close the business for lack of finances. With the approval of the creditors it was decided that they would have another try to recover from the difficulties that they had encountered. Thus a new firm evolved with William and Anthony the only partners. Known as A and W Arnold it became firmly established and was a leader in the trade for many years. In 1894 the men's union had demanded an end to all work being carried out at home by rivetters and finishers; this meant all work should be carried out at the factory. This meant the premises in Louise Road were not large enough. Accordingly new premises were acquired and rented in St Giles Terrace in 1896. This was the former factory of Messrs Allinsons who had moved to the top of Earl Street. This move was a big undertaking for them and meant one long struggle. At first they were making little headway, or so it seemed. Soon, however, the factory was established and became the permanent premises for A and W Arnold Footwear turning out quality boots and shoes.

William Arnold.

William Arnold was a man who realised that his personal religion played a great part in his business and ultimate success. He said: "I made up my mind that in my business, come what might, the result whatever it might be I would be most honest and honourable". He had continued to attend All Saints Church after turning Teetotaller but later went with his future wife to Mount Zion Baptist Church (later called Princes Street Chapel) - now demolished to make way for Princes Walk, Grovesnor Centre). Then there came a period of attendance at Doddridge Congregational Chapel during the ministry of the Reverend J J Cooper, followed by a time worshipping with the Salvation Army, for a number of years. In turn he tried worship with all different denominations. Remembering that he had no religious training when young he found it extremely difficult to make a choice but finally he settled at Grove Road Primitive Methodist Church (now Queensgrove) during the ministry of the Reverend George Parkin and later the Reverend Henry J Pickett. Both he and his wife worshipped at Grove Road for many years and he became a trustee, society steward and class leader. He said: "I consider that to Grove Road Church and the friends there, to my dear wife and to God, I owe everything; all that I am, my condition, my hopes, my life. When I look back and see how I have been led through difficulties and troubles and trials, I do not think there are any many living who have had more than I have. It is all very wonderful. I have always known that there has been a higher power than my own; no one ever told me, but I have known it. I am not able to explain it now, but I am still absolutely certain of it or else I should not be where

I am and what I am. I have been guided, guarded and led; how I do no know". What a wonderful testimony for a man who had no religious upbringing and whose early life was marred by drunkenness.

William Arnold had six sons Harry, Matthew, James, Alfred, William Junior and Thomas. All were associated with him in business and shared his religious interests. He also had four daughters a large family but not quite so large as his father's family. William's success meant that his family enjoyed a better standard of living into which he himself had been born. At a time when the boot and shoe trade was undergoing the greatest change since it became an industry, business for the Arnolds was prosperous. The poor little village boy had succeeded beyond his wildest dreams. After the 1887 lockout (the dreadful Jubilee Year), when all the shoe factories were closed; and there was fearful distress all over the town the Arnolds triumphed. When machinery was introduced after the dispute of 1895 they too began to get a strong foothold in the trade. William took the initiative making it a matter of prayer. Confident he was doing the right thing he speculated thousands of pounds on machinery, when truthfully he had not got a spare shilling himself. Time came when Anthony retired and William carried on the business alone. Happily he came through the experience and the factory prospered. After twenty six years of business trials and tribulations the name of A and W Arnold stood second to none in the trade; for honest dealing, good workmanship, an untarnished name, honourable and clean. Together with his sons he owned three factories, employing over 800 people and in 1915 were paying out a £1000 in wages every week. The factories were producing over half a million pairs of boots and shoes per annum and could claim to have customers in almost every civilised country under the Sun.

Two of William Arnolds Sons, Matthew and William junior, founded their own shoe factory on 1st January 1909 after working in their own fathers factory in St Giles Terrace at the age of twelve. William junior was standing at a clicking board for 54 hours a week. Their factory in Henry Street became famous for its Cathedral Brand of men's and women's shoes. William junior also became a devout Methodist and a well known local preacher. He was fond of music, radio, and was a keen bowls player. His son Malcolm Arnold is the celebrated musician and composer. Ever since the days when the old firm of Arnold and Company had the misfortune to call its creditors together, William Arnold's chief ambition was to repay all who had lost money. Finally by the Grace of God, the ability to do this was achieved and all creditors paid in full with interest. All claims against the old firm of Arnold and Company were repaid by A and W Arnold. The personal pledge that William had made years earlier, to always be honest and reliable was very much in evidence when this ambitions to pay those who had lost money was realised. Whenever he spoke of his achievements he always attributed his success to prayer, temperance and asking God's help. "It is not myself", he would say, "It is God above, and to Him I give all the praise, and all the glory. Not more than others I deserve; but God has given me more". From poor boy to humble shoemaker; from a shoemakers workbench to business man; William Arnold was truly a disciple of Saint Crispin.

"There's a Divinity that shapes our ends, rough hew them as we will".
William Shakespeare.

Chapter 13

The Boot and Shoe Trail

Before its redevelopment in the 1970's the whole area from York Road to Lady's Lane and Wood Street, and from the Mounts to Colwyn Road, Kettering Road and the Racecourse including Overstone Road, Dunster Street, and Clare Street were full of old shoe factories. After all the making processes became mechanised and the factory system replaced handsewn making and all outworking, the Eastern side of Northampton Town grew rapidly. In 1869 there were almost no buildings east of the Mounts but within twenty years this whole area was built up piecemeal fashion. The dates engraved on many of the buildings which remain will testify to this. The smell of leather was very prevalent as you walked through this area and although today that is not so a walk round these most interesting streets of the district of Saint Crispin will reveal many historical aspects of a bygone age.

The heart of the old Boots and Shoe area was thought to have been St Michaels Road. Two leather companies Berrill and Williams and Messrs Mathers were at 14 and 18. In the middle backing on to Lower Mounts just below the old Baptist Chapel was the leather factory of A E Rodhouse who was one of the Borough's best known citizens. He first established a business as a leather merchant in Kettering in 1903 and moved to Northampton in 1906 supplying good class sole leather to the trade. A public spirited philanthropist Rodhouse devoted much of his time to the public good. He was a life Deacon of Doddridge Castle Hill Congregational Church, President of Northampton YMCA and many other worthy charitable institutions especially Bethany Homestead of which he was the treasurer.

On the same side of St Michael's Road at number 56 was the factory of Pollard and Son, and at 62 still stands the firm of R E Tricker and the offices of Haynes and Cann. At the bottom was the British American Last Works and immediately opposite was the three and half storey Boot factory of H J Bateman with its overhead hoist which can still be seen. Also in St Michael's Road was the factory of Beale and Company. Founded in March 1887 by two brothers Walter Beale and T G Beale. Walter Beale was devoted to town welfare as a town councillor and deputy chairman of the Tramways Committee. The firm of R E Tricker and Haynes and Cann are both very old firms with much history; they are still turning out footwear today. The factory of the latter however is now in Overstone Road. The firm of R E Tricker Ltd was founded in 1829. It was originally a London firm which came to Northampton in the later 19th century. The factory in St Michaels Road was built in 1903 and the top floor in 1947. The firm which specialises in handsewn footwear, produced top quality mens shoes and also has premises in Regent Street, which is known as Trickers International, seven tenths of the firm's output being exported. About a hundred people are currently in the employ of this firm, and as recently as 1984 one of its longest serving and oldest employees, Arthur Nichols, retired at the age of 89 after 75 industrious years of service. Mr Nichols built up a lasting friendship with his employers, starting with the Company as an errand boy in 1909 working 56 hours a week for about four shillings. In those days the firm employed about six people and the factory was based in a small house. Since that time Nichols watched the Company expand from these very small premises and worked his way up from delivering messages through each department to be one of the Company Directors. This type of loyal service was to be found in many factories. Employees would spend the whole of their working lives with one particular Company and sons would follow their fathers into the trade. In 1993 Trickers, still a family owned shoemakers, celebrated the opening of a smart shop in the high fashion Aoyama Shopping Centre in the Japanese capital Tokyo. The store, modelled on a traditional English clubroom, features a four thousand pound carpet hand-woven in Japan, and is fitted out in teak. It is envisaged that a fifth of its total production is destined for Japan, where the company feel there is a strong market for high-class footwear with a brand image, which in Japan can cost the equivalent of three hundred pounds per pair.

The factory of Pollard and Son was established by E Pollard in the year 1857. In earlier days the work they produced consisted mainly of handsewn goods. When machinery was installed, high class welted goods were made which found a ready market abroad in Canada, the United States, South Africa, South America, Australia and Egypt as well as the British Isles. F W Pollard, who commenced work in the factory as a lad of 14, succeeded his father and his son A E Pollard joined his father in the year 1900. The success of this family firm was evident in as much as it was still making high class footwear until more recent years when it had to close down. If you were to walk along the alley way between 85 and 87 St Michael's Road, which leads to Dunster Street, you would pass the houses, which form part of Alcombe Terrace. Here behind the houses, workshops can still be seen where the early cordwainers were engaged in their craft. Nearby Dunster Street, however, was once full of firms making and selling sole leather but now only contains one footwear firm, that of G T Hawkins whose factory at the top corner of Dunster Street and Overstone Road extends into St Michael's Road.

The Boot Factory of G. T. Hawkins, St Michaels Rd/Overstone Rd, Northampton.

George Thomas Hawkins founded his factory in 1882 later going into partnership with H G White and H Edwards; they moved to Overstone Road in 1886 first taking only the Dunster Street Corner. G T Hawkins, the founder, lived at 19 Shakespeare Road whilst he was setting up the factory in Overstone Road and which today is still in business and occupies the whole corner block between Dunster Street and St Michaels Road. This Company is the only Northampton shoe firm to hold the Royal Warrant. The Royal coat of arms can be seen displayed on the factory building at the corner of St Michael's Road. The firm became a private liability company in 1915 when G T Hawkins was joined as fellow directors by H Edwards and H G White both who had worked for the firm throughout their business career. About 220 people are still employed in this factory which specialises in making climbing and riding boots and the "magazine" type boots used by servicemen working in ammunition stores. The firm in its early days did an extensive trade in both ladies and gents footwear, in all parts of the British Empire. Opposite Hawkins' factory stood the boot and shoe workers union offices and club and institute (known as the United Trades Club).

G. T. Hawkins.

The present tall Dutch style buildings in Dunster Street were previously used by leather merchants and curriers (leather dressers). At the Clare Street end of Overstone Road is Bodiley's high class shoe shop which has been in business there since 1919. Opposite the shop is the shoe factory once owned by Hornby and West, and later by J Dawson and Sons. This factory stood empty for many years but was bought after the Second World War by the Brevitt Shoe Company of Leicester. When remodernised about 180 workpeople were employed here making ladies' comfortable casual shoes. This factory moved in more recent years first to the Old Hutton Shoe factory in Vicarage Road (once A E Marlows) and later to the old John Marlow factory in St George's Street. The building in Overstone Road is now a snooker hall the remainder now being occupied by the Shoe firm of Haynes and Cann founded in 1919 under the title of Young Gents Ltd.

Near the site of the present Chronicle and Echo building once stood the factory of Cove and West their foundations being laid by John Cove in 1854. He was later joined by B E West. Later, the premises were taken over by A E Marlow in 1907 with W Parker as joint managing director, a former Saints scrum half and County gymnastic champion and a golfer of repute. His first job in the boot and shoe trade was when he sat on an office stool as a young man in the factory of John Marlow and Sons. The business became the Mounts Factory Company in 1922, Parker having been joined A D Tearle. The factory was also known as Parker and Tearle. The factory closed down in 1965 and the premises were demolished in February 1970 when the area was redeveloped.

Northampton's finest piece of industrial architecture, often called the Horton and Arlidge block, stood on Campbell Square opposite the Church of the Holy Sepulchre. The two factories standing together were built as warehouses in 1857. One of the buildings was built for Isaac Campbell, (who gave his name to the Square) and was used by Horton and Arlidge who were box makers to the shoe trade after 1910. The other building with its ornamental tower was built for the famous shoe firm of M P Manfield who eventually moved to larger premises in Wellingborough Road in 1892. These two buildings which stood until the winter of 1984 had been empty and derelict for a number of years. However, because of their historical origin and significance they were both protected as "listed buildings" by the Department of the Environment. Sadly, this the oldest purpose built shoe factory in Great Britain became the target of the property developer. An appeal to the Department of the Environment by Pennine Property Developments (who had already demolished the nearby Notre Dame Convent and School) was upheld and the buildings were demolished. In their place, there has arisen a modern office block. The Department of the Environment decision to allow the grade two listed buildings to be pulled down was described as "disastrous and disappointing" by Northampton Borough councillors and many local citizens who had hoped that the buildings might become a museum of the boot and shoe industry.

Almost adjacent to the old Manfield factory was the Lotus factory in Victoria Street and Newland. Nearby at the junction of Wood Street and Lady's Lane stood the factory of H E Randall Ltd whilst in adjoining Union Street was Birdsall's box factory. In the 1880's outworkers from as far away as Cowper Street and Talbot Road used to carry work to and from Manfield's factory in the Campbell Square building when the factory was little more than a warehouse. The idea of having a shoe museum in this very building seemed the natural choice, and an excellent idea to preserve the building. Alas, blocks of offices were destined to rise in their place and most of the nearby streets, which have already given way to new roads, car parks and the Greyfriars Bus Station.

The small factory situated at number 74 Cowper Street was used by H J Bateman before his move to larger premises in St Michael's Road in the 1890's. At the corner of Cowper Street and Shakespeare Road was a boot factory with the name of H Sharman and Son. This enterprise was founded in London in 1872 and came to Northampton in 1886, first to a small factory in Spencer Road removing later to Cowper Street. John Thomas Read and his brother William commenced a business in Duke Street in 1885 moving to Cowper Street in 1893 and later to a newly built factory in Billington Street and Adams Avenue in 1897. The brothers were both practical men and continued in partnership until 1910 when owing to ill health William retired leaving the business to be carried on by John Thomas Read, who in July 1913 was joined by his son, John William. Some time later the firm became known as Read, Myall and Read and were famous for their brand of "Hotspur" football boots, used by professionals and first registered in 1894.

A well maintained old shoe factory still stands at the Hood Street and Shakespeare Road junction. It was occupied for some years prior to the Second World War and afterwards by Haynes and Cann. This company incorporated the much older business of Roland Fisher whose factory in Bearward Street has closed down. For a time the building was occupied by R and F Closers and Shoemakers. Another small firm C F Tomkins and Sons was founded in 1883 in a small house in Shakespeare Road, subsequently moving to Exeter Road (now Exeter Place) and later Pytchley Street and Ecton Street. This firm made boots for "Home, Export, and Allied Governments".

Thomas Singlehurst.

On the corner of Burns Street and Shakespeare Road is an old boot factory. This building was the original factory of Singlehurst and Gulliver. The firm was originated in 1879 by Thomas Singlehurst who started as a boot manufacturer in Turner Street at the early age of 19. After a short time he was joined by James Gulliver and they moved to Burns Street as the partnership of Singlehurst and Gulliver. Successful business made it necessary to erect a new factory in Oliver Street, Kingsley Park. This building was ultimately extended as trade further increased and was known as the "Speedwell Works". In 1898 owing to ill health James Gulliver dissolved the partnership and the business was run entirely by Thomas Singlehurst. In the following year Arthur Singlehurst, only son of Thomas, started as a lad in the factory; he later became a junior partner. He was trained in various departments and then became a salesman making important journeys to the North of England to secure trade. In June 1911 he became a full partner with his father when the business became styled as Thomas Singlehurst and Son. In 1903 the management of the factory had been put in the able hands of Harry Blake, son in law, who became an important figure in the business. Besides supplying customers throughout Britain the firm also had a warehouse in France which was an asset to them. In wartime, they also turned out quantities of British, French, and Russian army boots. Thomas Singlehurst the senior partner led a very active life outside his business. He was a town councillor and an alderman for many years, resigning in 1913 owing to failing eyesight which led to blindness. He was a great worker all his life for the Temperance Movement and was a devoted Methodist and superintendent of one of Northampton's largest Sunday Schools (Grove Road) for over thirty years. He retired from business in 1929.

Number 119 Clare Street (just off the Kettering Road) was yet another shoe factory. Until the late sixties this building was used by the famous Northampton firm of Stricklands Ltd. A visit to Strickland factory was a step back into the past; it was the largest factory in the country devoted entirely to the manufacture of handmade shoes. Here the roar of machinery was unknown and each man the master of his craft. The men who were employed there were each individual creators knowing every stitch in every shoe they made. Each calculating his measurements like a skilled engineer to a fraction of an inch. No machines were used in the process. The men were seated at their benches carefully controlling the tools and materials of their trade producing fine shoes. A handsewn or fully handmade shoe consists of first beating up the welts, the welt being a strip of leather sewn round the shoe between the upper and the sole before sewing them together. "Welt-sewing" is sewing the upper along with the welt to an insole. Nowadays this is done by machine but at the Strickland factory it was an important part of the total handmade process. Although both handsewn and machine welted shoes are still made this superb craft is no longer a principal part of shoe manufacture. The majority now have their uppers lasted flat on the insole and the sole is stuck on with powerful modern adhesives or moulded on by an injection moulding process. Stricklands Ltd was founded by W F Strickland in 1912. He was joined in 1919 by his son Sidney who later became managing director. Sidney became a local councillor and was first elected in 1932. He was later an alderman and was twice mayor of the Borough in 1944-45 and 1947-48. Stricklands amalgamated with Tebbutt Taylor in 1965 until its closure three years later.

Travelling along Clare Street in a westward direction one comes first to Spencer Road on the left in which stood the small shoe factory of John Rogers who made ladies shoes. It was known as the featherweight factory. Also at number 26 was the business of Joseph Sharman. A little further along is Grove Road and here at the junction with Clare Street is a large factory building which was once the thriving business of G M Tebbutt and Sons who manufactured shoes from the 1890's to 1968. This building in 1993 housed a dress making factory. There were few firms with a longer record of service than G M Tebbutt and Sons which was founded in 1872 by G M Tebbutt (who was the Mayor of the Borough in 1878) and who left his fathers business to start on his own account, in Robert Street making best handmade goods. Tebbutt was a deacon of College Street Baptist Church and an active Liberal. The connection of the Tebbutt family with Northamptons staple trade goes much further for Alderman Thomas Tebbutt of King Street was also a shoe manufacturer who commenced business in 1844; his sons and grandson both followed his footsteps into the trade. The principals of this established firm (known after 1952 as Tebbutt Taylors) were a continuance of many generations. Before coming to Northampton the Tebbut family had lived at Earls Barton which was then a village but famous for its shoemakers. An ancestor of the family was Lord of the Manor at Whilton near Daventry.

Tebbutts factory was one of the first firms to instal the British United Shoe Machinery welting plant and finishing machinery. The firm became a private limited company in 1912 with G M Tebbutt J.P., managing director and A E Tebbutt, director and Alfred Tebbutt, secretary. Some extensions were carried out to their Grove Road factory in 1913 absorbing adjacent property. This extension looked out over the school playground of St Mary's R.C. Boys School. It was one of the finest factories in the town at the time, and the firm never deviated from the original plan to make the finest shoes. They sought little publicity relying upon "the good wearing properties of their footwear" for future recommendation. Their goods had a worldwide reputation for colonial markets and in the United States. The firm also excelled in a range of hunting and riding footwear for which they achieved a reputation unique in the trade.

G. M. Tebbutt.

Albert E Tebbutt succeeded his father as head of the business as managing director in 1923. During his sixty years association with the company he made a special study of shoe craftsmanship. He helped to found the British Shoe and Allied Trades Research Association and was one of the founders of boot and shoe courses at the former technical school on Abington Square (latterly a cinema). His ideas were brought into fuller fruition by the establishment of the larger and later College of Technology in St Georges Avenue (later Park Campus of Nene College) where there was an extensive Boot and Shoe department. Albert

Tebbutt was also one of the founders of Northampton Chamber of Commerce and President of Northampton Boot Manufacturers Association for four consecutive years from 1920-1924. He was greatly respected for his benefactions and his patience and concern towards others. He wrote a series of textbooks for students at technical college classes in the boot and shoe trade. He died in May 1939.

Former G. M. Tebbutt Factory, Clare St/Grove Rd, Northampton.

After this Factory closed we used it as a clothing Factory Welfar.

At the far end of Clare Street opposite Overstone Road are Hunter and Hervey Street; here was situated the firm of H E Browett which flourished at the turn of the century. At the next junction with Great Russell Street and opposite the Drill Hall was a public house (the Jolly Crispin) named after the patron saint of the industry. Probably one of the most significant buildings in the whole of the Saint Crispin ward was the Saint Crispin shoe factory at the junction of Clare Street and Earl Street. Once the premises of Allinson and Company this firm celebrated their centenary in 1980 but had unfortunately to close in October 1982. There was a history of shoemaking in the Allinson family as far back as 1820 when John Allinson was a shoemaker in Knaresborough, Yorkshire. His son Alfred worked as a travelling salesman for the firm of Willis's of Worcester before deciding to enter the shoe manufacturing trade himself. Mr Willis gave Alfred Allinson some of the capital to form a business, and Alfred purchased the factory and business of Edward Haynes in St Giles

Terrace. The Haynes factory only made ladies shoes and when it became the firm of Allinson and Company in 1880 Willis became a "sleeping partner". Alfred removed to Earl Street opening the Saint Crispin's factory in 1896. His son George F Allinson succeeded him and became sole proprietor.

George Allinson set about extending and developing the business on modern lines. They produced both ladies and mens high class footwear and also did their share in wartime, supplying boots and shoes to the British and Allied Governments. George Allinson took a great interest in local charities and was instrumental in raising large sums of money for benevolent funds. He was a former President of Northampton Town Boot Manufacturers Association serving in 1932. The Allinson factory was well known for its "Our Boy's Boots for School and Play, and the celebrated manufactured boot for Ladies and Gentlemen". In the third generation George Allinson was succeeded by his two sons and in 1950 he was joined by his cousin G Allinson. After more than a century of shoemaking this well known Northampton family firm closed down in 1983 and so closed another chapter of shoemaking history.

Former St Crispin Factory of Allinsons Ltd, Clare St, Northampton.

In nearby Connaught Street were a number of small boot factories, one being used by W T

Mark. Number 32 is now occupied by Crask and Slinn and Company, shoe mercers (merchants selling components used in the manufacture of shoes). For many years the far side of adjoining Robert Street was bounded by the tall walls of Northamptons Gaol now the site of the Police and Fire Headquarters and Swimming Baths. It is difficult to imagine what it looked like in the days when so many shoe workers occupied houses in surrounding streets. Old leather factories still remain on the corner of Connaught Street but are no longer used for that part of the shoe industry.

The Boot and Shoe factory first used by Stead and Simpson (who had a larger factory at Daventry) and occupied later by Walkers stood at the bottom of Ash Street between Bailiff Street and Barrack Road. This has long since been demolished. Nearby a more modern building on a small industrial estate was used by a firm who closed the uppers of shoes and was known as Scorpion Sports Footwear (part of Tebbutt and Hall Bros. Ltd). In nearby Campbell Street was the premises of C A Quinn, footwear finishing component manufacturers now demolished for road widening. It was situated between the Holy Sepulchre churchyard and the Old Bull Hotel on Regent Square. Looking down on Campbell Street across Regent Square into St George's Street one could see a tall domed building. This was the Phoenix Shoe works which was built in 1890 for John Marlow and Sons. The firm of W J Mark started in premises in Regent Street (off Regent Square) in 1886 moving to Lorne Road at the far end of Bailiff Street, around 1922. In Campbell Street opposite the motor cycle premises of Glanfield Baldet was the firm of Woodford Gubbins who specialise in Orthopaedic footwear. This was originally the shoe firm of C E Gubbins founded as early as 1868 and who in 1912 just prior to the first World War occupied premises in Clarence Avenue, Queens Park. The Bailiff Street Area besides having houses occupied by shoe workers or leather workers also had a number of small factories in which these workers earned their living. This included the streets known as Thomas Street, Oakley Street, Lorne Road, and Louise Road. James Holmes who was a holder of a bronze medal for pattern cutting and a City and Guilds London Certificate commenced a shoemaking business in Louise Road after having twelve years experience in London West End trade. During the firms existence in Northampton the business made gents' medium and better class footwear for home and export.

It would be true to say that few people today would realise that there are not many of the older thoroughfares of Northampton which did not at one time have factories belonging to the shoe or leather trade. In the central area of old Northampton many of the smaller factories can still be seen. When handworking was the rule and many employers only had warehouses, some of these small workshops in which clickers worked, giving out and receiving work from the outworkers, were the hub of the early shoe trade. Likewise the little workshops in which the shoes were actually made still exist in many back gardens. In fact many folk pass these buildings day after day without any possible knowledge of their former history. I wonder, too, how many of the present residents of Northampton's Victorian houses realise that the workshop at the end of their house or at the bottom of their garden was most probably a cobbler's shop. As we explore the streets of central Northampton we may realise afresh the extraordinary energy and enterprise which characterised its life in times past. Due to the entrepreneurial skills of the town's boot and shoe manufacturers whole generations were given employment in an industry which made the town's name world famous.

"Old age is a sunset and sunrise in one. We cannot climb the hills as in Youth
But we can mount up on Eagles Wings".

Chapter 14

Victorian Values and Edwardian Enterprise

Following the setting up of the very earliest shoe "factories" by men like Frederick Bostock in 1836 Philip Manfield in 1844 and Henry Wooding in 1861 there appears to have been rapid growth and expansion in the shoe trade over the next twenty five years. In fact the number gradually mounted up right until the turn of the Century. The number of firms established between 1866 and 1891 was at least ten and most of these became thriving companies whose name became famous in the industry. Many of these were in operation at the time of the First World War and beyond. At least four of the larger companies are still in existence today as major shoe manufacturers in Northampton. Although many of the firms founded in the Victorian era have of course long since disappeared they were indeed very much part of Northamptons heritage and occupied an important place in the towns industry during their years of solvency. No history of our shoemakers would be complete without recalling some of them.

A firm called Jonathan Robinson was founded as early as the year 1850 by Jonathan Robinson in premises situated in Bath Street which at that time was regarded as being part of the Central Area. He moved to large and more modern factory premises in Countess Road in December 1901. Such was the quality of their work that they supplied boots and shoes to the Royal Family and they had offices in London and Paris. The son of the founder J P Robinson became a partner and the firm flourished until well after the first World War. Simon Colliers was another firm which became well known. Founded in 1865 by Alderman William Collier who was a prominent citizen and later became a Mayor of Northampton. The Company later developed under the control of Simon Collier Senior and it prospered exceedingly. The firm occupied a large factory in Harlestone road, St James, extending from Spencer Bridge Road to St James Square with branches on Campbell Square and at the village of Kislingbury.

It was said that there was no finer judge of leather or on possessing more expert knowledge than Simon Collier. This undoubtedly led to his success in business. Other directors of the Company were Mr J V Collier and Mr Simon Collier Junior. The latter Director was a representative for South africa for which country they did a large trade. One of their triumphs was that during the Great War of 1914, this firm produced a million pairs of army boots at the rate of 15,000 pairs a week nearly 3,000 pairs a day. It was stated at the time, that had these boots been laid end to end they would have stretched 380 miles in length. In later years after the firm closed down the premises were occupied first by the Mettoy Toy Company and later by Wembley Sportsmaster Ltd. The whole building was demolished in April 1993 for new development. This site is now occupied by the Aldi and Iceland supermarkets.

James Branch had opened a factory in London in 1866 and moved into the Bective factory in Kingsthorpe Northampton in 1901. The London factory was sold in 1931 and in 1937 the company began an association with Rice-O-Neil of St Louis, USA. It was one of the first Anglo-American tie ups. The firm was also a victim of a take over in the years after the second World War when it became part of the Scholl Group and traded under the name of Scholl Footwear. The factory is no longer in existence and has been replaced by a row of shops.

In 1872 the firm of George Green and Son of Leicester established a branch in Commercial Street and with the introduction of machinery moved to a factory in Stimpson Avenue in 1892. This firm became a separate company in 1902. Two extensions were made to the building but a disastrous fire destroyed it on March 3rd 1913. Temporary premises were found on Campbell Square and business was conducted on a reduced scale. The factory in Stimpson Avenue was rebuilt and opened 1914 with Mr S H Green as Managing Director. He was supported by another Director Mr H Johnson who had joined the firm in 1905 after spending thirteen years in the United States. Another firm, founded in 1881 in the Central Area, was the firm of Latimer and Crick and Company. On the retirement of Mr Latimer in 1892 the firm became known as Crick and Gunn. When a few years later Mr Gunn also retired the business was conducted as Crick and Company. This firm also made high class Ladies and Gents footwear and during the First World War did large quantities of army work for both the British and Allied Governments.

The Unicorn Boot Company formed in 1887 by Walter Beale and T G Beale as stated in the previous chapter had a factory in St Michaels Road in the heart of the old Boot and Shoe area. This factory became well known and its proprietor Walter Beale was president of the Boots Manufacturers Association from 1904-1907 when he succeeded William Hickson. Two firms established in 1891 were W B Stevens and Company and A Jackson and the British Shoe Company (BSC) not to be confused with the British Shoe Corporation of recent times (also BSC). The firm of W B Stevens and A Jackson were known to have turned out a quarter of a million pairs of Army boots for British, Russian, Italian and Serbian Armies during the 1914-18 conflict. The British Shoe Company which was probably known better as John and G H Roe commenced business in a modest way in 1891 in St James Street removing to Gregory Street and Freeschool Street in 1895. They became multiple shop owners and exporters with branches in all parts of the country. They produced some of the finest shoes in Northampton. The year 1895 saw the founding of Abraham Lee's Enterprise Boot Company in Bective Road, Kingsthorpe. This firm was also still in being during the Second World War and became a Limited Company in 1942. It has since joined the ever increasing number of factory closure and the factory is now used for other purposes.

The boot and shoe trades journal of this period in history was often very critical of the men's output in the factories. On 30th April 1880 it stated "the election and the races, interfere with trade, and despite order to hand and the recent depression there's a strong disposition as ever on the part of the workpeople to avail themselves of every excuse for a holiday and to extend it beyond reasonable limits". The short period before Whitsuntide was always one of great rush in the industry. A report also in the Boot and Shoe Trade Journal of 23rd May 1885 said "During this rush period, it is difficult to get work done. The workers know they can have it ready when wanted yet they do just what they like and more. There seems to be no control over Rivetters and Finishers either indoor or outdoor workers as to how much they shall do or how long they shall work. They appear to have every licence to do as they like; while on the other hand, clickers and other indoor hands must expect summary dismissal if they are not at their work regularly and turn out so much per week. The manufacturers ought to have this opportunity of making up for the slackness which is sure to prevail after the holidays and his employees ought to make up for the loss of earnings during that quiet time. It is however a fact that in the majority of cases the workmen have no idea of the future".

Whether or not these comments seem to be justified it is hard to say but it must be remembered that some work was still done in home workshops and those who had gone into factories "indoor workers", as they were so often referred to, were not entirely happy with factory life. There was also a reluctance on the part of the employers to upgrade the men's wages in return for their eagerness to increase production and so expand their business. With the men's union now operating efficiently employers all looked toward a better future and to this one end the Boot and Shoe Union dedicated the whole of their resources. Just as the manufacturers sought to increase trade in their factories, and so make them profitable, so did the men's union strive to achieve better working conditions, sensible hours and living wages for all their members.

Shortly after this the Boot and Shoe Journal announced on the 18th January 1890 that the firm of Stubbs and Grimsdell became the first Northampton firm to concentrate all processes under one roof and this was followed by Philip Manfields revolutionary new factory in 1892. Meanwhile George Thomas Hawkins became the first Boot manufacturer to lay down a complete finishing department. Steadily the Boot and Shoe trade flourished and Northampton made footwear became known the World over. As the town expanded so it seems did its Boot and Shoe factories. The population of Northampton expanded rapidly form 61,000 in 1891 to 87,000 including Far Cotton and St James.

In the east of the town the Borough petered out on Billing Road around St Andrew's Hospital and between there and Weston Favell there was almost an untouched stretch of countryside. North of the town the Borough ended at the Cock Hotel with Kingsthorpe beyond, a village in open country. Franklin's Gardens in St James was the terminal point for the horse-drawn tramways on the western side of the town. To the east on the Kettering Road the Borough ended at the White Elephant Hotel, and the part of Kingsley Road towards the Romany public house and Kingsthorpe Grove, was known as Gipsy Lane and was also in open countryside. The greater part of the town's workforce were employed in the boot and shoe industry and the town "boasted" 240 public houses which attracted many of the town's shoemakers. Whilst the working class were still very predominant there was beginning to emerge a much stronger middle class. A substantial number of three or four bedroomed houses could be rented by shoe workers for around five or six shillings a week.

East of the Kettering Road many new firms came into business. Opposite Henry Street, the premises now occupied by J T Meadows and Son (Leather Merchants) was originally the Boot factory of Flack and Durrant. Meadows had the much smaller building at 76 Artizan Road. The buildings at the bottom of Henry Street were once used by an important footwear firm known as John Branch and nearby Arnold Brothers but only Charles Smith (Top Boots) remains. The small factory at number 74 was used by J H Bateman before his move in the 1890's to St Michael's Road. At the corner of Billington Street and Artizan Road the building now occupied by Tone Footwear was one of the many shoe factories used by James Branch Ltd and later by the high grade footwear manufacturers Crockett and Jones whose factory is now in Perry Street. John Branch formed in 1890 were also in London before moving to Northampton and were also in business in larger premises in Henry Street for many years. There were two large factories in Talbot Road: one was the factory of Arnold Brothers Ltd and is now occupied by a dress making firm; the other was Oakeshott and Finnemore, later Norvic Brand Footwear. On this site modern flats have been built. Two small upper making firms once operated from 43 and 94 Talbot Road.

The fortunes of the firm of Oakeshott and Finnemore are retold in another chapter as is the story of Messrs Crockett and Jones. Arnold Brothers however was an offshoot of A and W Arnold of St Giles Terrace. This factory in Henry Street also had a large frontage in Talbot Road. The business was established by William and Matthew Arnold, a partner in the firm of A and W Arnold. A year or two after the two brothers launched out in business for themselves they took over the large factory in Henry Street which was the company's headquarters from 1909 until they finally closed down. This shoe manufacturing business represented the third and fourth generation of a shoemaking family. As early as 1898 Will Arnold Junior had as a lad of twelve worked as a shoemakers apprentice in his fathers factory where he graduated to working at a clicking board. In the St Giles Terrace factory he had worked a fifty four hour week for the princely sum of five shilling. Clickers in those days earned twenty six shillings to twenty eight shillings a week. William Arnold Junior, like his father, was a prominent Methodist and an accomplished local preacher.

Various factories opened in the large area between Kettering Road and Wellingborough Road at the turn of the century and in the roads stretching towards Abington Park. Besides the large factories of Manfield, Crockett and Jones and the True Form factory all built within a decade. Prominent among others was the firm of Hornby and West who moved from Overstone Road to Wycliffe Road. This factory was destroyed by a disastrous fire in the late twenties. The factory of F W Panther in Barry Road was still in business in 1990 as part of the British Shoe Corporation and closed down in 1991.

Former Factory of Simon Collier, Harlestone Rd, Northampton.

The west end of Northampton, better known as St James, also saw many developments in the trade. In addition to the firm of Simon Collier and the "Progressive" factory of C and E Lewis "Jimmy's End" also became the home of Padmore and Barnes (now Church's Footwear) and A E Marlow. In the closing year of the 19th Century which was perhaps the most crucial year in that century in the history of British Boot and Shoe making; Albert E Marlow, first launched his business over a Butchers shop at the top of Overstone Road. (now Bodily's shoe shop). It was in the year 1899, a year when manufacturers in the county began to realise that there were rivals in the field more formidable than any that had menaced the trade in this country. America, for example, had then reached a high level of prosperity in the trade.

Albert Marlow was a go-ahead young man who had spent all of his working life working for his father John Marlow in his Phoenix factory in St George's Street. In July 1899 Albert decided to sever his connection with his fathers firm and started on his own account. Whilst his business progressed in a small way he was already negotiating with Lord Spencer's estate manager for ground belonging to the Earl in St. James, Northampton. The place was something of a wilderness and some distance from the town but he acquired the site which covered four acres and he built his factory in 1900. Like that of Manfields it was built on the "one floor system" with offices fronting Vicarage Road.

Albert Marlow appointed as his manager George Webb who was a life long friend and associate. Marlow also became proprietor of the Mounts factory which he acquired in 1907 with W. Parker. He also became Managing Director of John Cave and Sons of Rushden. Marlow became in 1905 the youngest Mayor of the Borough and Chief Magistrate at 33 years of age. He was an active business man who was never afraid to speak his mind. He became President of the Boot and Shoe Manufacturers Association during the Great War and a founder of St Matthew's Nursing Home. In 1936 the factory was acquired by Hutton Welted Footwear a new Company which also had premises in Countess Road.

The well known firm of Padmore and Barnes was formed at the turn of the century by W. Barnes who was joined in business later by George Padmore. Their first factory was in Thomas Street, off Bailiff Street, where Barnes produced boots by hand labour. When the introduction of machinery for welt sewing and stitching revolutionised the industry the partners were the first to install a complete plant and to adapt themselves to all subsequent new methods. So great was the demand for their products that the firm moved to larger works in St James in 1901. This factory after many extensions became one of the largest and best equipped in the industry. The firm was said to have installed the first sewing machine used in the closing room and it is reported to have been worked by a Miss Betty King. One of their longest serving directors was Sidney Davis who became a director in 1908 at the early age of twenty six. Sidney had started his working life as an office boy in the factory of G Dawson and Son in Overstone Road. When George Padmore retired in 1932, Davis became Chairman and Managing Director. A position he retained until his death on 4th January 1954 at the age of seventy two. Davis was President of the Northampton Town Boot Manufacturers Association in 1934 and his enterprise led to the founding of a sister company, the Moccasin factory at Kilkenny. The firm used a picture "on watch" as its trademark. It was of a Red indian in the famous headdress, with his eyes scanning the distant landscape. In 1954 a Company was formed to take over the factory and it became known as Moccasin Shoemakers. The chairman was P S Davis with joint managing directors, R Dunwell and C

G Davis. Moccasins became a well respected firm making high grade footwear which was said to have "secured a firm hold on British feet and with more of the World's surface covered by them than any other high grade boot made in Britain".

Another firm emerged at this time; Edward Green began making hand-crafted shoes for gentlemen in 1890 and quickly gained a reputation of making "the finest shoes in England for the discerning few". The firm moved to the "Westminster Works" in Oliver Street, Kingsley Park in 1904, premises which they still occupy. In 1983, John Hlustik took over the firm with the aim of reviving the shoemaking craft. Hlustik brought with him experience of designing and making shoes in Milan and Paris. Edward Green shoes are mostly hand-made and take six weeks to complete, being worked on by fifty-seven different craftsmen. Uppers are cut by hand from high quality calfskins, then are hand-sewn using a hog's bristle needle, rolled around Edward Green's own 7 ply waxed Irish flax/twine. The thread is pulled through a hole made by a flat awl thus making a smooth almost invisible hole in the leather. The shoe is then formed by pulling the finished upper over one of the original Edward Green "lasts", many of which are over 40 years old. Then the welt is stitched to the shoe, either by hand-sewing or using traditional machines which have been carefully restored. Finally, the soles, made from fine oak bark tanned leather are stitched to the shoe which is then trimmed, finished and "antiqued". This antiquing takes several days, with many layers of polish and wax being specially blended and worked in by hand to bring out the richness, depth and fine grain of the calfskin. Edward Green also make shoes to customer requirements and prepare special orders such as the Household Cavalry Officers' thigh-length ceremonial boots.

During the reign of Queen Victoria 19th Century Britain had witnessed time of industrial expansion bringing new techniques of mass production which in the early stages had created ill feeling and opposition rather than increased production and prosperity. The Diamond Jubilee of Queen Victoria in 1897 was a scene of great celebration especially in Northampton and marked the triumph of a sovereign who had given her name to an era and a particular type of society that was later described as Victorian meaning pompous and prudish. Even buildings of the era have long since been described as being of Victorian Architecture. Queen Victoria's reign came to an end in 1901 just after the turn of the century after sixty four years. She was succeeded by her Son Edward Prince of Wales who became Edward the Seventh. Edward was reckoned to be a flamboyant character, and his reign brought many changes too.

In Northamptonshire the boot and shoe industry seemed firmly established. The changes that were making themselves felt in the town were very obvious. For instance the first electric tramways appeared in the town in 1904, replacing the old horse-drawn-trams. Tramways became a favourite means of travel for shoe workers whose occupations were on the outskirts of town. The motor car was just beginning to emerge on the streets in small numbers but none were owned by the working classes. Those within walking distance of factories went on foot, others cycled. Many other things came, such as electric light, but the majority of homes, factories and shops were hitherto lit by gaslight or even by oil lamps where gas was not connected. The coming of electricity was to herald a new era. The introduction of the telephone meant better and easier communication for businesses and those private citizens who could afford it. Horse-drawn carriages began to disappear as cars and motor buses replaced them. All these things had a far reaching day to day effects on the lives of ordinary folk throughout the country.

During the Edwardian period for nine years the Borough of Northampton was to receive a number of distinguished visitors. Each of them were to make some impact on the nation's history and well being. There were also a number of important events one of which was the Coronation of King Edward the Seventh, an occasion for celebration in the town. The year 1905 was the year of the famous Raunds shoeworkers strike in which Northampton Union officers were involved. Also in that year the town received a visit from General William Booth, father of the Salvation Army who addressed a large meeting in the Corn Exchange, on Market Square. Twenty three years earlier he had also come to Northampton and had received a very rough ride indeed from shoeworkers of the Borough and was stoned by a mob who poured tar on his carriage. During 1906 Liberal politician Henry Herbert Asquith, later the Earl of Oxford, addressed a meeting in Northampton on June 16th and was heckled by suffragettes who were becoming organised in the crusade for votes for women. On 26th June. In the same year American Millionaire Andrew Carnegie who was Scottish born donated £15,000 to the town for the building of a library and hall. Another upheaval in industry was felt in 1907 when Northampton shoeworkers staged a general strike on 26th January. There was still a lot of dissatisfaction amongst workers not only about wage rates, but of disciplinary measures taken by foremen and the constant threat of dismissal because of poor productivity. The following year of 1908 saw the first ever motor cars in Northampton streets and on 9th April Mrs Sylvia Pankhurst, the leader of the suffragette movement, addressed a meeting in the town. On a lighter recreational note the well-known bathing place in Midsummer Meadow was opened on 26th July. For more than sixty years this venue was popular with shoeworkers and their families. In the later summer of 1908 crowds flocked to Delapre Park when the famous pioneer airman Gusta Hamel landed there in a Bleriot monoplane of the same type as that which the inventor Louis Bleriot had made history by completing the first air crossing of the English Channel on 25th July.

Business in the Boot and Shoe trade was booming again having begun to pick up during 1907 and factories were busy turning out their orders for home and abroad. The first ever court of arbitration appointed by the Board of Trade sat in Northampton on 7th January 1909 to rule on shoeworkers' union claims. The shoe industry despite increased trade was still having its problems and the mens union, ever mindful of the needs of its members, was very persistent in its efforts to secure successful arbitration. Industrial topics, especially disputes, never went unnoticed by the media and other local citizens; on 10th September 1910 the vicar of the Church of the Holy Sepulchre, the Reverend Charles Brookes, summed up the problems in quite a different though less graphic way. Writing in the Episcopal Visitation Return he said: "The strain of daily life nowadays, prevents, people form giving the time they used to do to religious exercises. Increasing strain and anxiety about daily life leads to a great yearning for excitement for a something that will relieve the monotony of a life spent at a machine".

Earlier in 1910 on 6th May the death of King Edward the Seventh brought another reign to an end and on 10th June the new library and Carnegie Hall were opened in Abington Street. This imposing building was erected on the former site of the stables used for the horse-drawn trams which had been discontinued upon electrification. The building is still Northampton's Central Library. With industry prospering and the town expanding the census taken in 1911 revealed a population of 90,000 people in the Borough. The Duke of York had succeeded to the throne as King George the Fifth and on 22nd June was crowned king with his queen Mary again there were celebrations in both town and county. For most people their lives went on as normal with a gradual acceptance of the changing scenes of life which seemed to be making a steady impact on the industrial and working life of the community. Many of the leading citizens had long cherished the hope that other industries would come to the town but sadly it was a hope that was to remain largely unfulfilled for more than half a century. The boot and shoe industry was, and remained for many years, the staple industry.

Politically the country had a Liberal Government under Asquith and the town Liberal members of parliament. Few working people realised that as the international situation changed and unrest grew that the whole of the country would soon be plunged into the worst crisis that had ever been known. On 27th August 1912 the county experienced great floods throughout the Nene Valley causing hardship to families. After recovering from this disaster the town prepared to welcome King George and Queen Mary who paid a state visit on 23rd September 1913. It was a great occasion for citizens orf both town and county. The King and Queen were welcomed to the Borough by the Mayor Alderman W Harvey Reeves. This important event gave a great boost to the town and its trade. However, almost a year later "dark clouds" began to appear over Europe. Events led to the outbreak of hostilities and by 4th August 1914 Britain found itself at the beginning of a war which was to claim millions of lives and change the social fabric of the nation. The pattern of life in Britain changed immediately as thousands of men were called to the colours and Lord Kitchner's famous poster "Your King and Country need you" appeared on the streets. On 1st September sixteen thousand troops of the Welsh Brigade were billeted in private houses in Northampton; the Borough virtually became a garrison town.

Whilst hundreds of shoeworkers left the factories to serve their country in the armed forces the war did in fact bring a certain amount of prosperity to the staple trade. It was announced that an avalanche of army boot orders for France as well as England had descended on Northampton. It was felt that not only would the town benefit by the influx of army orders but there was the probability of Northampton becoming a very important military base. By 31st October 50,000 pairs of army boots had already been manufactured for the allied armies. The French asked for two million pairs of boots, Britain 400,000 pairs for the army and 70,000 pairs for the navy. Thirty Northampton firms sent in tenders and all were accepted. The immediate prosperity brought by the war, however, was very soon overshadowed by the loss of shoeworkers into the armed forces as the men, some of them quite young, went to fight on the battlefields of Europe. There were many fierce battles, some raging for almost a whole year, and the loss of life was appalling. Some of the fiercest fighting of the war took place in 1916 in the battles of the Somme, and at Verdun in France. During the Battle of the Somme River alone the British sustained a loss of 171,000 troops. In that year in Northampton on 8th March German zeppelins passed over the town after dark and bombs were dropped on the outskirts. Between 26th and 31st March there was the worst blizzard in Northampton for forty years and over a million tons of snow fell within twenty four hours inside the Borough boundary. The Corn Exchange was turned into a recreation centre for troops during the war years. The shoe factories continued to turn out boots and shoes for the war effort and Albert Marlow said in praise of the industry: "Thirty years ago shoemaking in Northampton was just emerging from the domestic handicraft stage, to what is now a highly organised industry". Later, a letter to the President of the National Association of Manufacturers Owen J Parker, J.P. from Lord Kitchener, Minister for War said: "In carrying out the work of providing the army with its equipment employers and employed alike are doing their duty to King and Country equally with those who have joined the army for service in the field".

The long dark years eventually ended and on 11th November 1918 the Armistice was signed and an end brought to the fighting. But for many families who had lost loved ones there was great sadness. Peace celebrations were held in Northampton on 19th July 1919 and ended with a mass thanksgiving service on the Market Square. It was said that the conflict was "the war to end all wars". There were Victory parties in the streets and slowly people began to rebuild their lives. Gradually, as demobilisation took place, the battle weary survivors returned to their families, their homes and their work.

Former Boot factory of A. E. Marlow, Vicarage Rd, Northampton.

Pre 2nd World War Scene. Finishing room of Mentone Shoe Works (George Webb & Sons) Brockton St, Northampton.

"In the track of Great Armies, there must follow lean years".

Chapter 15

An Inspiration, Male Initiative and Mail Order

"You can tell a man's character - or a woman's by looking at his or her shoes". This is a saying that is attributed to an old cobbler and could be the inspiration behind the fascinating story of the Barratt Brothers, whose name was to become a household word and whose products were to achieve a world-wide reputation. William Barratt was born in 1877. His father was a silk weaver living in Desborough, who when thrown out of work walked to Northampton to learn the shoe trade, eventually opening a shoe shop in Abington Street. He had seven sons and two of the seven brothers, David and William, soon acquired a skill of selling boots both leaving school at the age of twelve and working in their father's shop.

William Barratt.

In those days little was known about the art of fitting shoes with understanding of sizes, widths and shapes meagre in the extreme. This condemned the owner of a large, wide, or slightly unusual foot to a most uncomfortable future. This problem later provided William Barratt and his company with a basis for making comfortable footwear a primary consideration. William migrated to London where he worked for some years in other retail shops selling boots and shoes. Here he gained human understanding as well as a complete knowledge of the feet. This all served to confirm his more youthful impressions whilst working for his father that the well-being of his fellow men and women was sadly neglected. Whilst serving this "apprenticeship" in London he married on a wage of seventeen shillings and sixpence a week and lived in one room in Islington. He returned to live in Northampton in his early twenties and opened a shop in the Drapery with his brother David. He became absorbed with the idea of selling boots by post. This method had gained ground in America but was entirely new in this country. This novel idea of supplying boots by post was really inspired by a speculation of David and William's elder brother Harry, who was then a foreman in a Northampton boot factory. Harry ventured to purchase several cases of shop-soiled boots and misfits at a factory in the county. As William had a shoe shop in the Drapery Harry at once suggested that Will should sell them. The offer was declined when Will discovered that all the shoes were size eight. But Harry with the pertinacity of the Barratt family inserted an advert in a London newspaper offering one pair of Glace Kid Boots

- misfits at a sweeping bargain of one guinea this was four times more than he had paid for them at the sale. The result was astonishing, for he was inundated with letters containing money from all over the country and the stock was speedily sold. This soon gave Will Barratt an insight into the potential of advertising boots by post. He told Harry, "If you can sell boots by post so easily, then there's a fortune to be made in developing the idea". William at once invited Harry to join him in launching his postal business on a large scale, but Harry hesitated and then declined as he felt settled in his employment as a foreman. He therefore missed the ultimate opportunity of becoming a shoe magnate on a big scale.

In his younger days William had been a keen amateur boxer which obviously endowed him with a spirit of adventure, and this, combined with a will to win, became the whole driving force behind the Barratt business. His enthusiasm was born of an intimate knowledge of working men from his early life of "ups and downs" of human existence which served to make him a born leader in later life. Finances were low but with enthusiasm and boundless energy David and William Barratt translated their inspiration into action. From a small idea in one room over the shop in the Drapery the Barratt "Footshape" business was born. Financial support for the first boots by post scheme came from Mr J Clarke of Messrs Jacques and Clark of Rushden (shoe manufacturers). This support was of a considerable nature. Another helper was Albert E Catt (a shoe machinery agent) who later became a director of the Barratt company. This help undoubtedly assisted the Barratt brothers to launch their enterprising scheme. Their first advertisement in 1903 blossomed out in the course of the years, into large adverts, under the "Walk the Barratt Way" slogan. The first advert for mail order shoes was an insignificant four inch single column insertion in the "Carpenter and Builder" offering workmen's boots of sound quality with stout uppers and thick soles at a reasonable price and in a large range of sizes and widths hitherto unheard of. Customers were required to draw an outline of the foot on a piece of paper. This method of establishing the size and shape of the foot still has adherents the world over. The writer remembers having a pair of shoes made by an Egyptian cobbler in wartime using this age old method. A perfect fitting pair of shoes was the result. The isolated village populations were particularly drawn to the new mail order scheme. In those days transport into towns was a long trek on foot or meant being squeezed into the horsedrawn covered-in "Carriers Cart". This mode of transport accommodated no more than six people after goods had been loaded for market.

Enquiries from the advertisement poured in to the Drapery shop and would-be customers enclosed money and a pencilled outline of the feet for which the shoes were required. It proved to be an outstanding success and only the two brothers did all the work, toiling feverishly and for long hours. They replied to correspondence without mechanical aids or secretarial help. Both executed the orders, packed parcels and prepared the other adverts which followed. Catalogues became necessary as a result of the many enquiries for walking as well as working boots. From the deluge of orders which followed the first advertisements the famous men's walking boot developed. This boot retailed at eight shillings and sixpence (42.5p) pair. The business prospered and large premises had to be acquired and additional staff taken on. Two other brothers, Albert and Richard, joined the founders. However, David who had helped William pioneer the project, ultimately sought new adventures elsewhere leaving William, Albert and Richard in control, a partnership that was to last for many years. With their fingers unerringly on the pulse of the public the Barratt brothers stocked their warehouses with comfortable widths and shapes such as had only been dreamed of by millions of foot sufferers who knew the precise meaning of "breaking in of a shoe". The personal attention given by the brothers to each of their individual customers earned for them a unique reputation which was to last for many years when they entered into manufacturing boots and shoes for themselves.

The advent of the first mechanical vehicle, the motor car, to appear on Northampton's roads spelled the demise of the carriers' carts. The idea of buying and obtaining boots by post started to wane and a new era of shopping emerged as people from the surrounding villages were able to travel into nearby towns and so get a personal fit and a better choice of footwear by visiting shops of their choice. With wise foresight the Barratt Brothers led by William decided to become manufacturers. Eventually their own new modern and ornate factory was built in 1913 on the site where William used to fish for "tiddlers" in a lake in the days of his youth. The factory built on Primrose Hill, Kingsthorpe Road, was aptly named "Footshape Works".

The Footshape Boot Works (W. Barratt & Co. Ltd) Kingsthorpe Rd, Northampton.

The building was a fine example of the architecture of the period, a palatial building with a fine stone front and a large clock set in the midst of the factory name. The building was the design of a Scottish architect A. E. Anderson. The factory was gradually equipped with the most modern machinery and skilled methods of production were used to carry out the numerous operations in shoemaking. These mass methods resulted in the operatives working at uncanny speeds, a strange contrast to the laborious awl and thread method of the handworkers of old.

Clicking Dept, (W Barratt & Co. Ltd).

Closing Room, (W Barratt & Co. Ltd).

Like the earlier modern Manfield factory described in a previous chapter the Barratt "Footshape" works was a model of comfort, light and hygiene. Four impressive extensions took place in the space of fifteen years. With the passing of time it became a limited liability company and there came the latest and most modern additions to air conditioning, fluorescent lighting, fan ducts to carry away dust and impurities, a workers canteen and "Music while you work" over the radio. In fact all the amenities were introduced which the Barratt Brothers considered necessary to make happy and healthy workers and incidentally good shoes. William Barratt was once asked by someone being taken on a conducted tour of his factory: "How do you, and those around you manage to work in such regal surroundings"? "Why shouldn't we be comfortable', he replied, "We spend most of our conscious hours at our business and we endeavour to make those hours as pleasurable and as profitable as possible".

The first branch shop was opened at 22 Cheapside, London in 1914 together with an ambitious programme of branches which only materialised after the termination of World War One. The success of Barratts was a supreme story of united effort. William Barratt gathered around him capable young men with a professional and progressive outlook who alongside his brothers showed enthusiasm in business. Their wisdom and experience was inherited by another three brothers, Norman and Dennis (the sons of Richard) and David (son of Albert). Norman remained a director of the firm until his death in 1984. The company was soon at the top of its profession employing skilful shoe designers and pattern cutters and, in conjunction with the directors, originated and designed "the fashions of tomorrow". Two brands named "Perm-arch" and "Footshape" were designed and made with a permanent arch support for customers who had fallen arches. These and other concealed joint-fitting shoes soon became popular with those who had problems with new footwear. Arising from the latter designs was another distinguished brand of Barratts called "Soft Spots" proclaimed as "high lights of luxury and super smartness for unlucky joints, albeit that they hide under their attractive exterior for there is ample room and a soothing chamois-lined pocket to protect the tender joint".

The policy of the Barratt Company was always a forward one with the continual growth of the retail establishments until almost every large town and city in the country had one or more Barratt branch. The huge stockrooms boasted as many as 70,000 pairs of shoes in stock. If anyone asked for a particular pair of boots or shoes they could be told in a minute whether or not their own particular size and fitting was available. Advertising continued to play an important part in the sales drive and the famous Barratt advert with its slogan "Walk the Barratt Way" was inspired and always written by William Barratt himself and his picture appeared in every advertisement. Each advertisement was carefully phrased and placed in the prominent pages of national newspapers and many foreign ones. The name of Barratt and its famous slogan became a household name not only in Great Britain and the Commonwealth but practically every part of the world was represented.

The familiar advert carrying the photograph of the founder of the firm William Barratt wearing the traditional English bowler hat was always followed by a personal message. It not only brought prosperity to the firm and works for its hundreds of employees but assisted to make the name of Northampton, the capital of the world's boot and shoe industry, known in every corner of the Globe. - A typical advertisement was as follows:

"It's become an old family custom...it must be fifteen years ago, Mr Barratt, that I bought my

first pair of your shoes and now here are my two youngsters being fitted out in the same branch. The rising generation doesn't always agree with its elders these days but they trust their dear old Dad, in his choice of their shoes.

WALK THE BARRATT WAY"

Barratts adverts were translated into most languages from Chinese to Arabic and drew correspondence and orders from people of all races.

On 10th September 1921 a letter was received at the head office from a person who by nature of his special profession knew the value of having boots made from prime leather. The letter came from none other than the distinguished explorer Sir Ernest Shackleton It read:-

"I wish to equip each member of the Shackleton - Rowett expedition with a pair of your double sole boots, particulars of which are attached. Will you please ensure that these are delivered by Friday next the tenth instant as the ship is due to sail next day".

Signed E H Shackleton

The boots were gladly supplied so on the "Quest" Barratts' boots travelled to the frozen wastes of the Antarctic and were worn on a voyage of discovery during which exploration the gallant pioneer explorer lost his life.

The Barratt brothers constantly sought to build up a reputation of quality and service to all their customers. This kind of reliability and consideration was no less reflected in their dealings with their employees. Every effort was made for the comfort and happiness of all their workers many who spent a lifetime of service with the company having been employed there from its inception. One of the welfare schemes of which the company could be proud was its benevolent fund for sick workers. Remembering that between the wars State sickness benefits were not as they are today. The benevolent fund was administered by a committee of management and employees with workers representatives in each department of the factory. Each employee could elect to make a small weekly contribution to the fund which was deducted from his or her salary or weekly wage packet. This contribution was doubled by management. The fund ensured that an employee had considerable financial assistance in the case of illness. In 1935 a non contributory pension scheme was inaugurated together with a superannuation fund. This non contributory pension scheme invested quite a proportion of its money in Barratt shares and many retired employees still receive pensions as a result of the wisdom of their employers. During the Second World War a payment of over £66,000.00 was made in grants to employees on war service.

The amazing success of William Barratt and his brothers was achieved without any of the advantages of early riches or of social position. The sympathetic concern for the welfare of his two thousand employees and the comfort of those working in his model factory and the vivid memories that will remain of his munificence (described in another chapter) and the personality that had become so familiar to newspaper readers through his conversational adverts, are a legacy that Northampton can be proud of. A record of public service enabled William to be returned to the Borough Council in 1929 as a Labour Councillor. He was a natural leader in the Labour Party and a supporter of the Socialist cause to the end of his life.

After five years on the Council and a Borough Magistrate he was adopted and fought Bethnal Green in London as a Labour Candidate. He was invited to stand again in 1935 but declined.

He was a great supporter of the Saints Rugby Football Club and followed its fortunes for forty years. In 1927 he was President of the club and donated £500 towards a new stand and helped the club in other ways. He was a very keen bowls player belonging to the County Ground Club and was a pioneer of motor cycle trials. In 1939 Richard Barratt died and it was felt that William never got over the death of his Brother. He too suffered a complete breakdown in health brought on it was thought by considerable overwork. Will had anticipated joining his brother Albert (who had retired from business earlier to live in the seaside resort of Clacton) anticipating a long period of convalescence before returning to Northampton. Sadly in the late Autumn a return of his illness occurred and he died in December 1939 aged 62.

Control of the business then passed to yet another generation of Barratt brothers, Norman, Dennis, and David, who with their fellow directors continued to maintain the high standards of expert craftsmanship inherited from generations of skilled workers combined with fine leathers and other materials. Each of these gave a consistently high quality and being among the basic factors on which this Northampton firm's reputation for fine quality shoes depended. The Barratt factory was taken over by Stylo Shoes of Leeds in 1964 and was closed down in 1971. After sixty eight years in business the name of Barratt as a boot and shoe manufacturer disappeared; the model factory is now put to other uses but its ornate facade is a reminder to all who pass by of its importance in the town's one-time staple industry.

"Some things come to the poor that cannot get into the doors of the rich, whose money blocks the way".

Chapter 16

The Custodians of Savile Row

"What would your reply be", said a friend, "if you were asked: how many soles might a shoe be thought to take"?

We who heard that question thought a little and replied with circumspection:- "It would depend", we said, "upon the condition of the rest part of the shoe". "That," said our friend, "might well have been a reply but now listen", said the narrator, "here is a surprise". My friend fetched me a pair of shoes that were but recently repaired. They were well used in the uppers and insoles but with newly attached soles they were sound and good for further wear. I was asked "How many soles do you think this pair had had"? I waited for him to give me the answer to his own question and it came. "This is the seventh new sole on that one pair and you would be interested to know that upon that pair of shoes was the name of the maker George Webb, Savile Row, Number 222".

The above story was retold in one of the Webb's News Bulletins, a monthly works magazine issued to all employees at their Mentone works in Brockton Street, Kingsthorpe Hollow, Northampton. This was a magazine that was originally sent out to all employees who were serving in the armed forces during the Second World War. Later it evolved into a regular works magazine. The incident quoted in this particular issue, referred to the name of Savile Row which was one of the many trade names of George Webb and Sons Limited and it became known as one of the leading brands of footwear sold in this country. The firm was renowned for its expert styling and very wide variety of fittings giving a choice of different cuts and colours as well as different shapes and leathers. The name of Savile Row made the name of George Webb famous for its men's shoes.

George Webb.

George Webb obtained his first experience in the shoe trade with a firm called Messrs Seaby in a small factory in Regent Street. In 1899 he was invited by a friend Albert E Marlow to become the works manager for the business he had just started. Albert Marlow, his brother John Marlow and George Webb were all fellow members of Henry Coopers Bible Class at Doddridge Church at the time. George Webb was also an ardent worker at the nearby Castle Street Mission associated with the Church on Castle Hill. Both George Webb and Albert Marlow were masters of their craft with the possessing of additional gifts of organisation and enterprising initiative. Some of the older manufacturers in the trade looked rather askance at the new methods and energetic enterprise that these comparative youngsters in the trade were introducing. However they forged ahead and the competition became wholesome and the whole industry began to benefit from the activities which the firm of A E Marlow brought into play. When Albert Marlow died suddenly in the Langham Hotel in London in 1922 at the age of 51 it was his close friend and manager George Webb who was appointed managing director of the limited liability company that was formed to run the business. With George Webb at the helm and with Albert's brother John Marlow as a fellow director a contract was signed to last for five years.

George Webb appointed as his works manager W H Hall who followed A D Tearle who left the firm to join W Parker in partnership at the Mounts factory trading as Parker and Tearle. A D Tearle was known to be a prominent churchman and was church warden at St James Church. Whilst in the employ of A E Marlow first Webb had introduced his two sons Dennis and Frank to the business. Both started at the Marlow factory when they reached the age of sixteen after leaving Northampton Grammar School for Boys where they both received their final education. Each of them was to learn the art of the craft of shoemaking under the watchful eye of their father, in a factory that had established itself as one of the towns leading firms of shoemakers. After being connected with the firm for a total of twenty-eight years and with his five year contract terminated George Webb decided to resign as managing Director to found his own business. His two sons Dennis and Frank resigned with him and both became partners in the new firm.

The former firm of George Swann had occupied a factory in Brockton Street in Kingsthope Hollow and after they moved to new premises in Adnitt Road the factory in Brockton Street had stood empty. George Webb acquired the premises and set about installing machinery and making it ready for production. The new factory of George Webb and Sons opened on 1st July 1927 and began production. The partnership got off to a resounding start and by the end of August were producing their first brands of footwear for the home market. From the outset the firm specialised in Good Year Welted and only made men's footwear.

Four staff employees who joined the firm at the beginning were Oliver J Farey (Ollie to his workmates) R A M Browning, J C Sparrow and W H Mott who all later occupied executive positions and were destined to complete long service. Farey was a craftsman of the highest order who was familiar with every aspect of shoemaking. His first position at the factory was that of Making Room foreman. Robert Browning was the first Finishing Room foreman. Both were first class operatives with a very high standard of craftsmanship whose work left the hallmark of quality upon George Webb Footwear. In fact George Webb had chosen only the best craftsmen to help him launch his factory and each of these early operatives was a specialist in his own field. The firm soon made its mark as one of the foremost manufacturers in Northampton, establishing several famous brands of footwear. Few appreciate how wide the range of styles and designs required in men's shoes. A walk through one of the George Webb factories particularly during the fifties would have enlightened many. For there, seen in production, were many hundred of different styles both for home and export destinations. Two operatives who also joined the Company in the very early years were Herbert (Bert) Comerford who joined school leaver in 1931, and Ray Wykes who joined the firm in 1932 as a pattern cutter. Comerford left in the Autumn of 1958 to take up duties as secretary of the Northampton Branch of the National Union of Boot and Shoe operatives and later became National President. Wykes became a designer who was responsible for countless styles of George Webb productions. He was a man of many talents, being organist of Gold Street Methodist Church and a Sunday School associated with the church in Gold Street.

George Webb & Sons, Brockton Street Factory, Northampton.

George Webb and his two sons built up a very extensive business making good quality shoes. Besides their famous Savile Row Brand of Shoes they introduced their popular Winter Warms in 1950. These were superb Chukka Boot lined with real sheepskin (tanned with wool on pelts). Another popular brand was a more flexible type of shoe known as Boundabouts. These lightweight shoes had a very flexible leather sole. It is noticeable that most of George Webb's earliest staff members served the firm until their retirement which is a tribute to the firm's organisation. A most outstanding record of service was that of Oliver Farey who in the first years of the company was promoted from Making Room foreman to Works Manager, a position he held until his retirement in November 1948 after twenty-one years of service. Farey made an outstanding contribution to the business, serving with loyalty, reliability and outstanding leadership particularly during the war years of 1939-1945. It was said of him then that he was not only a first class shoemaker but an able organiser capable of thoroughly tackling either problems of day to day routine or complete changes of far-reaching consequence that the war years brought. At the outbreak of war in 1939 Webb's like all other shoe factories in the town and county suffered the loss of manpower to the armed forces. Over one hundred and seventy men were called up in the first year of the conflict and by the time the war had ended almost four hundred men and women had served their country in the services and eight men paid the supreme sacrifice. A testimony of just one small portion of the boot and shoe industry of Northamptonshire involved in the wartime service of their country.

Dennis G. Webb.

Frank E. Webb.

Early in the war George Webb and Sons established the *Mentone Services Bulletin* for members serving in the armed forces. Planned to bind those away more closely with their shopmates in the factory it was the idea of company employee Herbert E Smith (known as H E S) He was a man of many parts - photographer, artist, free lance journalist, and the first editor of the bulletin who had also been in the employ of the firm since 1927. War had prompted factories to set up schemes for raising money to provide comforts for the troops and amongst the many ideas were concert parties, fetes, and jumble sales. One of the George Webb factory inspirations was the founding of a choral society which had much success in raising money for charity under its conductor A G Billingham and accompanist Ray Wykes. On one or two occasions the choral society linked with the "Footshape Follies" of the neighbouring Barratt Factory in charitable shows. George Webb died in April 1940 in his 70th year. He had been associated with Doddridge Castle Hill Church all his life and was a Sunday School teacher for thirty-two years and a Deacon for thirty-three years. In 1899 he had pioneered the founding of the first Company of the Boys Brigade in Northampton by an address he delivered at the church recommending the acceptance of what was then the first organisation of its kind for boys. The result of his proposal was that the first Northampton Company was formed with William Pitt as Captain. This eventually led to the establishment of the Northampton Battalion which both his sons, Dennis and Frank and his daughter Dora were to serve in different capacities over the years.

Women at work in the George Webb Factory. c1940-45.

Shortly after the passing of the founder the residence of Mr and Mrs George Webb which was situated in Kingsley Road was presented to the Y.M.C.A by sons Dennis and Frank and their sister Dora. (Mrs J W Stirling) The Y.M.C.A duly opened the house as a hostel providing accommodation for service men and it was known as the George and Amy Webb hostel for service men. Following the death of their father Dennis and Frank became joint managing directors of the firm. Frank was responsible for manufacturing and the organisation of the factory, and Dennis became responsible for sales. With a country-wide sales team under chief salesman Harold V Whitby he set up a reliable home and export market for their products. Dennis Webb travelled extensively, particularly in America and in 1946 Frank Webb toured the United States and Canada with a Federation Mission during which George Webb shoes were exhibited at the Chicago Shoe Fair.

George Webb & Sons' overseas markets. 1946.

In 1944 the Webb brothers took what was then rather a unique step in the shoe industry when they appointed W Ralph Rutter as personnel manager. This appointment was believed to have been one of the earliest appointments of its kind in the shoe industry. Rutter was given such responsibilities in company welfare and a wide range of other duties which later included editorship of the George Webb Bulletin. Rutter was a former minister occupying the pastorate of Regent Square Methodist Church. He served as personnel manager for fourteen years until his retirement in July 1958 when he returned to the ministry, this time in the Anglican Church.

As the war entered its final stages and victory was in sight the Webb factory together with their fellow manufacturers in Northampton looked forward to the return of their employees and set about planning for the future. They took what was regarded as another step forward in the formation of a works council in March 1945. The idea was to achieve complete understanding and co-operation on all matters for mutual good; constructive co-operation promoting the comfort and well being of all employees. The functions were advisory on matters such as working conditions, factory welfare, and those matters which were not covered by agreements between the firm and the trade unions. At the inaugural meeting of the council Dennis Webb described it as an invitation to all employees to participate in the business not only for craftsmanship but also for human fellowship which he considered so necessary in the industry. In 1946 further changes took place in the sales structure and Harold V Whitby was appointed sales manager, and one year later John B Rouse joined the sales team as assistant to Whitby eventually becoming senior sales representative. On Whitby's retirement in 1948 he became sales manager.

During the year 1946-47 the company took over the old premises of the Manning Brewery on Black Lion Hill, as a Branch factory with Robert Browning as general manager. Another landmark in the company's history was in September 1946 when the firm was established as a private limited company and became George Webb and Sons (Northampton Limited). Other branch factories were opened up, the first being a closing unit at Brigend, Glamorgan also in 1946 with George Norton as its manager assisted by S Barritt as maintenance engineer. Two other factories completed the group; one at Walgrave opened in 1951 and the other at Wellingborough which opened in 1960. Albert H Halestrap A.C.A who had joined the firm from Northampton Chronicle and Echo in 1945, as company secretary and accountant was appointed a director as was Ray Wykes. In 1948 Oliver Farey's son, J K L Farey who had joined the firm in 1939 and later served in the Royal Marines, was promoted to assistant works manager in December 1948 thus continuing a family shoemaking tradition. Of the many appointments made to enhance the firm's productions during the post war era one of the most significant proved to be the appointment of R Norman Bullock A.B.S.I as export sales manager in 1952. Bullock, formerly of W Barratt and Company Ltd, became a roving ambassador for George Webb footwear travelling the world to secure orders and promote business. He visited many parts of the world including Canada, U.S.A, Bermuda, the Bahamas, Norway, Sweden, Denmark, Saudi Arabia, Hong Kong, Singapore, Japan, and Australia. Bullock kept the company in touch with life in the countries that he visited and sent them regular reports which were always featured in the George Webb Bulletin.

The company organised a wealth of activities for all its employees, especially in various sports. Opportunities for taking part in football, cricket, tennis, angling and table tennis were among the pursuits of Mentonians as the firm liked to refer to its employees. Teams regularly took part in the leather trades competitions and other social activities were organised in the social club and canteen. Opened just prior to the end of the second World War on Tuesday February 29th 1944 by the then Mayor Councillor Alfred Weston J.P. the canteen had a reputation for good food and the Social centre under a management committee proved very popular. On 1st July 1948 the company's coming of age was celebrated and plans were put in motion to commemorate the event. Highlight of the year was on 27th September when two special trains were chartered to take all the employees to Brighton for the day. Organising secretary for the event was W Ralph Rutter and the factory operatives were entertained to luncheon in the Aquarium Ballroom by the directors. It proved to be an outstanding event with all returning to Northampton around midnight.

In 1952 the firm became a public company and was known hereafter by the title of George Webb and Sons Limited. Dennis and Frank Webb remained as joint managing directors supported by two other directors, Albert H Halestrap and Ray Wykes. The firm continued to enjoy a certain amount of prosperity. The fact that George Webb shoes were sent to faraway places applied in no less a degree to Northamptonshire trained (George Webb's) craftsmen. This was recalled to Mr Dennis Webb on one of his visits to America when he visited the factory of Johnson and Murphy of Newark, New Jersey. There he met Richard Davis a Northamptonian by birth who was a handfinisher trained under George Webb at the A E Marlow factory in Northampton from 1902-1907 when he emigrated to the United States. A sequel to this meeting was recalled in the George Webb Bulletin of January 1953 under the title "News of a Craftsmen". The article went on to say "it was an unexpected pleasure to welcome Mr and Mrs Richard Davis to our works recently when in the late summer of 1952 they visited relatives in Northampton. Mr Davis comes of shoemaking stock and has been in the trade all his life. He is a handfinisher, and worked with Mr George Webb before he left Northampton to live and work in the United States. At his emigration he took with him a reference in the form of a letter personally signed by George Webb. This was presented to Messrs Johnson and Murphy of Newark, U.S.A one of the most famous of the American shoe factories. The actual reference retained by Mr Davis was brought to our works when he called and it was for us to meet a fellow townsman after forty six years who brought with him news of close associations with our senior. Mr Davis...recalled to Mr Dennis Webb the strange coincidence that the two of them had met personally at the factory of Johnson and Murphy on one of Mr Dennis's earlier visits to America...Mr Davis has devoted himself to work which has kept the Johnson and Murphy factory in the top grade of American productions. The proprietorship of this company passed to the General Shoe Corporation in 1951 but the well known name of the firm is retained. They are shoemakers to the President of the United States and Mr Davis has been one of a team to make the President's footwear for over forty five years. Just prior to his retirement he was working on shoes for President Eisenhower...it is good to find such skill among men who come from our town and were trained in its craft".

A pension scheme for long serving employees was established with a gift of £10,000 by the Webb brothers and came into operation on 1st January 1955 and functioned quite successfully for about seventeen years. The branch on Black Lion Hill closed as a shoemaking unit in 1955 owing to changes in the type of shoes that were being required by the trade. This factory remained closed for productions until 1964 when after a complete re-organisation it opened with new production methods. The factory was re-equipped with new machinery which was designed to promote the smooth running of a new specialised process known as injection moulding; a process I have attempted to describe in an ensuing chapter. In charge of the new unit was James Stirling a nephew of the managing directors, with Patrick Jenkinson as foreman. Following the retirement of Ralph Rutter in 1958 Ray Wykes assumed the dual role of works manager and personnel manager with a secretary who was responsible for day to day personnel matters. Also in 1958 John Rouse, sales manager and head of the company sales team, joined the board of directors as sales director. In the autumn of 1960 Wykes was appointed technical (works) director and J K L Farey (following in the footsteps of his father) moved from the Walgrave factory to assume the role vacated by Wykes. It was Ken Farey who was to have oversight of other important changes in 1963 when the Webb factory took steps to come into line with new developments in the shoe trade. A further symbol of progress was the installations of a power driven conveyor in the Making Room. Believed to be among the first of its type in Northampton this was a three-tier track conveyor, seventy feet in length. The object was to replace the normal rack system and so speed up and improve production. I took shoes from the "pulling over" operations to "slipping in" about forty-five minutes as opposed to three to four days by previous well-tried methods.

Rough Stuff Room. George Webb Factory c1940-45.

Grading Insoles. George Webb Factory c1940-45.

Shoes had to be of the type which were tailored to the demands of high speed production. The various components were fed on to the trace at the right place and at the right time. The powered conveyor removing the manual feed from the job and high speed moist heat setting and drying cabinets were installed at different places to "set" the leather on the last; and to dry the toe puffs, cements in preparation for subsequent operations. The work was assembled on to the trace by means of one pair peg trollies. Each operator could control the flow of work by finger controlled stops. The conveyor track was intended for better supervision and improvement in quality and greater speed for production. Only seventy two pairs of shoes were on the conveyor at any one time making for greater economy in the use of lasts. These new methods of organisation meant another step in development in the shoe trade many different methods and types of conveyor were tried in different factories prior to the war and after, including non-mechanical track systems. Whether or not some of the early systems were entirely successful is a matter of conjecture. From my own personal recollections they were not initially welcomed by the operatives and were removed by some managements. In the Webb factory, however, conveyor systems were later installed in both the Closing and Shoe rooms.

In 1966 the business of George Webb and Sons Limited was acquired by the firm of George Ward of Barwell, Leicester with Dennis and Frank Webb continuing as joint managing directors. The union of the two businesses was effected in February 1966 and the new company was known as Ward-Webb Limited. The chairman of the new board of directors was W Jenner-Jobson with messrs H Y Timpson, R A Wykes, A H Halestrap, and J B Rouse as directors whilst Frank E Webb was also appointed a director of George Ward Holdings Limited. In September 1966 Dennis Webb retired and his brother Frank continued in the business until 1968 when he also retired from the industry, and John Rouse was appointed managing director. Both the Webb bothers had followed in their father's footsteps as serving members and Deacons of Doddridge Church Castle Hill and both played a prominent part in public life. Dennis was for many years the secretary of the Northampton Battalion of the Boys Brigade and later succeeded George Lewis as president. He was also a National Vice President of the movement and was an honourary vice president and life president of the Northampton Battalion. In 1986 he was appointed Elder Emeritus of Doddridge and Commercial Street United Reformed Church. Frank also served the Boys Brigade for many years as supervisor of the junior movement, the Life Boys. He served the town for a number of years as a magistrate, being first appointed a justice of the peace in August 1949 becoming chairman of the bench from 1962-1972. He was for thirty-two years honourary treasurer to the Bethany Homestead, a former President of the British Footwear Manufacturers National Federation and also of the Northampton Town Boot Manufacturers Association. He was also joint Chairman with Albert Hope of the Northampton Board of Conciliation and Arbitration for twenty years. He was also a director of Northampton Town and County Building Society (now the Nationwide)) of which he was chairman for five years.

Further executive changes took place in 1968 when E A Wykes retired and his position as technical director was taken over by J K L Farey. Two years later Albert H Halestrap retired and his place was taken by C Richards of George Wards of Barwell, assisted by Norman Blincow. On June 18th of that year Mr Ken Farey joined the board as a full director. During the seventies the George Webb factory like other firms in the industry had suffered severe setbacks due to cheap imports and expensive exports and a general fall off in home consumption. Further changes became imminent with yet another take-over. This was a bid by the ever-growing John White Group who succeeded in adding the company to their enterprise in 1972. The firm then became known as Ward White and the new board of directors at the Brockton Street Factory was as follows:- W J Jobson (chairman) S W Iliffe, T W Lucas, J B Rouse (managing director) as and J K L Farey (technical director) The works manager was T W Bounds. With the shoe trade generally experiencing difficult times experts within the industry had warned that if manufacturers were to beat off foreign competition they must put quality first. Accordingly the company launched a new quality drive. Despite all this the years which followed saw the closure of the Webb Branch factories one by one, the last being the one hundred employee factory at Walgrave. This factory had been turning out 7,500 pairs of welted shoes a week and after a spell of short time working of four months the unit closed on 10th July 1980. John B Rouse retired as managing director the following year and his place was taken by P Joseph with chief executive J G Dodson, and J K L Farey and M T W Bounds as directors. However, the life of the factory at Brockton Street which had been making shoes for well over half a century was short lived and the blow finally came on 10th September 1982 when the factory closed. Remaining employees joined the long list of redundant shoeworkers, and the familiar signature of George Webb which had appeared on all their brands of footwear disappeared forever.

Console Operating Machines, Making Room, George Webb & Sons Ltd.

"I was accounted a good workman and recollect Mr Old keeping a pair of shoes I had made in his shop as a model of Good Workmanship".
William Carey - recalling his time as a shoemaker's apprentice.

Chapter 17

East and West of the Nene Valley

Whilst the County Town of Northampton can always claim to have been known as the capital of the shoe industry we must not overlook the fact that the craft of the shoemaker had long been established in other parts of the county. Shoe manufacturing sprang up in such places as Bozeat, Burton Latimer, Cogenhoe, Daventry, Desborough, Earls Barton, Finedon, Higham Ferrers, Irchester, Irthlingborough, Islip, Kettering, Long Buckby, Raunds, Rothwell, Rushden, Stanwick, Wellingborough and Wollaston. As in the county town in the early days much of the work would be done at home and the shoemakers would carry their shoes to and from the factories where some of the processes were carried out. Although in the late eighteenth and early nineteenth century a considerable weaving industry existed in the eastern part of the district, especially around Kettering, Desborough, Rothwell and surrounding villages, these trades had not brought prosperity as had been expected. Kettering, for instance, had known desperate poverty and on several occasions the whole structure of the town had been threatened by the overwhelming number of poor. In 1817 there was an appeal to parliament for aid. One person in every three was receiving Parochial Relief and the problem was temporarily solved by borrowing £500 and setting the poor to work making linen and sacks, raising a few crops or even quarrying stone.

With the rise of the boot and shoe trade and the coming of the Midland Railway links were forged with towns in both north and south of the country thus putting Kettering and other county manufacturers in touch with thousands of eager customers. A new more prosperous era arose from the days of adversity and by 1870 the number of shoe factories in Kettering alone had grown to twenty one. In all parts of the county outworkers were busy toiling in their tiny workshops. Every member of the family was involved ranging from the young children who fetched the leather to be made up transporting it from the warehouses in sugar boxes on wheels and returning the completed shoes, to mothers and daughters who did the "closing" while the men specialised in lasting and finishing. The life of all shoemaking families was hard and frugal but there is little doubt that it built character and ability. Many of these men and women rose to be manufacturers themselves and many of these same folk have paid tribute to their early training helping fathers or uncles in those little back garden sheds. The gradual increase in the use of machinery in the latter half of the nineteenth century in the county soon spelt an end to the happy go lucky way of life of the handsewers and their families just as it did in the county town. Kettering, along with the rest of the trade in Northamptonshire, said goodbye to the old methods in 1894 when the union had demanded the end of outside labour throughout the county. By 1911 the town had grown to 30,000 people and became the second largest producer of shoes in the county. Much of the prosperity that this and other towns had enjoyed had sprung from the shoe trade.

Northamptonshire has very early connections with the shoe industry as records show. Bozeat, for instance, was said to have belonged to the King of Scotland in the twelfth century. In the Border Wars ownership changed hands may times. In the Reverend J H Marlow's history of Bozeat it is recorded that among the former village officials of the seventeenth century was a leather searcher who had to see that leather was lawfully tanned and duly sealed. A record of 1768 mentions one Thomas Blason, a cordwainer, and in 1849 there were two shoemakers in the village apparently local bespoke makers. During the early years of shoemaking in Bozeat the factories were lighted up by means of paraffin lamps and it wasn't until 1913 that two factories decided to go over to electric light whilst another chose gas which was produced on the premises.

In the mid nineteenth century **Burton Latimer** had only one shoemaker, ten farmers and ten glaziers. Its main industry was a large carpet mill which employed 400 people and produced 16,000 yards of carpet a week. But in the later years of the century when shoemaking in mid-Northamptonshire began to develop rapidly Burton Latimer was one of the villages which did "outwork" for some of the town firms. Later, when the factory system began in earnest many operatives travelled from Burton Latimer to Kettering, walking the three miles to work and three miles back. One of the best known Burton Latimer businesses in 1896 was started by two partners Joseph Henry Whitney and Frank Roland Westley, both aged twenty-nine, who invested their slender savings and by ceaseless hard work built up a very prosperous concern. Their first factory was a cottage in the village. They employed five workers and step by step the business developed. Between the first and second world wars there were about six factories producing footwear for men, women and children. Local prosperity thus owed much to the boot and shoe trade.

Desborough, a small industrial town, had no fewer then five shoe factories at one time and it had factories which also produced lasts for the industry. It has been largely concerned with boots for men and boys although a fair quantity of ladies shoes were made. The shoe trade in Desborough really grew from a very small nucleus of handsewn makers for, early in the last century, like Kettering the main industry was weaving. Benjamin Riley founded his firm in 1868 (B.Y.Riley) When he died in 1894 his son F.T.Riley took control, building up a sound business producing good class boys' boots and men's rivetted footwear. Their export trade was large and included contracts for British, French, Italian, Serbian and austrian armies. F.T Riley was a keen and alert businessman yet he found time for public affairs being a member of the district council and other civic bodies. The factory closed in the mid 1930's. In 1888 B. Toone & Co started and became noted for the Little Duke boys' footwear and Seagull ladies and Pearl Maiden shoes. When first established the company was a branch of the Toone & Black firm of South Wigston and employed about twenty people. By 1914 they were turning out 8,000 pairs of shoes every week and employing 400 operatives. Frome 1914-16 they made 170,000 pairs of army boots. The firm was taken over by George Ward of Barwell in the 1970's and closed in 1981. Other Desborough firms were: Crompton Footwear Ltd, a cooperative production society which closed in the 1970's; T Bird & Company which came under the supervision of Groocock's of Rothwell, and closed in the 1930's; W.Barnes & Co, closed in 1952; the Desborough Shoe Company which still produces men's rivetted, welted and moulded footwear. This firm was originally under the Yeoman's name but was taken over by Ellington and is now part of Griggs & Co of Wollaston.

Finedon was once the property of Queen Edith, wife of Edward the Confessor and she would hunt deer in nearby Rockingham Forest which once extended thus far. It has been claimed that the queen stayed at the Bell Inn, one of the oldest inns in the country but historians regard this as uncertain. Of more certainty is a story of the duke of military fame who gave his name to the Wellington boot. On an old Toll House on the Thrapston Road is the inscription "Panorama of Waterloo Victory" June 18th 1815. The Duke of Wellington visited the place and on descending remarked "That is exactly like the field of Waterloo - the lie of the land is the same". Shoemaking in Finedon for local needs was carried on from early times but it was not until the nineteenth century that there was much development in manufacturing. In the 1860's John Langley was prominent combining the trades of shoemaker and maltster. At first the work was handsewn and the men stitched the soles and the women sewed the uppers. When treadle sewing machines came in men and women and girls were to be found in little workshops in the village. Work would commence at 7 a.m. and finish at 7 p.m and the wage would be about seven or eight shillings a week. The first army contractor at Finedon is believed to have been George Frederick Claypole whose business flourished between 1870-1890. During the first world war army work was called for in abundance whilst in the 1939-1945 world war many varieties of service work were produced. The heavy army works was the mainstay of the old days but eventually gave way to production of men's and women's welted footwear.

Not far from Finedon along the Thrapston Road lies the village of **Islip** where for years the factoring of footwear made its name widely known. In its old-world surroundings this pretty village represents what was the very eastern extremity of the county's shoe trade.

Only an imaginary border line divides the ancient borough of **Higham Ferrers** from the town of Rushden. Higham is one of the oldest boroughs in the whole of England situated on a rocky elevation half a mile from the banks of the River Nene. Although the two towns are practically merged each retains its independence. In 1951 the Festival of Britain year the borough celebrated the 700th anniversary of the grant of its first charter. One of the citizens name in this charter was Ralph the Cobbler. In the court Polls of Higham Ferrers which in bygone days boasted a castle there is a reference to the office of Leather Searcher and the oath which had to be taken. It states "you shall well and truly behave yourselves in all things that shall appertain to the office of the Leather searchers of this Borrowe of Higham. You shall see Leather dulie searched whether that it be lawfullie tanned according to the statute and the seale it and you shall see that no leather be here sold befoe it is searched and sealed and you shall do those things without any meede. Favour or affexion and all other things belonginge to the office of Leather Search so helpe you God".

There is also a record that in the Sixteenth Century tanners were brought to account for selling "illegitimate leather" (i.e. not properly tanned) and taking excess profit; fines were imposed. In the early seventeenth century shoemakers at Higham were fined for making shoes with insoles of dry red leather, and later one man had to pay a fine for selling shoes on a Sunday. Such were the efforts in those days to uphold the quality of craftmanship, standards which today are to some extent taken for granted. Higham Ferrers became quite an important centre for the shoe industry, built on centuries of craftsmanship that has been handed down from father to son and family to family over generations. This ancient borough goes on producing fine shoes including welted and cemented types of footwear. It is also supported by a progressive leather industry supplying the highest quality goods form calf and kids, upper and lining leathers and other shoe components.

Although little is known of the history of the neighbouring town of **Rushden** it is a town which has made surprising progress. Whilst adjoining Higham basked in its ancient glory Rushden grew and flourished. It is difficult to say with absolute accuracy who was responsible for the shoe trade in the town but it is believed that the families Denton, Calridge and Cabe were the original pioneers of the shoe industry. In the early part of its career as a shoe producing town Rushden devoted its attention to making men's boots and shoes of a less expensive kind than those made in Northampton. For many years it devoted itself to producing footwear mainly for the wholesale trade and Rushden's shoe productio was second only to the county town. Factories specialised in boots and shoes for men, women and youths and work was produced both for sport and play, even riding boots and jodhpurs. In wartime full use of Rushden's adaptability was made by the Ministry of Supply when boots and shoes were sent out by the million. It was once said: "Ask for anything in men's footwear and Rushen could produce it. The operatives are no mere machine minders but the true successors to the handsewn bootmakers of the past". In the 1860's Rushden was in the throes of growing from a village into a town. Few roads were in existence and it was not an uncommon sight to see women going to church on a Sunday in their patterns. Well before the end of the last century when a lad entered the industry he would start as a half timer, school in the morning and work in the afternoons or vice versa. For the job of eyeletting he would be paid eighteen pence a week. Lads would be working full time at the age of twelve and would then receive a "real wage" of two shillings and sixpence a week. This was before the factory system was fully established and the cut uppers and bottom leathers were handed out over wicket gates at the employer's premises. The closing of the uppers and the inking and finishing of the shoes were all done by outworkers.

Raunds is in this same part of the county and is synonymous with the word "Rand" (a shoe term itself relating to handsewn footwear). In the Domesday book it appeared as Rande and it was possible that the town was established by raiders striking up the Nene Valley in the fifth century to be founded as Rand (Teutonic) meaning the end of their journey. So the "rand" of the handsewn shoemakers who founded the fame of Raunds as a boot and shoe centre can never be lost though today these craftsmen are few. The supply of military footwear helped to build the fortunes of the town, but the shock decision made by the government in the 1914-18 war to abolish the use of handsewn boots was a blow to the trade. But the trade was resilient and local firms had already anticipated changing needs. Raunds as a shoe centre began to follow other manufacturers in the county by adopting modern methods of production. The town soon became well ahead in technical developments and besides producing a wide variety of service footwear its ranges of boots and shoes for civilians included welted footwear, safety footwear and boots and shoes for sports. Raunds was the scene of the famous strike of 1905 when the operatives marched to London to lay their grievances before Parliament. Since that time no major dispute has occurred in the town or district. Neighbouring Stanwick which is part of Raunds for local government purposes also followed a similar pattern of trade.

Rothwell was probably more closely identified with the shoe trade than any other in the county. It supported half-a-dozen flourishing shoe firms run by members of families who had strong links with the Free Churches; down the years they contributed greatly to the social well-being of the town through their untiring work on the local authorities and through their churches and societies. Avalon Footwear of Rothwell started from small beginnings in a building in Fox Street about 1892. A more extensive factory was erected in Littlewood Street about 1899 and this was later enlarged. An even more extensive factory was built in Cross Street when all old machinery was discarded, a welted plant installed and the factory modernised. It functioned as a cooperative production society in which the employees were shareholders. The business closed in 1983. Other Rothwell firms were: J T Butlin & Sons, a family business formed in 1869 making men's rivetted, welted and moulded footwear and taken over by C & J Clark in 1955 but closed in 1980; W I Butlin, a family business which closed in 1920; S E Gamble & Sons, a family business which started about 1890 making men's rivetted and moulded footwear and closed in 1973; another family firm of Chamberlain & Co which closed in 1922; Eaton & Co which ceased trading in 1929; Taylor & Sons, taken over by John White of Higham Ferrers and closed in 1976; S Sergeant & Co, closed in 1973; and the family firm of T Groocock, still making men's rivetted, welted and moulded shoes and ladies' footwear.

Wellingborough is an old market town that obtained its name from the famous wells which formerly existed in the locality. One of the most important mineral springs was known as Redwell the water of which was heavily charged with iron. There is evidence of the existence of some shoemaking in the fifteenth century. Wellingborough certainly had a shoe manufacturing business in 1749 and in 1817 a shoemaker advertised that an apprentice had run away from his service. A reward of two guineas was promised for the apprehension of the runaway. It has been said that the town later failed to make full use of the advantages it possessed when the shoe trade began to emerge into a large mechanical industry. Had it done so it may well have outrivalled many other centres which did not possess the same natural facilities. Nevertheless it was boots from Wellingborough which shod members of the ill-fated Arctic Expedition led by John Franklin in 1845. Impetus to the boot trade in the town was given following the outbreak of the Crimean War in 1854. In 1873 there were twenty-three boot and shoe manufacturers with a great many more outdoor closers. Prior to the 1914 war the town had twenty boot factories of considerable size. Caleb Archer in his Recollections of Wellingborough recalls the story of how John Askham the shoemaker poet of Wellingborough (1825-1894) would pick up a piece of leather to scribble his verses upon it if paper was not to hand. He tells also of how for many manufacturers the leather was cut in the factory and given out to workpeople who closed the uppers and made up the boots and shoes in their own homes or in small outhouses with shops adjoining. When the trade was good they worked fairly hard five days of the week for the majority of them always observed "Saint Monday" when they visited each others homes and shops and took their walks abroad calling in at their favourite pubs for a pipe and a glass. Most of the younger men wore long hair with narrow leather fillets across their forehead to keep the hair from falling over the face when bending over their work. Although Saint Crispin was honoured weekly there were others who were men of deep religious feeling who would keenly discuss church matters with each other. Gaiters and leggings formed a large part of the output of the Wellingborough factories. It was even claimed that the town was the birthplace of the gaiter. Even up to the end of the First World War the making of gaiters was a major industry. The chief product made in the factories after the 1914-1918 war was welted footwear closely followed by slippers, sandals and winter sports goods. The urgency of the war had encouraged enterprise and laid the foundations for wider manufacturing interests which were firmly laid. Changing fashions however soon led to changes in production but in the mid fifties the large boot and slipper trade dwindled leaving only bespoke and surgical wear.

A few miles from Wellingborough is the village of **Irchester** which was once a Roman settlement. Towards the end of the last century the village was busy with handsewn production of footwear. Trade did not expand at the rate of some of its near neighbours because land for development was not easily available. South of Irchester, the village of Wollaston also has an interesting history. Roman and Saxon settlements were known there. The shoe trade here sprang up from the old workshop system and the first factories were in use in the 1870's. In 1873 Wollaston had two boot manufacturer, one machine closer and three shoe agents. At that period in time agents worked in the village and towns in the boot and shoe producing area to collect work and distribute it to the outdoor workers. Wollaston produced men's, youth's and boys' boots, women's casuals and children's sandals, and was considered to be an integral part of Northamptonshire footwear industry.

North East of Wellingborough on the A6 lies the town of **Irthlingborough** is thought to have begun as an Anglo-Saxon military enclosure as the Danes came marauding along the River Nene. Irthlingborough can boast of having the factory of the oldest shoe firm in the county; having been founded in 1820 at Higham Ferrers it was carried on in that borough until 1856 when a move to Irthlingborough had to be made because it was impossible to obtain land for building. This firm was John Spencer and Company (Irthlingborough) Ltd one of the town's two noted manufacturers.

There is a record of the early nineteenth century which is worth recalling to demonstrate the changes which have taken place in the industry. At a time when London employers had boots made in the country where labour was cheaper there was a law with penalties for workmen who worked at home and who took in similar work from two employers. One bootmaker discovered that two of his men at Irthlingborough were working at the same time for another in London. When prosecution was threatened one man made peace with his master by signing a confession of neglect by attending to London work. "Whereby I have incurred a penalty of from one to three months imprisonment" and the other man ran away. The man who stayed expressed public thanks for the withdrawal of the prosecution and made a promise not to offend again. An interesting paragraph featured in the boot and shoe trades Journal of 10th December 1892 gives the views of one Irthlingborough worker who was critical of the Union for agreeing with employers for speeding up the tempo of change from handwork to machinery. It said: "The men do not thank the Union for doing so, they do not want their liberty meddled with as they have shops to work in and leading men will not go with their sons into such places as they know they will be. Some will leave the Union if they do not stop so much interference". This remark was an indication that there were still men who were (despite Union encouragement) reluctant to leave their home workshops for the larger factories. Irthlingborough was a town in which the production of leather was as extensive and important as the shoe trade. The good water supply was the original attraction for the tanners and the huge output of full chrome producers coupled with the activities of the dressers. Footwear produced was best quality medium grades of Goodyear Welted shoes for men, youths, and women and children's shoes. Boots and shoes for football, golf and skating were also made.

It is interesting to note that most of these towns and villages in central Northamptonshire are situated on or very close to the A6 trunk road. Their development as centres of the boot and shoe industry owed much to the communications, especially in the development of the railway in the second half of the nineteenth century. This led to large-scale population growth and resulting expansion of trade. In the next chapter we turn to the county's second leading boot and shoe town, Kettering. Later we shall also study Daventry, Earls Barton and Long Buckby, other important and distinguished centres of the boot and shoe trade in Northamptonshire.

"People will believe in you, if you set them an example".

Chapter 18

Every Step, One Step Forward

Situated almost in the centre of England, Northamptonshire with its shoe manufacturing towns boasted some of the finest and up to date factories. They were directed by some of the county's most capable men and manned by operatives whose skill was and still is unquestioned. Many of the smaller towns and villages of Northamptonshire had their cordwainers; simultaneously with the growth of the industry in Northampton the progress of the trade was apparent in no small measure in practically every hamlet around the county and along the Nene Valley. Until the last quarter of the eighteenth century when the shoe trade in Kettering was really launched Kettering (the largest town next to Northampton) had been solely an agricultural and wool town. Its rise to importance as a shoe centre of nearly 40,000 people was amazingly rapid. Over a century ago there was only a population of 5,000 and among them only a dozen shoemakers. Only one was listed as being a shoe manufacturer.

Kettering is supposed to be derived from St Katharine who is said to have a well somewhere in the town. The true deviation is no doubt to be found in the Old Anglo Saxon names of Cytringan and Cytringas. In the latter part of the seventeenth century the wholesale manufacture of boots and shoe was going on apace. A description of the town in 1849 read: "Kettering consists of several streets and is curiously distinguished by some of their names. One is Pudding Bag Lane, because there is no outlet at the bottom of it. Two are named after Public Houses, Nags Head Land and Swan Street. One is called Bakehouse Hill because the old and formerly chartered Bakehouse stands there another is Parkstile Lane but nobody knows why". In those days Kettering was without a railway this came in 1857 and caused a transformation. Up to about 1860 shoe production in the town had been mainly in the hands of the bespoke shoemakers; most of the manufacturers were in Northampton. There was only one shoe manufacturer of note in Kettering, Thomas Gotch, and those men who learned the shoe trade with him began to use the new railway to leave the town to visit others and form their own businesses.

The launching of the shoe trade in Kettering was therefore due entirely to the enterprise of Thomas Gotch who had arrived in the town in about 1770. At the age of twenty-four in 1772 he married and with his wife and child lived in a house in High Street. Gotch was the son of a farmer, but reluctant to work on the land sought work in the town becoming apprenticed to a shoemaker. Later he began in business on his own account with a small amount of capital allowing the profits he made to accumulate. By this means he was able to provide funds for further expansion. In 1786 James Cobb, a Kettering ironmonger, entered into partnership with Gotch and in 1794 with the graduation of his son John Cooper Gotch gained a third partner. Thomas Gotch's son was twenty one years of age and had completed a full course of training in the trade. As early as 1778 the Gotch family were said to have executed orders for troops sent to fight the American colonists in the American War of Independence. After 1793 the business was carried on in a workshop in his house in Lower Street and in adjoining barns. Later, Gotch branched out to curry and tan his own leather. By 1837 he held an unchallenged position as the most extensive boot and shoe concern in the whole of Northamptonshire. The buildings adjoining his home and which had been his factory lasted until 1857, a period of some sixty years.

After about 1850, shoemaking became the chief occupation in Kettering. Most of the normal processes of manufacture other than cutting out uppers and soles were carried out by shoemakers and their apprentices in little workshops in their own homes. William Carey, the Baptist missionary, who was born in Paulerspury in 1761 was apprenticed to a shoemaker at Hackleton. Later, when his family moved to Moulton, he became on of Gotch's early apprentices. He used to deposit his work in Kettering once a fortnight and return home to Moulton with the uppers and sole leather. Carey is Northamptonshire's most famous shoemaker. Appointed in 1787 to be minister at the village of Moulton he became a leading spirit in founding the Baptist Missionary Society, and in 1793 went to India where he translated the Bible into many Indian Languages. The time that Carey went to India was the period when the business of Thomas Gotch began to prosper. It must have been very gratifying to him to know that one of his trained shoemakers had become such a distinguished servant of God. Gotch had generously supported Carey in his early training.

Another interesting facet of history which was to make Kettering so well known in the shoe trade in later years is to be found in the record of the trade in the 1850's. It states that William Timpson at the age of eight used to carry boots for outworkers from Rothwell to Gotch's factory in Kettering. As an employer Gotch seemed ready to make use of both women and child labour at a time when this type of labour was exploited. He also employed apprentices at an early age. An apprentice usually began between the age of ten and fifteen generally for an apprenticeship of seven years. Whether or not William Timpson later became an apprentice under Thomas Gotch is uncertain but there is no doubt that the long established firm of Messrs Gotch and Sons ultimately became William Timpson and Sons. The work of the firm was mainly in government contracts making shoes for the military. Shoe machinery came to the town in 1859 although it was a decade before Kettering became established as a machine town.

Thomas Gotch was a family firm until 1888 when it was taken over G H Jones. Eventually the name of the firm disappeared for good. A great grandson of the founder, David Frederick Gotch, joined William Timpson in partnership and so the story of another enterprise began. In 1857 Messrs Gotch and Son had been like Gulliver in Lilliput, one large concern amongst a handful of small businesses. The establishment of the boot and shoe trade in Kettering owes its origins and progress to Thomas Gotch's enterprise. It is upon these foundations that the Kettering industry was built and so ably carried on by his successors the Timpson family. Kettering shoes soon became known throughout the world. Manufacturers adopted machinery as soon as it was introduced and moved with the varying needs of time building modern factories and establishing a class of footwear entirely their own.

William Timpson was born on the 20th May 1849 in Rothwell. At an early age one spring morning he left Rothwell and walked to Desborough in order to get a train to the great city of Manchester where he hoped he would make his fortune. William had two brothers, Charles who lived in Manchester and Anthony who had settled in Ashton-Under-Lyne. William decided to live with Charles and his wife in Manchester but found his brother very strict. By the age of twelve he was delivering boots on a sackbarrow to a firm called Millroys in Pendleton. He managed to complete his education by attending night school and Ashley Lane Church and Sunday School in Manchester. He eventually realised he was not getting on with his brother and found his freedom restricted. He decided to return to his native Rothwell where he learned the art of shoemaking from a real old fashioned cordwainer John Thomas

Butlin. He became quite a clever shoemaker and when Butlin died William carried on his business.

Timpson realised that whilst it took a week to make a pair of boots it only took a few minutes to sell them. These thoughts led him back to the city of Manchester and together with his brother-in-law, Walter Joyce, opened a boot and shoe shop at 298 Oldham Road at Easter 1865. In May 1870 he started in business himself at 97 Oldham Street where he rented premises at £200 a year. He found instant success and in the early days became a retailer. However, about 1880 because of poor health he returned to Northamptonshire to live in Kettering, travelling to and from Manchester to give oversight to his business. It was a time when the boot and shoe trade was beginning to grow in Kettering and this made him determined to make boots for his Manchester shops. He began by starting his first factory in a shed at his home which was then Withington House. In 1884 he purchased a small factory building in Market Street which was a silk weaving mill. Four years later he took David Frederick Gotch into the business as a partner; unfortunately Gotch's health broke down and he resigned. Timpson continued to build up his business and opened several other shops in Manchester. In 1896 he was joined by his eldest son William Henry Farey Timpson. The firm remained a family concern until 1912 when it became a limited company. About 1905 a repairing factory was also established and old premises belonging to the company were reopened in Clopton Street, Manchester.

The foundations of the men's footwear Business of William Timpson Limited was undoubtedly laid by William Timpson senior. He had an absolute insistence for a high standard for his goods; no shabby cheap-jack shoes appeared in his shops. His elder son Will was to extend the skill of his father to others and, in turn, his son Noel became similarly experienced in the needs and requirements of the trade in ladies' footwear. Both father and son never deviated from the good value and straight forward methods of the founder. At the beginning of the century the firm's shops were only established in Manchester, Kettering and Wellingborough and three Lancashire towns. Later, shops were opened in other cities such as Nottingham, Leeds, Liverpool, Sheffield, Hull, Birmingham and London. Other centres followed both in England and Scotland. Establishing a chain of shops in those days was a hard task but William Timpson was extremely skilled at the task. His knowledge of shopkeeping was gained by personal experience and he tramped the High Streets of practically every town in the kingdom observing the people and the shoes they wore. He watched what type of shops they went into, saw what they bought and found out how much they wanted to pay; and that was how he built his business up. In 1929 the firm had 136 shops and just prior to the outbreak of World War Two in 1939 there were 191 and in 1946 - 197 with a growing shoe repair business. Timpson had a close relationship with his employees. He knew everyone of his managers and assistants as though they were his personal friends. He became one of Kettering's most successful citizens. He was a dedicated Nonconformist having been brought up as a Congregationalist. Later he became an enthusiastic member of the Fuller Baptist Church in Kettering and was an accomplished local preacher. Politically he was a dedicated and prominent Liberal. He died on the 23rd January 1929 and was mourned by a great concourse of local townsfolk.

The remarkable achievement of the factory in Market Street, Kettering was due to the work of Thomas A Mursell who, whilst a young man, took over the control of the factory in 1896. In the factory only men's and boys' boots and shoes were then produced. After the uppers had been cut in the clicking room they were sent to be stitched together in the closing rooms which were then in Wellingborough. About 1896 the Market Street factory was enlarged and most boots were made entirely on the premises. About 750 pairs a week were produced, rising to a weekly total of 1,250 in a few years. This climbed to a total of 5,000 pairs a week by 1914 and 7.000 pairs a week in 1919. A new factory was then built at North Park Kettering and opened in 1923. During the First World War Timpsons Limited began to manufacture Ladies Shoes. It was the making of wartime boots for female munition workers which inspired Mursell to produce ladies' footwear. The new factory at North Park when built was magnificent in conception. Standing in its own gardens it also boasted Bowling greens and Tennis courts for use of the employees. It was built with an extensive area of glass (and nicknamed "The Crystal Palace") and also had efficient heating and air conditioning systems. Great pains were taken to keep the whole building clean and working conditions pleasant.

Tragically the dreams of William Timpson and his very able manager Thomas Mursell were to be shattered soon after fulfilment. Not long after the new factory had opened Mursell was taken ill and died in November 1923. The management of the factory was taken over by Alan G Timpson, the youngest son of William Timpson, and Ewart T Hawthorne under whose guidance business continued to prosper. By 1939 over 17,000 pairs of shoes a week were being made. During the war the Timpson factory made thousands of pairs of army boots, a repetition of the Kettering war effort in 1914. After the war thousands of pairs of demobilisation shoes were made. Timpsons also began exporting after 1945, first beginning in the United States and eventually to many other parts of the world.

During the dark days of the early 1920's and the disastrous industrial depression of the 1930's many businesses stumbled and fell, but William Timpson Limited never faltered. It survived a most difficult and precarious period of company history to prove ultimately successful, becoming a public company in 1929. In 1933 the repair factory in Cropton Street, Manchester was move to Addington Street and other repair factories were opened in Sheffield , Birmingham, Stockport, Middlesborough, and Oldham. Within six years there were eleven repair factories in operation. One of the strongest features of the Timpson business was the way the company attracted the descendants of the founder. From 1929 the younger brother of William Timpson, Noel Mursell Timpson, took an ever increasing share in the responsibilities of the business; whilst F J Noakes, a grandson of the founder joined the company in 1929 as a ladies' shoe buyer and becoming a director in 1936. Noakes was responsible for the start of the export business. Noel Timpson became deputy managing director in 1929 and managing director in 1949. He was awarded the O.B.E. in 1959. The firm was noted for the large number of its long-serving employees. In 1956, to mark the occasion of the Diamond Jubilee of W H F Timpson (eldest son of the founder), 441 employees with twenty-five years or more of service were presented with a gold watch. Similar awards followed each succeeding year and the centenary year, 1965, the number of watches awarded totalled 628. Many retired employees had served the company for fifty years or more. In its centenary year the company was still being led by members of the Timpson family. Two grandsons of the founder, W Anthony Timpson as chairman, David J Timpson as managing director with and Geofrey Noakes O.B.E., D.J.P., vice chairman.

During the late 1960's heavy losses resulted in the Kettering manufacturing division of the Timpson Group being reorganised. In 1969 the company purchased another kettering shoe factory, Tite & Garfirth (T Shoes). The whole operation of this firm moved into the North Park factory, and the workforce was trimmed from one thousand to six hundred and fifty; at the same time output was stepped up from 18,000 to 22,000 pairs of shoes per week. Jeffrey Redding, a manager from Charles Clore's British Shoe Corporation, was brought in to haul the factory out of the doldrums. Almost immediately Geoffrey Noakes was appointed the group's managing director, having successfully built up the firm's repair side. The Kettering factory then became known as Tite & Garfirth and operated as a subsidiary of William Timpson Ltd. The company had to fight for survival with every means at its command. Yet despite vigorous management the company continued to make losses until 1971. The acquisition in April 1972 of the shops of Norvic Retail took Timpsons into an important new segment of the footwear market, dramatically increasing its number of retail shops to five hundred. Simultaneously Timpsons announced its decision to discontinue its Kettering-based manufacturing operation in order to concentrate on retailing.

The firm ceased manufacturing in December 1972 when six hundred and fifty operatives were involved. Timpsons was hitherto a business of 262 shops, 210 repairing units and a factory producing 20,000 pairs of shoes a week. The closure of the North Park factory was quickly followed by two other units, one at Corby employing 130 women and the other at Maltby, Yorkshire where 70 women lost their jobs. These redundancies, in the wake of the closure of major Northampton firms like Barratt's, brought much bitterness and hardship to families who had spent most of their working lives in the trade. The MP for Kettering, Sir Geoffrey de Freitas, declared: "This is very sad news...the Government is always talking about increasing employment in the country as a whole...Footwear will remain our most important industry"> The Mayor, Ald. David Thompson, also pledged full support to save the jobs of the shoe workers. Together with Sir Geoffrey, Herbert (Bert) Comerford the General president of the Shoe Workers Union (Nuflat) and other union officials met the firm's chairman, government officials and local employment officers. All was to no avail; jobs were not saved. So ended with a note of irony another family business, the achievement of which originated in the journey of a small boy from Rothwell to Manchester in 1860 and which had attempted to maintain to the end the tradition he laid down: "Every step shall be one step forward, and never must one step be backward".

Timpson's North Park Factory (N'ptonshire Evening Telegraph 2.12.74)

Chapter 19

Neighbours of Arbury Banks

The town of Daventry in the western part of the county has seen rapid development and expansion in the latter half of the twentieth century, mainly as an overspill for the city of Birmingham. Hitherto it was known for its familiar radio station whose giant masts towered over the countryside west of the Roman Watling Street. Further south west is Arbury Hill, an ancient earthwork once known as "Arbury Banks". Daventry has also played a considerable part in the shaping of the boot and shoe industry. During the Victorian era cobblers (cordwainers) from many of the surrounding villages walked either to and from Daventry or Long Buckby where they worked for long hours making boots and shoes in small workshops.

Not all factories had their origins in the town of Northampton or the county towns. Some had their roots in other places and then moved to Northamptonshire because it was generally recognised as the home of the industry. One of the most notable of such companies was the firm of Stead and Simpson which opened a factory in Daventry in 1844. The founders were Edmund Stead and Edward Simpson, two shrewd Yorkshire men. Both had sound business ideas and were endowed with perseverance and determination. Stead was a hard-headed man of stern character and keen enterprise and was the senior partner. Simpson was a different type of man, extremely far-seeing in his approach to business. He was equally Wesleyan in his beliefs and a very prominent member of that particular church. The business had actually began in 1834 in Leeds in premises in Horse and Trumpet Yard, Upperhead Row, first as leather merchants and curriers. An office was established at 132 Kirkgate, Leeds and they became well known as tanners and curriers. Later on the partners added a japanning shop for the production of patent leather. They began to make boots and shoes in large quantities in the Sheepscar factory. The business flourished. The premises at Kirkgagte were extended to employ between five and six hundred workers; this included about fifty girls employed in the machine (closing) room using the newly invented sewing machine. The business then reached heights of considerable importance it emerging boot and shoe industry. Due to the difficulty that the firm was experiencing in getting sufficient workers in Leeds to become shoe operatives it was decided to look elsewhere for premises. Finally it was agreed that sites in Northamptonshire and Leicester were most suitable.

Thus the Daventry factory was opened in 1864 under the supervision of Edmund Stead. At the time the factory was opened no machine goods were made there, but Daventry was noted for being a district where large numbers of handsewn shoemakers lived. In the early days large contracts were taken for boots for the Royal Navy and the regulation "Blucher" boots for the army. Besides this large quantities of men's boots were made for both home and export, notably Australia. Large quantities of long and short Wellington boots were also produced for shipment to Rio-de-Janiero. In 1856 a small factory was opened in Cank Street, Leicester. This factory specialised in the manufacture of handsewn, water-tight, navvies' boots, the boots being supplied to agents in Melbourne, Australia for men going to the gold fields. In 1860 a larger factory was built in Belgrave Gate, Leicester and in 1866 a modern one storey building was built in Daventry.

The two partners, Edmund Stead and Edward Simpson, had in 1863 introduced their two Nephews into the business. This was beginning of a long line of family association with the firm. Richard Fawcett was the Stead's nephew and H Simpson Gee Simpson's nephew. Richard Fawcett acted as a traveller and salesman working from the Leeds warehouse whilst H Simpson Gee took charge of the branch factory in Leicester and the control of the new factory in Daventry. Between 1885 and 1903 the firm owned premises in Ash Street Northampton. This may have been a closing room but no records are available to confirm it. Along with Freeman, Hardy and Willis, the retail shoe distributors, Stead and Simpson were the first shoe company to have retail shops. This trend was copied by many other manufacturers to market their own brands of footwear. In the late 1870's the first retail shops were opened in Carlisle, Whitehaven, South Shields and Sunderland. The Northampton Shoe Museum has in its possession an account for their Whitehaven Shop dated 1857.

In his early days with the company H Simpson Gee was supported by his manager at the Leicester factory, Joseph Griffin Ward, who was eventually taken into partnership. Under the auspices of both Gee and Ward a substantial shipping trade was added to the business. Large export orders were completed and shipped to Australia, South Africa and South America. In 1878 changes were made in the partnership; the title of the firm was altered to Stead, Simpson and Nephews. In April 1891 it was decided to abolish outworking in Daventry and make provision for executing all the work inside the factory using modern machinery. In 1892 the tanning and currying of leather business in Leeds which had been so successful for so many years was discontinued in order to finance a further extension of retail shops.

In 1890 Joseph Griffin Ward was elected president of the newly formed Boot and Shoe Manufacturers Association and took a foremost part in framing the Terms of Settlement by which a lengthy dispute between the manufacturers and the operatives trade union was brought to a satisfactory conclusion. Ward showed conspicuous ability in conducting the negotiations and he was one of the signatories to the terms of settlement. This agreement has been the basis upon which the manufacturers and the National Union of Boot and Shoe Operatives conducted their negotiations over many years. It secured for the industry a long period of industrial peace which has remained to the present time. In 1928 the company purchased eleven acres of land in Daventry to lay out a sports ground. A pavilion was also built and furnished as a sports club for the benefit of employees. It was similar to the one formed earlier in 1924 for the Leicester based employees. The Daventry Sports Ground was formerly opened on 31st May 1930 by the Mayor of Daventry Captain G W Stopford. The cost of the venture to the company was £6,200.

The total number of people employed by Stead & Simpson in its centenary year of 1954 was: factories 1,067; warehouse and clerical staff 168; shop managers and assistants 1,130; the total number of employees being 2,365. It was noteworthy that the firm even after it became a Limited Company preserved the unbroken record of family continuity. From its foundations to its centenary year and beyond the control of the business remained a family affair. Unfortunately the factory in Daventry closed down in 1971 although the business is still very much alive and standing by the objectives laid down by their founders in their circular of 1835: "To supply every article of sterling quality at the lowest rate of profit".

"None have less praise than those who hunt after it".

Chapter 20

The Craft village

Throughout Northamptonshire there is much evidence to show that in each village there were cobblers whose activities were centred on their home workshops. Mechanisation took time to reach the villages. Long Buckby, some ten miles from Northampton and lying between Daventry and Rugby was well-endowed with craftsmen; it was a noted centre for woolcombing and worsted weaving yet in 1777 the village had six cordwainers. The rise of the boot and shoe trade in the village was thought to be linked with nearby Daventry. It was a Daventry manufacturer, Thomas Lee, who first introduced the trade into what was then his native village, probably as early as 1812. Around 1860 the firm of Stead and Simpson of Daventry recruited work from the handsewn craftsmen of the village.

Around that time there were only two successors to Thomas Lee who were known as manufacturers, namely James Hill and Richard Swift. The latter employed a former employee of Lee as his manager. Some of the handsewn men also continued to work at home making handsewn boots for Pollards of Northampton. They carried their work into town on foot or sent it by carrier cart. Two small factories emerged later beginning in cottages owned by two brothers, Alfred and Joseph Howe. Eventually Alfred built what was known as the Castle Factory in King Street. Another factory, the American Boot Factory was owned by William Sanders. He was born at Gloucester and was apprenticed to a shoemaker in Bristol. During his late teens around 1860 Sanders emigrated to America with another youth where, in typical pioneer style, he traded with farmers of the American Prairies often in danger of molestation by Indians. In the Federal War of 1861 Sanders had to assist in building bridges for one of the armies. About 1873 he decided to return to England and secured employment with a firm called Blakeys. He then married and shortly afterwards in 1866 opened a shoe shop in Great Charlotte Street, Liverpool. Following a further short visit to America Sanders took over a larger shoe shop in Liverpool as a result of which he decided to return to Long Buckby to manufacture boots and shoes at his newly opened American Boot Factory in the Square. By this time he had opened other shops at Birkenhead, Manchester and London.

In 1871 Samuel and Carter Davis and Thomas Bishop (a former manager of a Co-operative Long Buckby Manufacturing Limited, established in 1867) founded two firms which lasted late into the nineteenth century. Another two brothers, John and Thomas Eyre, became partners with John York Howe in 1869 and built a factory in the Market Place. In 1870 there were three factories and by 1884 eight, reaching a peak in 1890 with twelve. Alfred Howe first appeared as a manufacturer in 1875 or 1876. The Castle Street factory appearing between 1875 or 1876. Pollards of Northampton continued to send work to the village in 1889. At that time a laster earned twenty-six to thirty shillings a week, but the average wage of other workers ranged between nineteen and twenty-two shillings. Prices for handsewn shoes varied from three shillings and threepence to five shillings and eightpence a pair.

It was William Sanders who made the greatest impression on the trade in Long Buckby in the latter part of the nineteenth century. He took over Eyre's business and established it as his own American Boot Factory. He was an enthusiast in dealing with the problems of correct foot fitting. His boots were made in four widths to one length. In 1881 at the

International Exhibition in Frankfurt he was awarded a medal for "Electric Ped" Boots which were intended to banish malformations due to badly designed footwear. One of his schemes was to give a spare pair of calf shoes with every pair of boots. He was the first to establish a travelling repair shop and when customers so desired the repairs were executed whilst they waited. He had an independent mind and his original and energetic methods were thought to be due to the experiences gained in America. His Blake sewn boots were made of the best possible leather and enjoyed a good reputation. Sanders died in 1899 but he left his mark on the village. Although his factory has long since disappeared a row of houses which he built for his workers and an assembly hall remained long after the factory had gone. His Independence Band, formed from his workers, played in towns where he had his shops. As the band advanced it became known as the Town Silver Prize Band.

Other small factories appeared in the village such as Parkers, Marriotts, and Muscatt, and Frank Eyres Central Boot Factory in 1909. Six years earlier with the building of the South Place factory at the top of Rockham Hill in Station Road a new phase in Long Buckby history had begun. The building was occupied by the London firm of Frederick Cook Limited who employed 200 workers. Established by Cook in 1896 the factory in the village was built on the Bourneville style and was called the "factory in the garden". This led to a new area of the village being developed when houses for foremen and workers employed at the factory were built. Frederick Cook's became the largest manufacturer in Long Buckby during that period and many handsewn men went to work there forming a handsewn department. Most of the work however was machine made. Long Buckby was always noted for its handsewn footwear and much of the Cook handsewn work was exhibited at the Shoe and Leather Fair regularly in London. A report published in the shoe and leather record of 1909 tells of the firms "offering a selection of high grade footwear such as has never been brought together" at the fair. The Long Buckby employees were invited to attend the exhibition. Cook paid their railway fares, giving them free tickets for the fair and providing tea. There was also a reimbursement of wages for time lost at the factory to attend the exhibition. On this occasion the staff presented Cook with a silver rose bowl and the employees a silver spergne.

An extract from the *News Chronicle* of 21st February 1933 provides the answer as to why Long Buckby was chosen as the home of this factory: "Here then is the village of Long Buckby, the centuries old cradle of the Shoemakers craft. In Long Buckby the old stitchmen have sat through the years in their workshops making boots by hand. From father to son the craft has been handed down. Sometimes generation after generation had sat in the same home workshop on the same old stool. This pleasant factory, South Place, on the outskirts of the village deliberately came to Long Buckby in order to capture the unequalled skill of the village craftsmen and graft it on to modern production". A H Hollister J.P., one time managing director of Frederick Cook Limited and a former President of Northampton Boot and Shoe Manufacturers Association from 1927-1931, said: "Long Buckby makes only high grade shoes and we decided to bring our industry here to the home of our craft". In 1933 Messrs Cook Limited were obliged to close down and many operatives had to find work in Northampton. Others took new work in Rugby or Coventry. Many travelled each day to and from the village to work in the Northampton boot factories.

The factory was reopened in 1935, however, by the Kettering firm of Bryants whose Kettering factory had been destroyed by fire. The managing director at that time was B W Cunnington who had started work with C and E Lewis in the 1920's. The name of the firm was changed to Long Buckby Shoes and many of the old hands returned to work in the factory. During World War Two this company produced army boots and many men from the county who were in the armed forces were wearing boots stamped "Made in Long Buckby England". During Coronation Year 1953 the firm made and supplied boots for Her Majesty's Horse Guards and supplied shoes to Simpsons of Piccadilly. The company remained in business until 1959.

The old Castle Factory in King Street built by Alfred Howe became the well known factory of George York and Son. Another well known factory, that of Harry Tomlin, turned out fine specimens of surgical footwear. George York and Son were handsewn boot manufacturers and the founder was head of the firm for more than half a century. George York was only twelve years old in 1890 when he joined William Sanders local Temperance Band, an association which was to last sixty years with fifty of them as bandmaster. York founded his business at the age of twenty-six in 1904 and the firm celebrated its golden jubilee in 1954. Frank Eyres central factory closed down in 1983 after seventy four years of trading; one of the last in the village to go.

At the beginning of the century there were as many as 200-300 handsewn men in the village. This was reduced to about two dozen in the years immediately following the Second World War when no younger men seemed interested in learning the craft. Whilst Long Buckby made shoes which drew the attention of all who attended the Shoe and Leather fairs it will be best remembered as a village of cordwainers, and will be remembered as "the centuries old cradle of the shoemakers craft".

Frederick Cook.

"We do not lend money on Balance Sheets, we advance money on character".
An old London Banker.

Chapter 21

Shoemakers of the Fourth Generation

Seven miles east of Northampton and four miles to the West of Wellingborough lies the village of Earls Barton. Situated just before the confluence of the rivers Nene and Ise at Wellingborough the village nestles peacefully in the midst of the Nene Valley. Dominating the village is its most famous landmark, the Church of All Saints built, in the late 10th Century and one of Northamptonshire's fine Saxon Churches. Most villages in the county owe their origins to the Anglo Saxon period. Earls Barton was favourably situated close to good pasturage and Rockingham Forest which stretched across much of the county. The forest gave rise to many industries, especially bark extracting mainly from British Oak, used in the tanning of leather. Local soils were highly suited to the digging of vats for the tanning of hides; so Earls Barton became noted not only for its Saxon Church but for its long association with the boot and shoe industry.

The Right Reverend George Townley, one time Suffragen Bishop of Hull and a native of Earls Barton, worked in the industry as a youth after attending and studying at Technical Schools in Wellingborough and Northampton. In 1913 he was awarded the highest prize then available in town and county, the honours stage silver medal. As part of Earls Barton Millenium Festival an exhibition of shoemaking was arranged and the Rev Townley published the story of shoemaking in Earls Barton. In it he stated that the excellence of leather tanned in Northampton was recognised in the reign of Edward the First and that it was recorded that in the 13th Century an Earls Barton shoemaker bought his leather in Northampton and so may have been responsible for founding the village industry.

The church registers make early mention of cordwainers and shoemakers in a thriving community. It was also known that William Carey the famous missionary who apprenticed himself to Thomas Gotch of Kettering had intimate links with Earls Barton. His father was parish clerk at Paulerspury but William became a journeyman shoemaker at Hackleton. During that time he was converted to membership of a Dissenting Chapel and in 1782 was invited to become Lay Pastor to the Earls Barton Baptists who worshipped in a tiny thatched meeting house, opposite the Parish Church. Carey walked twelve miles every Sunday to preach to the Rushden mat weavers who worshipped there but who could not pay him enough to cover the cost of shoes and clothing worn out in their service. Yet from this humble beginning this most famous of the shoemakers of the county developed his preaching scholarship and zeal to become the foremost missionary of modern times.

In 1801 the population of Earls Barton was 729; it rose to 1097 in 1841, and 2602 in 1891. This growth indicates the change from a mainly agricultural village into a considerable boot and shoe manufacturing centre. The first shoe manufacturer in Earls Barton was Thomas Dunkley who was born in 1802. His son William along with F Dunkley, W Arnsby, and George and Elijah Rogers were listed as shoe manufacturers, with a number of independent shoemakers, in the 1849 Directory. There were also many handsewn craftsmen or cordwainers who in fact persisted in their own little workshops in Earls Barton until the end of the century. In 1851 William Dunkley employed fifty men and twenty women. In the 1866

Directory there were seven shoe manufacturers and one currier. In 1877 thirteen were listed, and in 1891 these had grown into sixteen firms. During the nineteenth century at varying times there were more than thirty manufacturers in Earls Barton.

Like many homes in the shoemaking areas of Northampton, Earls Barton houses that were built before 1900 still have a workshop built either behind the kitchen or in the back yard where the shoemakers worked. Earls Barton has the reputation of being the first place in the country in which the pegging of boots was carried out. This was a system which held mastery for waterproof footwear until the Wellington Boot came in, and it was all due to one man, Josiah Walker who originally went to the Unites States to better himself. His prospects did not immediately improve but he noted that in one of the factories there wooden pegs and not rivets were used for sole attaching. He returned to Earls Barton with his newly acquired knowledge and his high boots and thigh boots, which were completely watertight, found a ready market.

When Walker's boots were finished they were tested for their waterproof qualities. The old trick of the trade used by the handcraftsmen was remembered prior to the First World War when the village still produced pegged seamen's thigh boots. They were filled up overnight with water and if any came through the seams they were rejected. These boots were hand closed outdoors with a have grain leather for the uppers. Many of the outworkers in Earls Barton did not even have a workshop but worked in the living rooms of their homes. Some factories had empty cottages where lasters worked at their benches in the lower room and finishers on their stools in the upper rooms. In the earlier period one or two rooms sufficed but later, as in Northampton, three storey buildings were erected with a Rough Stuff Room where sole leather was cut and a Clicking Room where uppers were cut.

The sixteen factories at the end of the last century were natural successors of earlier firms. Pioneers like W Arnsby and Elijah Rogers disappeared as did firms like Abel Dunkley, Samuel Clifton, G Barker, Andrew Austin, John Austin, Joe and Ambrose Dayton, William Miller, Owed Miller, William Simpson, and Willis and Simpson. Ward and Sheffield became a dominant firm during the second half of the century. Ward continued to farm while Daniel Sheffield became a public figure as a county alderman and J.P. These firms were followed later by Abraham Allibone, Charles Dunkley and several other employers. Workers gave conspicuous service in both village and county. Josiah Walker was a great character who partnered John Abbott, formerly of Morris and Abbott, and was churchwarden for many years.

One of the most famous names for shoemaking in Earls Barton is that of Arthur Barker and Sons who have had continuous growth and who have family links with the Dunkleys and Ward families. It is one of the few great family firms in Northamptonshire which have not succumbed to the clutches of the large financiers. It is a well established firm built up by five brothers, which has not only survived but expanded. The name Barker is synonymous today with high quality footwear, but few people realise that its derivation is itself very apt to the trade as a barker was one who stripped trees of bark. The process began with the felling of the chosen tree and the lopping off of "mains" and "secondaries" among the limbs and branches. The bark was first "raced" with a bill hook, then barking iron (locally called a "spud") was inserted into the incision so the bark could be eased off in strips and coils. These were then carted up and taken to the tan yard. From this occupation of being a barker came the occupation surname we know today. It is a name which is still so prominently represented in the area.

Crude heavy peg boots were the products of A Barker and Sons Limited before the turn of the 20th Century. From such beginnings has grown a world wide reputation for quality shoes. For over a hundred years Barkers have overcome setback and disappointments. In 1880 Arthur Barker had been making shoes in a very small way before he decided to form a company. He first carried on the business rather like a cottage industry, handing out orders to be made up by craftsmen in their own homes. Barker was known affectionately by all the succeeding members of his family as Great Grandfather Barker. He was a man of great reserves and tenacity of purpose. He had begun his working life as a shoemaker working in a workshop situated at the bottom of the garden of a house in North Road. After a time he moved his business to a small factory in Station Road but before 1900 he had become one of the nine manufacturers in Earls Barton who produced Pegged-Sole Boots. This type of boot found a ready sale in Liverpool in particular. Originally handcut and baked in local ovens the little pegs were soon being imported ready for use, and the replacement of conventional construction methods with pegging gave a good hardwearing boot for seamen, firemen and brewery workers. They were also worn by others who job meant working in wet conditions the pegs merely swelled to make the boot waterproof.

As gradually more machines were built that were capable of revolutionising the shoe industry Barker installed new shoe machinery in the premises he had built in Station Road.The Company became established despite an up-hill struggle with the founder working with very little capital. By about 1905 his three sons had joined him in the business, but after his eldest son Charles left to become a leather importer his other sons Ernest and Arthur Junior worked on with him during the First World War, fulfilling contracts for army boots. Ernest and Arthur continued the policy of development towards one end - the product of high quality shoes. Wartime shortages on the home front led to a demand for wooden-soled footwear or clogs. To overcome the flexibility of the sole Barkers designed a specially incised one, which bent with the movement of the foot in walking. These, together with the orders for army boots, were the basic production during the war years.

After the war had ended there came a return to making traditional footwear and the Barker theme was a family firm of shoemakers with a love for beautiful shoes. This was coupled with an incentive to continually strive towards better footwear. During the early 1920's a large export trade was started with South Africa. This business increased to such an extent that within a few years an astonishing 75% of Barkers output was being sent there. The firm had always been an export house, even from its early beginnings. In 1921 Arthur Barker, the founder of the Barker enterprise, died leaving his two sons to carry the firm onward. In 1933 a new branch was established in Capetown, and several workers from Earls Barton emigrated and settled there thus taking their expertise to a new and distant land. This redoubtable band is still referred to today as "the pioneers". In 1934 Arthur Barker Junior went out to South Africa to take charge of A Barker and Sons (South Africa Proprietary) Ltd. He was helped in the running of the business by his son Ray who subsequently took up the reigns and ran it until 1965.

Shortly after the war of 1939-45 Barkers considerably expanded the Earls Barton factory. A new one was designed and built in Station Road for the making of ladies' footwear. This enabled the older factory to be re-developed and to concentrate on making men's boots and shoes. In the early 1950's Barkers Shoe (Sales) Ltd was formed to sell direct to retailers from an in-stock service, and in 1955 the firm celebrated it 75th anniversary just seven years after the third generation of Barkers had come into the company. These were brothers Albert and Charles Barker who took over the company in 1948. The former became one of the world's finest shoe designers. This is not surprising for a flair of art and design runs like a thread through the Barker generations. The business is now in its fourth generation under the control of William Barker as managing director; he is also a respected shoe designer. As in many of Northamptonshires shoe factories the firm has known many loyal employees who have served the company faithfully all their working lives.

Today Barkers have additional small production units in Wellingborough and Northampton as well as the village complex, and in 1985 a new high technology factory was constructed to take over from the Victorian factory in Station Road. The £2.4 million project was completed in 1986 and includes an octagonal stone clad building for sample display of the Barker range of footwear. This new factory, one of the most modern in Europe, was officially opened by Her Majesty Queen Elizabeth the Queen Mother on 7th May 1987. As a memento of her visit the Queen Mother was presented with a hand-made pair of court shoes. A very noticeable quality of Barker's shoes is the suppleness of their Leather. Much of it is best calf, obtained only a few miles away at Olney, Buckinghamshire, one of the country's few remaining sources for such fine material. Genuine quality and individuality is increasingly rare these days but one can be certain that the Barker family will always maintain the very highest standards of shoemaking as they have done for over a hundred years. Their shoes are nationally recognised as being in the forefront for fashion, style and quality.

Earls Barton has long ranked highly in the boot and shoe industry; in 1850 it was said to be third behind Northampton and Daventry, whilst in 1900 it was level fifth with Kettering, Wellingborough and Irthlingborough. Today, Rushden and Higham Ferrers are higher in production but Earls Barton is still an important shoe centre for its size. The village has not only exported boots and shoes but also skilled workers, designers, foremen, and managers, overseas and to many shoe centres in the United Kingdom. Possibly it could never have absorbed all the skilled workers it produced so other Northamptonshire villages and even Northampton, Wellingborough, and Kettering have employed Earls Barton men to their advantage whilst other craftsmen have set up as shoemakers or repairers in many other cities and towns. Despite the decline in the industry there are in addition to Barker's four other firms which have survived and even expanded together with the leather factors, Nene Valley Leathers.

It is significant that Barkers and Whites were the first to operate fully integrated factories in Earls Barton where all shoe work was produced under one roof. The name of W J Brooks continues as a thriving firm. The business of H Clifton and E Knight prospered for years but later divided. During the present century T and C Partridge took over the Allibone factory. New firms by B Hagar, F Simpson and T Blackwell were founded, another Dunkley family came producing children's footwear, and later there was Botterill's. The slump around 1930 took its toll of Earls Barton firms and today the five survivors are Barkers, Whites, Brookes, Partridges and Botterill's.

114

Arthur Barker.

Heel Attaching. A.Barker & Sons.

Sole Cutting. A Barker & Sons.

Welt Sewing.

The Queen Mother opens Barkers new factory 7 May 1987.

It was in the year 1883 that the brothers Alfred, Ernest and Walter White joined in partnership making boots in two rooms in a house on the Square, Earls Barton. By the year 1893 the business had grown to such an extent that the first single storey factory was built on the present site in Doddington Road and in 1898 two younger brothers, Arthur and Frank, joined the partnership. During the years 1900-1902 further making capacity was required and additional land was purchased to facilitate the building of an extension to the original factory. The business became a private limited company in 1938 the directorship comprising the two remaining partners, Walter and Frank, together with the next White generation Percy, Fred, Godfrey and Harold and Bert Miller. In 1942 the third generation entered into the business and between the years 1959 and 1964 Percy, Fred, Harold and Godfrey White in turn retired. Each had contributed the whole of his working life to the business totalling well over 200 years between them, a remarkable record of service. The board of directors which followed comprised Bert Miller, Don and Keith White and Bob Fairhurst. More extension and modernisation to the factory was completed in 1965 and with demand for the company's products both at home and abroad steadily building up further production capacities meant a future to be approached with confidence and continuing business prosperity.

A. H. White.

J. E. White.

W. White.

B. F. J. White.

Another firm closely associated with Earls Barton District was the firm W Botterill and Son Limited. Now known as Botterill (Sports) Limited and making various types of sports shoes, mostly under the nationally advertised and increasingly important brand name of Gola. Established in 1895 by the grandfather of the present directors the first workshop was sited at Wollaston. By 1900 premises were built at London Road, Bozeat on the site of the present factory, being a small single storey building adjacent to the founder's home. In 1967 it was found necessary to increase the lasting and making capacity beyond what was possible at the Bozeat factory. To meet this demand the old factory of Ward and Sheffield at Earls Barton was rented for three years. The venture was successful but it was impossible to lay out a satisfactory production line so the present new 5,000 square foot factory was built off the Wellingborough Road. This provided for another 15,000 square foot extension to be added as required. Initially working boots were mainly produced with some football boots being manufactured in the 1920's. However, working boots were finally phased out in the early seventies and now production is devoted entirely to sports footwear with over 12,000 pairs of sports shoes being produced every week.

The early shoemakers of Earls Barton divided into those enterprising men who could organise the skills of other shoe workers and develop the factory system and those who continued by themselves in their own little shops. Of the former one such firm was that of Harry J Briggs which was founded in 1899. Harry Biggs specialised in the manufacture of baby and children's shoes. Harry employed his three sons Herbert, George, and Harry Junior. Laster he moved to premises on the square and business prospered and the number he employed rose to about sixteen. When war came in 1914 Harry's sons answered the call to arms and served in France. Later Herbert and Harry Junior left the firm altogether and their brother George continued alone in one workshop which was part of the original factory in Station Road. George carried on until 1944 when ill health forced him to retire. The firm then passed to his son Albert who took over in 1945 upon his return from war service in North Africa and Italy.

The demands for repairs in a rapidly expanding business and the tradition of first class workmanship kept the business going into the seventies. On the shelves and racks one could still see some of Harry J Biggs original tools and the tiny lasts which produced the miniature footwear upon which the fortunes of the firm depended for so many years.

In 1889 William Brookes, another Barton shoemaker, entered into partnership with his brother-in-law Mr Austin and built a small factory on a site at the corner of King Street. In 1906 the whole concern was sold to William Cox and Thomas Pateman. High legged boots had been made for years, the closing of the large uppers being given out to women who were skilled in handclosing some of whom lived in the stone and thatched cottages having only candles for illumination at night. During 1914-1918 army boots were made and also high legged boots for Russian Cossacks. The legs of these were made so big that the riders could stuff straw inside for extra warmth. After 1918 trade fluctuated in Earls Barton. Directors grew older and Harold Cos and Frank Pateman were appointed to the board, Pateman eventually becoming managing director. After the early death of Harold Cox the company secretary, Miss Dorothy Pateman, was also appointed to the board of directors finally retiring from active work after forty nine years of service with the firm. During 1939-45 army boots were again made and shortly after the end of the war Jean Edwards (nee Cox) was appointed to the board and was subsequently followed by Richard Pateman (as factory manager) and Miss Eileen Cox. Further alterations and improvements have been made to the Brookes factory since the war and a wider range of
footwear is now made including ladies' bootees, men's fashions shoes and motor cycle boots.

The fifth Barton firm still operating today is the firm of T and C Partridge and Company Limited. In 1914 Owed Partridge came from Irthlingborough to purchase the existing business of Abraham Allebone for his sons Tom and Cyril Partridge. During the 1920's a variety of constructional methods were employed including staple welted, rivetted and stitched, screwed and stitched, and good year welted. In the early 1930's the firm undertook the manufacture of ladies sahara sandals on a large scale. In 1934 T and C Partridge Limited had the pleasure of supplying sandals to their royal highnesses the Princess Elizabeth (now the Queen Elizabeth the Second) and the Princess Margaret. Upon the outbreak of war again in 1939 the firm was also heavily occupied with the production of footwear for the three services and specialised in the production of commando and jungle boots. After the war the company concentrated on the production of men's goodyear welted footwear. Fashions demanded an increasing variety of light and flexible styles of footwear in the fifties and in

1959 a cement lasted plant was introduced. The need to increase exports during the following years meant that T and C Partridge have supplied men's footwear to no less than twenty different foreign countries.

An Earls Barton manufacturer in the 1920's commented that if he could label his shoes "Made in Northampton" instead of Earls Barton he could demand higher prices. Today, however, "Made in Earls Barton, Northamptonshire" means a mark of the highest quality made by men and women proud of an historic village which is a thriving centre of the county's shoe industry.

Preparing Uppers (A Barker & Sons).

The Lasting Room (A Barker & Sons).

"Old age is a sunset and sunrise in one, we cannot climb the hills as in youth, but we can mount up on Eagles wings".

Chapter 22

Establish the work of our hands

One of the most remarkable stories in the industry in the county is that of the founding of the firm of John White became part of the thriving Ward White Group of footwear manufacturers, a firm which began in a little shed in the town of Higham Ferrers in 1919 and grew into a single company later employing 2,500 men and women producing 120 million pairs of shoes. Much of the history of this company is told in John White's autobiography. He was born in 1884 of a strictly religious family, the youngest of nine brothers and sisters. Like many of his contemporaries he was brought up in Christian surroundings his parents being members of the Calvinistic Baptist Church.

John White.

As a boy John White spent a great deal of time watching the shoemakers of his hometown at work. His own father, also named John, was an experienced cordwainer. John junior used to sit by his father whilst he made shoes and read to him from his favourite story books. John's father always had a Bible and hymnbook at the side of his bench from which he would read extracts during the day. Each day after breakfast he would adjourn to the family parlour where he would spend half an hour in prayer. Against his father's wishes John decided to leave school at the age of twelve to enter the shoe trade. He began work at one shilling and sixpence a week, with a promise of another three pence a week after six months. His first job was working alongside another youth inserting eyelets in the uppers. One boy would punch the holes in the uppers whilst the other would put in the eyelets and clench them. They did about two gross pairs a day. When he reached the age of sixteen John joined his brother-in-law in a family firm making shoes. There was no machinery save for a machine which cut the soles. At that time no factories in the area had a stitching machine. The job of stitching the soles to the uppers was done by an "outside" trade sewer. John would take the work to the sewer one day and collect it the next. In 1902 he joined the firm of John Shortland as a clicker and went to work at a factory called the Express Works. He stayed with the firm for eleven years and at the age of twenty one he was earning twenty-two shillings a week.

When the great Raunds strike came in 1905 more than a dozen firms in this Northamptonshire village were engaged in government contract work; one firm alone employed 400 workers and there were more than 1000 engaged in the trade. Workers came not only from Raunds but daily from other nearby villages. Whilst handsewn work and outdoor working were still the prominent features of the trade in the area there was a change in the policy of the War Office towards machine-made boots. . This obviously meant the introduction of more machinery and new systems of work. The men in Raunds who were making army boots were on very low pay and they struck for higher wages. It was a by-product of the machine age and the government's unwillingness to purchase hand made boots. The end of the Boer War had also reduced the demand for army boots and this had hit the Raunds area very hard resulting not only in low wages but a considerable amount of unemployment. John White remembered how bitter this dispute became; it was one of the most significant in the trade at that time. The dispute commenced on 11th March 1905 and lasted until 31st May. The union entrusted its management to their organiser, Jimmy Gribble, who led the men on a march to the Houses of Parliament in London where after some difficulty in getting a hearing he was evicted from the House.

It is interesting to recall some of the various reports of the march that Jimmy (nicknamed General) Gribble organised. There were over three hundred volunteers and from these the fittest one hundred were selected. It was a spectacular march to London and one man, John Pearson, accompanied the marchers even though he had only one leg. Many of the members were said to be ex-service men and Jimmy had marshalled them into six companies. The column was headed by a local band and a cycle corps of three had been formed; they preceded the marchers and made preparations for them at each resting stage. In addition, a staff of three union officials and two St John Ambulance men accompanied the men who marched four abreast. Each man carried an overcoat and rations on his back and accepted the authority of their "Commandant" on all matters. The route taken went through Bedford, Luton, St Albans and Watford. Local newspapers in the area of the march reported that almost everywhere the strikers were welcomed with interest, sympathy and support from the public. It became commonplace for inns and cafes to offer refreshments. The Northampton Daily Chronicle in its editions of May 9th and 11th reported some of the arrangements: on the first day of the march strikers lunched at the Falcon Inn, Bletsoe where food-laden tables were provided along with cans and buckets of beer and several cases of mineral water. Then at Harpenden on the village green a delightful picnic had been prepared spread out on tables beneath the shade a lunch was waiting. The scene was a most charming and picturesque one and in such good spirit were the men after the feast some of them danced on the village green with local maidens who had previously waited at their tables. The break was altogether one of two hours at this delightful spot. At three thirty after a vote of thanks cheers and tunes form the band the march was renewed. The public gave generously to collections made along the route to finance the march. the collectors going out in front rattling their white boxes before all who passed. A man in a motor car came to a stop and dropped in a shilling,a horseman was seen to reign up and finger his waistcoat pocket, old ladies on the footpath slowly produced their pennies and from wayside cottages children sometimes ran out with their father's coppers. It was stated that one car driver who passed contributed a sovereign to the funds. The whole march and its organisation was full of similar stories and aroused much interest and yet despite its setbacks a settlement was eventually reached.

John White, himself a worker during the bitter dispute, said that it was the men's resistance and the insistence of their trade union leader Jimmy Gribble for a right to be heard which resulted in an agreement being established. Known as the "red book" this raised the wages considerably and made lower wages an offence. From White's own wages of twenty-two shillings a week he gave his father ten, saved ten and spent two, allowing himself a packet of ten cigarettes a week. At this time he had become quite disillusioned with his working conditions and longed to get away from the temperamental and sometimes cruel foreman at the factory. He made up his mind quite firmly that he wanted to be and intended to be his own boss. In 1906 he broke away from the Calvinistic Baptist Church considering their standards too rigid. He joined the Wesleyan Chapel in Park Road, Rushden meeting the girl who was later to become his wife and lifelong partner Nancy Darnell. They were married in 1911, a partnership which lasted for over fifty years. Another change of employment took place in 1912 when he went to work for Charles Horrell of the adjoining town of Rushden as a clicker. He worked very long hours at his job and by 1918 had saved £100, a considerable sum, and he made the decision to leave his job and start on his own. He started making shoes in an old paint shop close to his home. To save costs he built his own workbenches, shelves and racks for the shoes. He bought a clicking board and enough upper leather to produce 500 pairs of uppers and some leather to cut soles. He cut all the uppers himself and sold them to another manufacturer. Business soon boomed and he then recruited twelve ladies to do closing on their own machines and he employed two other clickers. In 1919 he bought a sole press and began producing shoes as a manufacturer. By the end of that year he had a staff of four including himself.

In 1920 White took over the business of a young shoe manufacturer who had failed badly. This firm was situated in a typical three storey building. The owner being in difficulties had left everything and abandoned the business as it was. John White bought it cheaply and his wife, keen to share his ambitions, engaged a body of women to clean the factory up. Shoe factories in those times were not always the cleanest of buildings. The finishing room of this factory in particular was a health hazard. Only sacks were attached to the scouring machines to collect dust. It was a most inefficient method. White began by installing a complete dust extracting plant in the Finishing Department. In just two years he was turning out over 2,000 pairs of shoes a week but it was a long time before he had the complete machinery to make shoes from start to finish. He engaged scores of employees but still had a lot of men making shoes for him outside. In this his first real factory he delegated the top floor to his clickers, the middle floor to the sewers whilst in another room a team of men made shoes by hand. In 1921 yet another firm went out of business with premises in Newton Road which John White purchased for £4,000. This factory had machinery but no lasting machinery and 125 veterans made shoes by hand. Extensions to this factory were carried out with further additions in 1925, 1927 and 1928. By 1925 the output was growing at such a rate there was continual progress and full employment. From that day White never looked back. To keep up with constant demand it became no longer possible to make enough shoes by hand and so consolidated lasters were installed. All key handworkers were found jobs operating the new processes. John White had such faith in his ability to go forward he was an enterprising and cost-conscious man who was not afraid to do a heavy day's work himself. In fact in the early days of his business he spent long hours at his clicking board cutting uppers for his shoes. His motto was "Keep believing" and it can be readily understood that when he decided to launch his own brand of shoes in 1930 he chose the brand name "K.B". In that year 1,250,000 pairs of John White shoes were made.

John White's main factory in 1931 when production was, 250,000 pairs a year.

White found that competition was very keen as there were then many other notable names on the market particularly those made in the town of Northampton. At this stage he decided to take a leaf out of the books of some of his rivals and launch an advertising campaign in the national press. To coincide with this he launched another new brand name which was eventually to become famous the world over, that of Impregnable. The first advertisement was something hitherto considered of a publicity risk. It was a full page advertisement on the front page of the Daily Mail for John White Impregnable Footwear.

Advertising continued to play an important part in the fortunes of the firm and in 1931 the first big extension to the factory was carried out. The company was then spending £80,000 a year on advertising. In 1934, on recommendation, White appointed Basil Lindsay Fynn as financial director and a limited company was floated with £250,000. When Sir Isaac Wolfson took over the Great Universal Stores White sold him his first batch of shoes and in 1937 was

**John White as
Mayor of Higham Ferrers.**

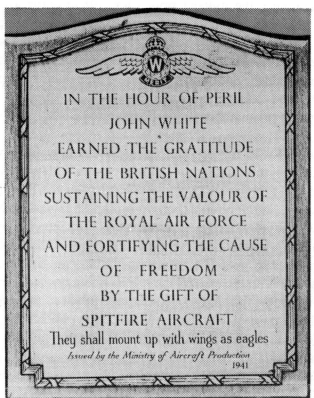

IN THE HOUR OF PERIL
JOHN WHITE
EARNED THE GRATITUDE
OF THE BRITISH NATIONS
SUSTAINING THE VALOUR OF
THE ROYAL AIR FORCE
AND FORTIFYING THE CAUSE
OF FREEDOM
BY THE GIFT OF
SPITFIRE AIRCRAFT
They shall mount up with wings as eagles
Issued by the Ministry of Aircraft Production
1941

Plaque to John White 1941.

Spitfire donated by John White.

supplying him with nearly 300,000 pairs a year. Always known as "Jack" White to his employees the founder prided himself in being known personally to every man and woman at his factory. He recalled that he could never remember sacking anyone. His company was known for providing constant work with high wages and total security. The factory at Higham Ferrers was built in 1936 and was reckoned to be the best shoe factory in the district. During the Spanish Civil war of 1936-39 this factory supplied boots to both sides. 100,000 were supplied to General Franco's troops with a further 100,000 being supplied through a London agency presumably to the Spanish royalists.

Just prior to the Second World War a new factory was built in Lime Road, Rushden. By 1941 there was a total of nine factories with a staff of 2000. These factories also turned out boots for commandos and the R.A.F., for the Royal Navy and for British, Russian and Greek troops. Attention to exporting brought business in North America and as a result of a visit by John White Maceys store of New York and Eatons store of Toronto became two of John White's largest customers and importers of their footwear. Visits were made also to Chicago and Miami visiting various American shoe factories to study their methods; impressed with them White introduced them into his factories. As a result of the tour John White footwear was soon exporting 4,000,000 pairs of shoes to America alone. This was reckoned to be 90% of all shoes exported from this country. When the Festival of Britain took place in 1951 the Company took 2,600 employees to London in 86 buses. They cruised down the River Thames in a fleet of barges and had seats booked for them in all the West End theatres. In Coronation year 1953 a similar outing was arranged when a special train was booked to take all the employees to the capital. The export trade in the 1950's covered 56 territories established in every continent, and in 1954 a factory was acquired at Corby specialising in closing of uppers for the other factories. This closing factory employed 250 women. White was honoured by his local council by being appointed Mayor of the Borough on two occasions, the second time in Coronation Year in 1953 when the present Queen was crowned. He had been created a Freeman of the Borough of Higham in 1952. On reaching the age of retirement in 1962 every member of his organisation of about 2,000 employees subscribed to a gift and a presentation of a leather-bound book inscribed with the name of every worker.

The company which still flourishes can remember many distinguished visitors to its Lime Street Factory in Rushden. The Dowager Duchess of Gloucester, Princess Alice when Duchess of Gloucester, Lord Woolton a wartime minister in the Government and Hugh Gaitskell the Labour leader. Nowadays the company embraces many other firms including Wards of Leicester and at one time controlled the firm of George Webb and Sons, Northampton Limited. It also has embarked on financial interests in other businesses and as recently as 1985 acquired control of the Halford Chain of cycling and motoring accessory stores. The company's growth would not have been possible but for the energy, enthusiasm and expertise of its founder who came from humble origins of a Christian family to give his name to a brand of footwear still being sold all over the world. A plaque in the hall of the Higham Ferrers headquarters, designed by Professor Sir Albert Richardson quotes a favourite passage of John White taken from the Book of Psalms. This, together with his family motto, "Keep believing" seals the history of John White footwear in one sentence: "Let the beauty of the Lord our God, be upon us; Establish the work of our hands; Establish Thou it".

"It never was loving that emptied the heart, nor giving that emptied the purse".

Chapter 23

Other Stalwarts of the County

It is not possible to cover the history of all the firms operation in Northamptonshire for some have long since disappeared. Of the few that remain it has been difficult to obtain complete records of their history but the small number that I shall mention can claim to have pioneered the industry in the county. Where a further or complete history has been available this has been the subject of separate chapters as with Earls Barton, Higham Ferrers and Kettering firms who became well known manufacturers.

The growth of the industry led to the development of a multitude of firms making components and accessories. There were the makers of machinery, lasts and a whole range of products ranging form cut soles and built heels to embossing dies and even cartons and boxes for the finished footwear. Some of these firms were firmly established in Northampton such as Chrome Tanning, W Pearce & Company, Wren Polishes, Boston Blacking, Miller and Whitton Lasts and British United Shoe Machinery Company; many others were spread around the county. The machinery houses were concentrated mainly in Kettering, Rushden and Wellingborough. Last making in Kettering and Northampton and at Higham Ferrers, fibre stiffeners, fibre boards and press blocks. Rushden specialised in protective steel toe-caps for miners and industrial footwear. Desborough, Higham Ferrers, Kettering, Raunds, Rothwell and Rushden built heels of leather and pulp. Many other centres in the county cut soles, welts and socks, or made inks, stains and polishes and manufactured waxes, solutions and dressings. In short, there were very few things that went into the making of good footwear, or to its repair, that were not produced in the county. This meant that a thriving shoe industry was totally surrounded by a multitude of specialist undertakings ready to supply whatever it needed. A thriving industry it was, and as in Northampton, firms began springing up in all of the principal villages and small towns. They were supported by the various component manufacturers and had a ready market for the boots and shoes that they produced. Shoemaker's factories expanded and the villages and towns along with them. Factories expanded and the villages and towns along with them.

Probably the oldest shoe firm to be founded in the county traded under the name of John Spencer and Company. Founded in 1820 by the late Charles Spencer in Higham Ferrers the firm moved into Irthlingborough in 1856. John Spencer, the son of Charles came into the business in 1849 on leaving school, and when his father retired in 1850 he assumed full control and responsibility. The business rapidly developed and to meet growing requirements extensions to the front part of the factory were built in 1858. It was then considered the finest in the district. The opening was quite an event being celebrated by the rendering of The Messiah in the new building, Irthlingborough at that time being full of musical talent. From 1849-85 John Spencer managed the whole business himself and the firm converted into a private company in 1909. He took a prominent part in public affairs and was a chairman of the Urban District Council and a county councillor for some years. He was one of the initiators of the great retail house of Freeman, Hardy, and Willis and was a director of the group for fourteen years. He was a director of eight or nine other companies including the Northampton Machinery Company. The firm of John Spencer specialised in army contracts but also produced some sound, reliable medium class footwear. During the great war of 1914 the firm was then under the capable management of J W Turner. It survived the Second World War having traded for more than one hundred and twenty years.

A factory with a good reputation was that of Charles Parker of Higham Ferrers. First founded in 1874 business boomed and in 1886 a larger factory had to be built to meet increasing demands. This factory was destroyed by fire in 1905 but it was quickly rebuilt in 1906. During the period of the Great War of 1914-18 the head of the firm was Owed Parker J.P. who was one time a president of the National Federation of Boot Manufacturers.

The number of factories in Rushden increased and Nurish & Pallett was founded in 1890. In the same year George Sellwood & Company started in premises at the back of Sellwood's house. The business grew and flourished; a new factory was built in Harborough Road in 1893 and in 1910 a branch factory was opened in Higham Ferrers. A thriving trade was pursued throughout England, Scotland, Ireland and on the European continent and in the colonies. The firm of John Cave of Rushden was thought to have been founded as early as 1846. During the First World War they turned out army boots by the thousand. At one time the managing director was A E Marlow J.P. a Northampton manufacturer who was supported by two county J.P.'s, C Pettit and H Morton. Another firm appeared in 1894; this was C W Horrell and Company, a father and son team whose factory was in production for some fifty years. The Cooperative Wholesale Society factory in Rushden was established in 1900. It was one of many CWS factories making their famous brands of Wheatsheaf men's welted and machine sewn footwear. It was an extensive factory and specialised in making boots for the British army, Russian infantry, Cossacks and Italians. One of the best equipped factories in the trade it owed its early success to its manager, Leonard Tysoe. The factory was modern with large airy workspace and clean white bricks to line the interior. Yet another Rushden firm was that founded by Harry and Frank eaton whose Irchester Road factory did a thriving trade with South Africa, India and the colonies. The company still has a reputation for good footwear. The Technic Boots Company of Rushden, whose present day factory is in Bedford road, was established in 1914. The principle founder was first employed by the Northampton firm of Church & Company for four years and later for five years as superintendent of the clicking department of W Green and Sons of Rushden . The first works manager was F J Tarry who was for some years employed by Crockett and Jones and W B Stevens in Northampton.

One of the oldest shoe firms to commence in Wellingborough was that of Ekins, Son and Percival, a firm that really grew from one first established in 1749 by an ancestor of H P Sharman J.P. of Swanspool, Wellingborough. He became head of the firm in 1868 and appointed John Ekins as his manager and whom he took into partnership in 1871. When the firm became Sharman and Ekins later J Edward Ekins was taken also into partnership. When John Ekins retired the firm was joined by Harry Percival and the style of the firm became Ekins Sons and Percival, the third partner being Robert E Ekins. Another early Wellingborough firm was R Rudlen & Company which was commenced by Robert Rudlen in 1862. They exported footwear to various parts of the world and built a larger factory in 1892. Both of these firms were operating during the First World War. In 1885 Hawkins & Company was founded in Wellingborough by William Hawkins. Although no longer in existence this firm was quite a thriving concern and was still in business in 1940. William J T Glover founded the popular firm of Glover Brothers, Wellingborough in March 1886 in Alma Street, removing in 1888 to larger premises in Grant Road. They were engaged in making their famous Laurel Glove and Phit brands of footwear. Another Wellingborough firm was that founded by Arthur Cheyney in 1890 as Messrs Denton and Cheyney. They were still in business in 1913 when the factory came under the sole proprietorship of the founder. The Walker brothers founded a small factory in Century Road in 1892 having first commenced in business in nearby Wilby in 1890. They soon outgrew their first Wellingborough factory and moved to new premises in Midland Road and the joint owners were J K Walker and Thomas Walker.

East of the county at Wollaston the firm of A W Partridge was established in 1864 by John Walker. His son Pratt Walker succeeded him in 1889 and carried on the business as Pratt Walker. It was thought to be the oldest boot manufacturing business in the neighbourhood of Wollaston doing an extensive trade in both home and export markets. Mr Pratt Walker retired from business in 1908 and the firm was offered as a going concern to his manager Mr A W Partridge as a reward for diligence and long and faithful; service. Mr A W Partridge had been in the firms employ from boyhood and had a thorough and practical knowledge of the business. He immediately set to work re-organising the whole factory adopting the best known modern methods with a view to attaining the highest stage of efficiency int he production of mens medium class footwear. He adopted a principle that would ensure once a customer always a customer.

One of the firms currently enjoying a surge in prosperity is the Wollaston group of R.Griggs Ltd who manufacture the famous Doctor Marten's Boot. Invented by a German, Doctor Claus Maertens, in the 1940's as an orthopaedic shoe this footwear with its air-filled soles, has remained the same since the 1960's. The sole is known as Airwair and Griggs own the patent. The success of the boot, especially in the United states, has been largely due to the sole which is practical and versatile. It led to a Queen's Award for export for Airwair ltd, the export division of the group. The workforce in this section has increased to 500 and turnover doubled every year between 1988 and 1992 when £28 million was reached. The Doc marten boot points to a fascinating development of an item of footwear that developed from an orthopaedic application to become industrial boots for policemen, traffic wardens and other workers, to "bovver" boots for the Skinheads of the 1970's. At the present time they are seen as stylish and popular with fashion designers. This has brought a welcome upsurge oif trade in a section of the shoe industry which employs some 2,200 workers.

Robert Coggins founded a shoe factory in Raunds in 1892. Its continued success is a tribute to the memory of a very capable man. He established his firm in very modest premises in Coleman Street and it met with unqualified success. A more up to date factory, the Nene Works, was erected in Marshalls Road in 1909. Another of Raunds most popular firms that is making shoes at the present time is Tebbutt and Hall Brothers. Founded in 1885 T T Tebbutt, W Hall, and J P Hall this firm has a splendid record.

One of the early firms in the Nene Valley was that of T C Mann and Sons of Cogenhoe. Founded in 1874 this village firm made only the very highest quality men's handmade footwear mostly for elite London customers. The village workers of those days were among the finest of skilled craftsmen. The firm of T C Mann and Sons continued through these generations and finally closed after the deaths of William Mann and Thomas Mann junior in 1950 when the business amalgamated with Stricklands of Northampton.

The village of Bozeat had its shoe factories and still does. The firm of John Drage was established in 1861 by John Drage who was succeeded by his son William Chambers Drage and later his two sons F C Drage and C Drage. This firm did a large home and export trade including South Africa and India.

The well known firm of Botterill Sports makers of the famous Gola Sports footwear of Easton Maudit Lane, Bozeat added another Shoe firm to this village when it was founded in 1896 by Mr W Botterill. I have referred to this firm connection also with Earls Barton. For many years it trade under the name of W Botterill Limited. At one time there were also two other factories in Bozeat the Bozeat boots Company and the John Drage Shoe Company. The footwear produced included mens and womens welted, youth machine sewn and rivetted, veldthschoens in various colours for children and sandals. Heavy boots, sports footwear, including football boots were also made in the village. There was a considerable export trade to Australia and the Pacific Islands, West Indies, the Middle East and Canada.

The founder of the firm of John Shortland of Irthlingborough was formerly with Messrs William Shortland and Sons when a dissolution took place in 1899. New works were built and a capacity of 10,000 pairs a week was reached. This firm became noted for its "Wearra" brand of footwear. this brand of multiple fitting shoes was first launched on July 13th 1939 and on January 22nd 1947 the name of Wearra shoes Limited was incorporated to protect the trade mark of John Shortland Limited.

In Burton Latimer Henry Whitney and Joseph Westley started making shoes in a small cottage in 1897 and they employed five workpeople. Their first factory was built in 1902 and they extended it in 1910. They turned out 7000 pairs of shoes a week and supplied half a million pairs for military purposes in the 1914-18 war.

The village of Finedon was another shoe making centre. One of the earliest firms to be established there was that of Arthur Nutt. Founded in 1893 the firm became a Limited Company in 1908. Over in Rushden another firm appeared the following year of 1894. This was C W Horrell and Company founded by C W Horrell who was assisted by his only son, W M C Horrell.

Sudborough brothers limited was first established in Burton Latimer in 1885 and moved to Findeon in 1904. It was founded by John Sudborough but the firm eventually moved to Wellingborough in 1906 and occupied premises in Oxford Street. Later they moved to Park Road where they had an extensive works producing 1,500 pairs of shoes a day for all markets. The Sudborough brothers were joined by their sons H J Sudborough and E H Sudborough. In nearby Wollaston F Pitts founded the firm of F J Pitts in conjunction with his brother Alfred.

Avalon footwear of Rothwell started from small beginnings in a building in Fox Street, Rothwell about 1892. They built a more extensive factory in Littlewood Street which was subsequently enlarged. Later, an even larger factory in Cross Street and Crispin Street became vacant and was taken over. All old machinery was thrown out and a welted plant installed and the factory brought up to date; F Tebbutt became the managing Directory of this new factory. The company has built up a reputation for fine footwear over the years. Other shoe firms in Rothwell were: J T Butlin & Sons, a family business formed in 1869 making men's rivetted, welted and moulded shoes, and taken over by C & J Clarke in 1955 but closed in 1980; W I Butlin, a family business which closed in 1920; S E Gamble & Sons, a family business starting about 1890 and making men's rivetted and moulded shoes which closed in 1973; Chamberlain & Co closed in 1922; Eaton & Co which closed in 1929; Taylor & Sons, taken over by John White of Higham Ferrers and closed in 1976; T Groocock & Co and related to the Desborough Groococks and are still making men's rivetted, welted, moulded and ladies cemented footwear.

Desborough has been associated with shoemaking since the mid-nineteenth century. Benjamin Riley founded his firm in 1868 known as B Y Riley of Desborough. When Benjamin Riley died in 1894 his son F T Riley took control. He built up a very sound business their production being mainly confined to good class Boys boots and mens footwear. They also had a large export trade and did contracts for British, French, Italian, Serbian and Austrian armies. F T Riley was known as a keen and alert business man who developed the business on sound lines for delivery to many parts of the world. Yet he also found time for public affairs and was a member of the District Council besides other bodies connected with the district. John Cheaney and Sons Limited of Rushton Road, Desbororough began in 1886. This firm is now part of Church's (Northampton) Group. Another Desborough firm followed two years later in 1888 and this was B Toone and Company who were famous for their well known brand of Little Duke boys footwear and Seagull ladies and Pearl Maiden Shoes. When first established B Toone and Company was a branch of Toone and Black of South Wigston, Leicester and employed twenty people. By 1914-18 they were turning out 8,000 pairs of shoes a week and employing four hundred people. During 1914-16 they produced 170,000 pairs of army boots.

Other Desborough firms were: the Crompton Footwear Company, a cooperative production society in which the employees were shareholders; this firm ceased in the 1970's; T Bird & Co, which came under the supervision of the Groocock family but closed in the 1960's; Bosworth & Co, a family business which closed in the 1930's; W Barnes & Co which ceased in 1952. But still turning out men's rivetted, welted and moulded shoes is the Desborough Shoe Company Ltd, originally trading as Yeomans, taken over by the Ellington family but now part of Griggs & Co of Wollaston.

Few firms still manufacturing in the county today are better known in the trade or have a wider reputation for making high class footwear than the firm of Loake Brothers of Kettering. This firm of shoemakers was founded in the year 1880 by John Loake who was their first chairman. He was supported from the outset by his brothers W F Loake and T Loake. Later the three of them were joined by C M Loake, E W Loake and G A Mayes. The factory was known as the Unique Boot Works and the reliability and reputation of their products became known far and wide. At first the Loake Brothers began in a very small way and specialised in men's and youths' best medium footwear. By steady perseverance they have grown to be one of the largest factories in Kettering still in existence. The factory continues to manufacture men's best and medium quality footwear. They regularly exhibit at the Shoe and Leather Fair.

Charles East of Kettering was a business established as long ago as 1854 by Charles East as a boot upper manufacturer. It was notable that soon after its foundation the first sewing machine ever to be employed in the boot trade was introduced. It led to strikes and other industrial troubles but the machine was used in spite of all opposition. On the death of the

Thomas Loake.

William F. Loake.

founder in 1875 the business was managed by his sons Walter C East and Frederick East. In 1903 the firm became a limited company. Later the son of Frederick East became a Director. The original factory which was built in 1863 and known as Britannia Works was enlarged in 1890. The company supplied footwear throughout Great Britain and the Colonies. Their earliest pairs of boots were marked "rivetted" and the firm pioneered this type of footwear. The house of East saw more developments in the trade than many in the district being always ready to adopt the many inventions and machines which in later years revolutionised the industry. Charles East and Company played an important part in the marvellous output for which the town of Kettering became well known. This business continued well into the forties.

Another Kettering firm was that of Thomas Bird J.P. who started business in 1862 in partnership with George Abbott. The Abbott & Bird partnership was dissolved in 1891. This firm was one of the oldest and best known manufacturers in the trade being noted for their reliable, sterling, and stylish boots and shoes. During 1914 they were producing as many as 7000 pairs a week. Yet another of Kettering's oldest shoe firms was Bryan and Son Ltd which was founded by J Bryan in 1859. He built a factory in Ebenezer Place which was occupied until 1886 when larger premises were built and a capacity of 10,000 pairs of boots a week was reached. They specialised in gents smart welted goods for both home and foreign markets, South Africa, India, Australia, New Zealand and Egypt. The firm also produced naval and military boots. One village firm in the Kettering area was that of Stephen Walker of Walgrave, Makers of heavy nailed boots. This firm was acquired by George Webb and Sons Limited for the production of Injection Moulded footwear in 1951.

The year 1895 brought another two firms on the scene in Kettering. Frank Wright and his brother Harry founded a shoe firm but this partnership was dissolved in 1903. The business was then carried on by Frank Wright and his son. A new factory was built in Carey Street in 1900 and was enlarged in 1913. The firm at that time were turning out 10,000 pairs of footwear a week. This house produced superior medium class lines in machine sewn and welted footwear and were still in business during the Second World War.

The business of Rice and Company Limited of Kettering was established also in 1895 by Earnest E Rice during the year of the shoeworkers strike. They began in a small place in Gordon Street, Kettering removing to larger premises in Wellington Street. When this factory proved inadequate they moved to a larger building at the corner of Rosebury Street and Shaftesbury Street. After a few years land was purchased in Durban road where a new factory was erected this was twice enlarged. The firm of Rice and Company made large quantities of footwear for the Government during the whole period of the First World War and the became a Limited Company in 1914.

Two popular Kettering firms founded in 1896 were Allen and Caswell, and Gravestock Limited. The former was founded by F Allen and H W Caswell in Albert Street premises. As business progressed, H W Caswell and his friend F T Allen found that the steady growth soon necessitated an early removal to still larger premises. A move was made to a new factory in Northall Street in 1900 and from thence they moved in 1905 to still larger premises in Sackville Street. Their final move before the first World War was to a more commodious factory in Stamford Road in 1908. It is a tribute to their founders that they are still in business making shoes today in Cromwell Road. The present firm incorporates Allen and Caswell founded in 1896 and the Drage Shoe Company founded in the 1920's and Safirst footwear founded in 1954-5. Allen and Caswell became a Limited Company in 1923.

F. T. Allen.   **H. W. Caswell.**

The firm of Gravestock is no longer in business but was still functioning in the 1970's. It was originally founded by George Cattell but in 1915 became known as E C Gravestock Limited. Its directors at that time were E C Gravestock J.P., E C Gravestock Junior and A W Gravestock. E C Gravestock Senior was also in partnership with George Wright of Kettering who had established a factory in School Lane in 1891 and later in Tresham Street in 1894. This factory became Gravestock and Wright in 1910. In 1914, however, Gravestock's shares were purchased by George Wright and his family and became George Wright (Kettering) Limited. E C Gravestock was famous for many years for its "Avenue" brand of shoe. E C Gravestock senior was a chairman of the Company and also a chairman of Kettering Urban District Council.

Three county firms started manufacturing in 1910 and the latter two of these are still in business at the present time. Perkins and Bird of Irthlingborough, Eaton and Company of Rushden, and G W Shelton of Wollaston. The firm of Eatons, who today have a factory on the Sanders Lodge Industrial Estate, was founded in quite a small way by Harry and Frank Eaton and their first large factory was in Irchester Road. In the early days of the business a large export trade was built up with South Africa, India and the colonies. G W and R Shelton of Wollaston also commenced in 1910 but its name dates back as far as 1886 when a W Shelton was in business in the village. Their factory which is situated in St Michaels Lane is still making fine footwear.

We can see from the number of firms quoted that there was a considerable growth in the industry throughout the county from the formation of the very first firm of John Spencer in 1820; a long period of active shoemaking. Many of the firms were family firms passing on skills from generation to generation.

Many of these firms were in business after the First World War, some at the outset of the Second World War in 1939 and afterwards. Their names can be identified in the Kelly's Directories of the Leather Trades of 1922, 1929, and 1940. Other firms followed in the early twenties and later such as Albert Hulett and Munn and Carver, (later Munn and Felton's of Kettering). Incidentally it was Munn and Feltons whose workers formed the Champion Brass Band which was later known as the G.U.S band and more recently as Rigid Containers Band. The Coxton Shoe Company of Rushden was another. Bignell, George Fox, Yorke Brother and Craddock and Martin of Wellingborough, R Griggs of Wollaston and T Groocock of Rothwell. Of these firms only the following are still in business today:- Hulett Shoes Limited, George Cox Limited, Craddock and Martin Limited, Yorke Brothers Limited, R Griggs and Company Limited and T Groocock and Company Limited. This represents a substantial core of the staple industry that has survived the rigours of the recession of the last decade.

The productive capacity of the boot and shoe trade after the Great War broke out in 1914 had been a surprised to the most experience of manufacturers. Taking into account the number of men leaving the factories for the army and the large amount of labour involved in the making of army boots it must have been reasonably supposed that to produce large quantities of army boots would have been impossible. But millions of pairs were turned out in Northamptonshire factories and in addition a fair proportion of civilian footwear. This was an exercise that was to be repeated during the 1939-45 war. Despite the two world wars the slump of the thirties and a number of other crises it is amazing that so many shoe firms have survived the storms and are still making footwear that Northamptonshire can be proud of today.

"When the lord leads, He provides shoe leather".

Chapter 24

I walked the Barratt Way

The title that I have chosen for this particular chapter was the famous slogan of the Barratt brothers which became a world famous phrase and could be seen printed in their advertisements in the national press almost every day. This slogan became a reality for me in the early 1930's when I first started working in a shoe factory and did actually "Walk the Barratt Way" from my home every day. As a schoolboy I had witnessed much of the hardship and insecurity that was caused by unemployment and short time working in the shoe trade and the slump which came during the years prior to my entering the shoe trade in 1934 at the age of fifteen. During the years of the slump my father was one of hundreds of Northampton shoe workers on short-time working as many firms lost much of their export trade due to the exporting of machinery to many countries who had hitherto been their largest customers. There was at the time little other industry in the town and it meant that the only likely employment for a boy or girl leaving school was when a vacancy occurred at the benches in a local shoe factory.

This sad state of affairs had prompted the M.P. of the Borough of Northampton, Colonel L'Estrange Malone, to make a statement in the press in March 1930. He predicted a decline in the family business of boot and shoe manufacturers. He said he was "of the opinion that the old family business system on which the prosperity of the boot and shoe trade was founded was doomed. Already", he said, "the sons are seeking wider fields to conquer with their inherited wealth. More often on the golf links than in the factory. On the other hand certainly signs indicate that outside financial interests are anxious to capture the trade. An outstanding example was the attempt of a certain financial group to buy up Freeman, Hardy, Willis of Leicester and Sears (True-form) of Northampton. This was averted by Sears but nevertheless it indicates forces are at work. Seeing these tendencies and noting also the general adoption of rationalisation on every hand I fear that the next ten or twenty years will see changes which may have disastrous effects on the workers in the industry if not carefully watched and guarded against". - History has proved Colonel Malone's words to have been prophetic. As I write this text many factories have gone and of those that remain most have been engulfed in great monopolies whose boundaries know no limits and whose tentacles have, like an octopus, reached out far beyond the shoe trade amidst so much uncertainty.

With such a similar fear of unemployment I found myself in 1935 at the age of fifteen having to accept that the only job likely to come my way was to enter the shoe industry. I well remember that it was the wish of my parents that I did not enter the shoe factory for they did not see any prospect in doing so. Neither did I have the desire at the time to become a shoe operative for I had visions of being tied to some humdrum job which had little future. I recall that I was one of countless thousands who left school at the age of fourteen at a time when there was a considerably high degree of unemployment. My first job had been a most unsatisfactory one with the local co-operative society and a temporary one with a sweet manufacturing company. After my first twelve months in work a period of unemployment loomed when suddenly through my brother I was offered a job in a shoe factory and reluctantly I accepted. The childhood vision of the shoe factories I had formed when I peered through the windows of some of the towns older factories soon diminished. It was the day that I entered the very modern factory of W Barratt and Company Limited in Kingsthorpe Road. Entering by Monarch Road (named incidentally after a brand of shoe machinery) one passed through a small open yard and ascended about four flights of stairs to find oneself in a large cloak room in which were heated rails from which men collected their "smocks" and hung up their coats before entering the factory. At this time the firm provided a warehouse type of coat which had replaced the traditional shoemaker's apron.

Just outside the cloakroom and on the factory floor one encountered the time clock. Prior to the starting time of 7.30 a.m. men could be seen "clocking in". This was done by means of a large clock which was surrounded by numbers and a handle which could be spun around. Each employee had his own number and he would turn the handle round clockwise until he reached that number pressing the pointer into a hole at the side of the number when a bell would ring. This action would stamp the exact time of arrival at work on a roll on the inside of the clock. Each employee was allowed two minutes "clocking in" after which his entry would be stamped in red and he or she would be deducted fifteen minutes pay for being late. This was known as "losing a quarter". Those employees who were a minute or two late would be pushing to get into the remainder of the queue to punch the clock. A dodge very often used by operatives who were on the borderline would be to punch the clock extra hard. This practice would sometimes result in the mechanism stamping the sheet back one minute. The general procedure in most factories was to clock in first thing in the morning, first thing after lunch and before going home at night. Not all firms used the same type of time clocks. Some factories used a system in which the employee took a card from a rack, inserted it in a space in the clock and punched the card.

The factory in Kingsthorpe Hollow was open planned and one could see from room to room on each floor. It was light and airy and, contrary to what I had expected, remarkably clean. There was little overhead shafting and despite the strong smell of leather and chemicals the standards of hygiene and safety were very high indeed. I was first employed in the Finishing Room, a long narrow room which rang alongside the Roughstuff Department and was reached by passing through the largest room in the factory, the Making Department. Little is known of the men who pioneered all their lives service to the industry by improving some of the early practices in shoe manufacture and the perfecting of the various machines and different processes in shoe construction. Over the years their productions exhibited supreme artistry and the greatest beauty. Thanks to their skill there has been benefit to all, both shoe workers and the public who wear the finished product. It was not very long before I became aware of these seemingly wonderful processes for here in the modern and up to date Footshape Works more than three or four hundred machines were running, sometimes with comparative noiseless speed, worked by electric power. Frequently one could hear the noise of the heavier machinery and the intermittent sounds of the thunder-like revolution presses of the Rough Stuff or Bottom Stock Department. I could also see these great presses in motion as the operator pushed under the huge sheet of leather and cut out and shaped the soles of the shoes with thick and strong knives. Whilst from the adjoining Making Room one could frequently distinguish the whining sounds of the pounding machine.

This modern shoe factory was full of the greatest marvels of machine invention, and the saving of labour by using machines was very evident. Admist all this mechanical activity it was not long before I became familiar with the general processes of shoemaking. Frequently a trip to another department of the factory or a visit to the general store which was situated on a lower level would ensure a view of the many varied operations in shoe manufacture. Sometimes a word with the operator who manned a particular machine would enable one to get a close look at a single operation. Each operative would be working on a rack of twelve pairs of shoes and its journey through the factory would take about three weeks, but the operating time spent on each shoe would only total an hour or so. Teams of men would be working on some parts of the shoes in the early stages at the same time.

The pattern room, clicking and closing rooms of the Footshape factory were situated at ground level and could be reached either by lift or staircase from the side of the Making Room. The Pattern Room specialised in making the intricate patterns for the clickers to use and here skilled and experience designers were at work, producing up-to-date designs for new styles of footwear. In the adjoining Clicking Room about a hundred men stood at benches. Each had a clicker's board on which the skin would be stretched. The clicker first examined the skin for any blemishes and when he was satisfied that it was perfect he began to cut round his pattern with a short knife using his skill to get as many parts of the upper from the skin he was using. The variation of stretch, quality and substance in every skin made this a very highly skilled job. Little is known of the origin of the word "clicker". One theory is that it was derived by the sound made by the knives on the boards; there being no machinery in this room at that time this was the only noise to be heard.

Along side the Clicking Room was the Closing Room where the section of the uppers which had been cut out by the clickers were joined together. In this room over two hundred women were to be seen operating rows of sewing machines each performing a separate operation, and here quickness was evident. No time was spent in winding spools or taking off the thread. The two or three rows of stitching required for the vamps were done at the same time. Some nine or ten buttonholes could be strongly and neatly worked in five minutes. This one operations will give some idea of the speed the girls were capable of. The work of the fitters was generally with very great skill by holding and turning the section of the upper under the needle until the stitching of the upper was finished. Other machinists were sewing on buttons and fixing eyelets and beading on some styles. The upper were then considered completed, labelled and passed to the Preparation Room which was a part of the Rough Stuff Department. The staff of the Preparation Department then selected the heavier but suitable bottom leather according to the descriptive label which was a duplicate of that used in the Clicking and Closing rooms. This, of course, enabled the work to be prepared at the same time as the uppers were being assembled. The bottom leather was then accurately matched for thickness and quality and the soles, insoles, welts, heels and stiffeners were paired with the uppers which had arrived from the Clicking Room and Closing Room. Finally all the components were assembled on racks which then proceeded to the Lasting or Making Room where the building of the shoe began to take shape.

The racks normally used to transport shoes through the factory were constructed of wood and were made to hold twelve pairs of shoes with room for lasts in the bottom. The Last Store was a series of "bunks" in the corner of the Making Room and was popularly known by employees as "the last cubs. When the rack was complete with the lasts the racks were taken together with all components to the Making Room proper. It was here that the tops and bottoms were fastened together. If the shoe was to be machine-sewn the upper was attached first to the insole by permanent tacks instead of sewing and as there was no welt the stitches that held the sole passed through the upper and insole. It was necessary to clench these fine tacks and for this purpose the bottom of the wood last had a plate made of steel. The upper was then "pulled over" the last the insole having been lightly tacked to the last. The shoe then proceeded to the lasting machines where the toes and heels were "wiped in" by two plate sowing like mechanical pincers with a scissor like action. The upper was then tacked down to the insole by the automatic machine with tacks and staple operated by an experienced workman who did the rest. The fastening of the sole to the upper may be done in one of many ways such as sewing as just described or by rivetting or cementing.

In addition to machine-sewn footwear one of the most widely used methods in operation was and still is the Goodyear Welted method of constructing a shoe. For this method a specially prepared insole is used having a raised rib near to the edge. During the "lasting" process soft staples secure the upper temporarily to this rib. A narrow strip of leather, called the welt, is sewn by chain stitch to the upper and the rib of the insole thus making a horizontal seam. The cavity in the insole is then filled up with compressed cork (known in the factory as "bottom filling") and the outer sole is then fixed in position. The sole and welt edge are then trimmed to shape and a channel cut in the former to receive the sole stitching. This sole stitching permanently attaches the welt to the sole with a lock stitch and these are the stitches that can be seen at the end of the finished shoe. It is worthy of note that when a shoe is made by this method the inside of the insole is perfectly clean and free from tacks or stitches. Shoes thus made are quite flexible. The heels which consist of layers of leather already fastened together and compressed are then attached to the shoe. Although rough in appearance the shoe is then completely built.

After the shoe had been through all the processes in the Making Room the racks of shoes passed to the Finishing Department where the edges of the soles and heels were trimmed and pared by teams of machines operators, first on edge trimming machines, waist trimming ("knifing up") machines, all at lightning speed. Other teams of men operating rotating machines scoured the heels and bottoms after which men working burnishing machines with hot irons then set the edges of the sole with hot wax. Next step in the journey through the Finishing Room was to the operators who coloured and polished first the heels and then the bottoms or foreparts of each shoe, giving it a "finished appearance". Lastly the shoes were then "slipped" off their lasts (by hand or machine) and then sent on to the Shoe Room where teams of girls added the final gloss and shine. Each pair would then be "treed" (ironed) so that they appeared untouched by hand or machine. Finally the girls put in socks stamped on the maker's brand name which in the case of Barratts was "Footshape". The whole of this room operation was described as being "shoe-roomed". The shoes were then put into boxes, labelled with the size and style, and after a final examination the finished shoes had passed through a hundred or more operations. All finished shoes when boxed were sent to the Despatch Department for onward transmission to the shops or placed in some of the company's hugh Stock Rooms at the side of the factory which adjoined Freehold Street. This building also housed the factory's own Repair Department which dealt
with returned goods from the shops and also customers' repairs.

Working life in a shoe factory did not really vary from factory to factory for modern processes were of the same pattern. Operatives could move from one factory to another and be employed on the same machine operation. Pay rates were generally agreed locally between managements and the union. Only the conditions of employment were different, for some factories were older and did not offer the same amenities as others. It was significant that many operatives remained with one firm for the whole of their working life. Conditions of employment at the Barratt factory were such that there were many long serving employees. As I resigned myself to factory life I had little thought at the time of finding employment elsewhere. I found that there was a great comradeship amongst most of the men and a deep sense of espirit de corps and often a helping hand when one was sick and off work. The company operated both a very efficient benevolent and a holiday fund. At holiday times each employee would receive a fixed sum from the holiday fund. At that time holidays with pay as we know it today did not apply.

During my first years in the shoe industry hours of work were forty eight hours a week with a commencing time of 7.30 a.m. and a lunch break of one and a quarter hours. Most of the employees went home for a midday meal. Special buses were operated by local transport for those not within walking or cycling distance of the factory. Few working men owned cars in those days and those who remained in the factory during the lunch break took sandwiches and made tea in what was known as the Rest Room or the canteen. No factories possessed the type of canteen facilities that have become a feature of most industries today. Sometimes during busy periods overtime hours would need to be worked. The normal practice would be to work one hour per day half an hour earlier in the morning and half an hour later in the evening. Overtime working was always at the discretion of the foreman of the department. Saturday morning was at that time part of the working week and work would commence at 7.30 a.m. and terminate at 11.45 a.m. All machinery would be switched off at 11.30 a.m. to allow all operatives time of fifteen minutes for a "cleaning down" period. During this time all operatives would clean their machines and bring them to a very high standard, each worker taking particular pride in his or her machine. The rooms would be thoroughly swept and all refuse taken to a tip and incinerator at the side of the Making Room. The factory always seemed to take on a special appearance at midday on Saturday.

Most shoe operatives were on "piece work", that is to say they were paid by the results of their labours. Each operation was costed and a price per dozen pairs agreed between management and the union. If an operation was adequately priced it gave incentive to the employee to work hard and thereby increase his paypacket. If a job was badly priced a worker would be deemed not able to "earn his money" and this created problems resulting in the operative complaining to his union who would then arbitrate for a better price. Workers not on piece work were known as "day workers" and each received a statutory wage also agreed between management and union. This wage varied according to age; the commencing wage for a youth at that time was about twelve shillings and sixpence. The piece work system often caused arguments between operatives on the same job operation. There was always the odd worker who would try and outsmart one of his mates when choosing work. Obviously some lines of work were easier to manipulate than others. Often there was dishonesty and cheating as each operative was required to take work in the order in which it came to him. When his operation was completed he would book the number of the ticket on a sheet provided; it was handed to the foreman at the end of each week, for submission to the factory Cost Office. This system had been in operation in most boot and shoe factories for many years. It was, however, to my mind a system that was open to a lot of failings and often created ill feeling. Day work wages were tied to the cost of living and meant that small increases in wages were awarded should the Cost of Living Index rise. This appeared to be a very satisfactory agreement to operate and avoided some of the large wage claims of other industrial workers. However, shoe workers ranked amongst the lowest paid in the country.

I have spoken of the comradeship which seemed to prevail in the Footshape factory and I think that by and large this was evident throughout the shoe trade. It would seem that the high qualities of workmanship were handed down from father to son and family to family. I would go as far as to say that the majority of shoe operatives took a pride in their work. There was a great deal of humour and the introduction of radio into the factories and the BBC "Workers Playtime", which was relayed throughout the factory, often encouraged operatives to sing whilst working. At other times it was amusing to hear a multitude of voices singing "Why are we waiting" or some of the popular tunes of the day such as "Roll out the Barrel"," Please release me" or" We'll never walk alone"; tunes which expressed in song the feelings of the moment. Other factory reminiscences include the ten minute "lunch break" which was around 9.30 a.m. This usually coincided with "Workers Playtime" and all machines were switched off so that workers could eat the sandwiches they had brought to work and drink tea from their thermos flasks. Milk was also served in half pint bottles with a straw and those operative who drank milk purchased tickets at the beginning of the week. Many shoe workers ate little breakfast before coming to the factory so the bringing of a "lunch packet" was a common practice. The drinking of milk was encouraged amongst workers because it was felt that in the dusty environment of the shoe factory it helped prevent tuberculosis. The Footshape factory was kept as dust free as possible by powerful fans which sucked the dust into huge pipes and carried it out of the factory. The Barratt brothers often came into the factory and would sometimes stop and talk to some of the operatives. They were generally concerned that the cleanliness of their factory should be of the highest order. Richard Barratt was heard to say on one occasion when he observed some dust near to a machine that it should be as clean as his drawing room. Every effort was made in this direction and permanent "sweepers" were employed to keep each department as free from waste as was possible.

Many operations in a shoe factory are done in teams. There were teams of Lasters, Puller Overs, Heelers, Sewers and Stitchers in the Making Department. There were teams of Edge Trimmers, Bottom Scourers and Bottom Makers in the Finishing Department. Often a boy starting work in a factory would be assigned to work for a particular team. In my own case I was first employed to do work for the team of Bottom Makers in the Finishing Department; about six or eight men whose skill put the finish on the soles of the shoes. They were a friendly bunch of men and would be quite generous at the end of the week and always at Christmas with their tips. Although I soon knew all of them by their Christian names I found that one or two of them were known by a nickname. As I became aware of this it seemed very much that the shoe factory was the birthplace of the "nick name" for a lot of the men were known by some very odd pseudonyms. Among those I encountered in the Barratt factory were Acker, Baggy, Barrell, Boner, Bubbles, Buck, China, Darkie, Digger, Drummer, Ginger, Hoppy, Polo, Slug, Snogger and Tuck, besides the more familiar Nobby Clarkes, Dusty Millers and the more traditionally known names.

In the "heyday" of the boot and shoe trade quite a large proportion of male workers were ardent supporters of the local football club, the Cobblers. This often led to a football outing being arranged by some of the men. On these occasions coaches would pick them up from the factory on a Saturday when work ceased at 11.45 a.m. If there was a particularly important away match in some distant town management would be co-operative and allow a half day or work to terminate early. Shopkeepers in nearby Kingsthorpe Hollow and Monarch Road would be kept busy during the lunchhour and often at the end of the day because most operated a system of "open all hours" and welcomed the trade from the factories. Those who sold sweets would have their regular customers. Nevertheless, it was always possible to purchase certain things within the factory brought in by men or women who had relativeS with shops. There was in Footshape works a man who made and sold humbugs, an employee who could supply bars of milk chocolate and an operative who ran a weekly club for socks, shirts and clothing. It was, of course, possible to purchase boots or shoes at the factory because each employee was allowed to buy footwear at special discount prices. This was a great advantage, and after applying for a paper at the office one would be able to go along to the huge stockrooms and select goods that had not passed the high standard required for selling in the shops. Over the years new machines were installed; some were tried and retained, others discarded. Individual motors were fitted to all existing machinery doing away with all overhead shafting. This not only prevented waste for valuable electric power but machines were able to be switched on or off at the will of the operator. New methods of speeding production were also tried in 1938 including the installation of a track system which did away with the conventional racks. The operator pushed a small trolley along a metal conveyor after finishing his operation. This particular type of system was found to be inadequate in many respects and caused bottlenecks.

Life in the shoe factory became very routine and progress was slow. In the late thirties trade seemed to pick up but in the world outside there was political unrest and talk of war. Little did we realise at the time that thousands of shoe workers would soon be called to serve their country in the armed forces and factories would return to making army boots. Following the invasions of Czechoslovakia and Poland there came that dreaded day of 3rd September 3rd when Britain found itself at war with Germany. Some shoe workers at the factory, realising that war was imminent, had joined the Territorial Army. Under the Conscription Act of June 1939 all were immediately called up for war service. Call up for other males was at twenty years of age and being in this category I found myself one of several of Barratt's employees being called up for military service in December 1939. We wondered how long our war service would last. Many shoe workers believed that the conflict would be over within twelve months but they were proved to be short-sighted for the war was to last five years. Week by week staff at the factory became depleted as more and more men, and later women, were called up for military service.

With so many employees on active service the firm's directors were quick to establish a fund where small weekly grants were paid to wives, parents and families. This financial help was available for use or could, if desired, be retained in the form of savings certificates. The fund continued throughout the war years. At the same time remaining employees contributed towards a "comforts fund" from which parcels were frequently sent to colleagues in the forces. With end of hostilities in 1945 there was a gradual return to normal in the factory as men and women slowly returned to civilian life. One of the tragedies of this, however, was the fact that although jobs had been kept open the machines had to continue operating during the years of conflict and this was done by employing what became known in the trade as "green labour". When skilled operatives were called up their places were taken by older men or women over military age or non skilled personnel not liable for military service. After the war rehabilitation in former jobs became a nightmare to employers with the result that some workers left the factory and took up other employment. The return to one's own particular job was often long and hard often feeling like a displaced person being moved from department to department.

Following the War welfare standards hitherto accepted in the boot and shoe trade were considered inadequate and prompted investigation into the need for improved working conditions. Comfortable seating for women operatives was immediately apparent. Also considered was the effect of working fatigue and its efforts on the rate of production. In consequence the idea rapidly gained ground that working fatigue could to some extent be controlled and its onset retarded by the cultivation of better working postures. It was demonstrated conclusively that posture could be improved for women operatives and that it was affected by chair construction. It was felt that in the closing rooms in particular permanent improvements in working posture could be obtained by providing adjustable chairs of a design and construction suitable for all heights of workers. I have related in these recollections of the high standards attained in the Footshape factory and one would have assumed that little needed changing, yet Barratts were among the pioneers of many new ideas and sought always to have the highest possible standards of welfare for their workforce.

After my return to civilian life I spent a further five years "Walking the Barratt Way" until I became disillusioned with the industry and what it had to offer. I felt the need to seek new environs and challenges. However, I have never felt ashamed that I was once a humble shoe worker for I found in the factory many friends whom I have long since been proud to be associated with. Although many of the huge rooms behind the ornate facade of the Footshape factory in Kingsthorpe Road are now silent and empty this impressive building with its clock, a timepiece for all who pass by stands as a lasting tribute to the Barratt brothers and the employees who served there; I was glad to be one of them. The Footshape factory was very much part of a town in which thousands of people were and many still are skilled in the art of making boots and shoes and whose ancestors made them for generation after generation.

It's become an old family custom

It must be fifteen years ago, Mr. Barratt, that I bought my first pair of your shoes. And now, here are my two youngsters being fitted out in the same branch. The rising generation doesn't always agree with its elders these days. But they trust their old Dad in his choice of their shoes!

Walk the **Barratt** way

Barratts, Northampton—and branches throughout the country

Walk the Barratt Way.

Working the Barratt way, Clicking Dept.

"Remedy your deficiencies and your merits will take care of themselves".

Chapter 25

Philanthropists and Good Samaritans

The industrial revolution during the late eighteenth century and early nineteenth centuries not only brought changes in working conditions but prosperity and wealth to many employers. Yet there emerged from time to time men and women whose names became synonymous with their munificence and their desire to use some of their newly acquired wealthy for the benefit of others. There were to be found in Northampton those disciples of St. Crispin who showed that same concern and who through various charitable institutions gave of their time, talents and energies to raise large sums of money for worthwhile causes. Both owners and operatives in the shoe industry have acquitted themselves with honour in this field of benevolence.

One of Northampton's most charitable institutions was the General Hospital which, prior to the introduction of the National Health Service in 1948 by the then Labour Government, was maintained by voluntary contributions. The raising of money to support the hospital was one of the many annual events which called for the support of all citizens of the Borough. Shoe trade workers were very much a part of these efforts. All contributed weekly from their wage packets to a Hospital Fund the beginning of which is part of this story. There was the organising of the Hospital Sports each year when athletes competed with one another on the County Ground. There was also the great annual event of the borough, held on a summer evening, the annual Hospital Carnival which for years was popularly known as the Cycle Parade. The event was so known because of the many decorative cycles although there were also decorative floats and the whole parade was led by a carnival queen. Many shoe firms were entrants with floats whilst shoe workers who were not entrants in the parade would be out with collecting boxes or selling programmes. Doctors and nurses from the hospital would also ride on some of the floats collecting money thrown to them by the spectators. It is significant that most of the known charitable work and gifts have been in connection with and for the Northampton General Hospital and its annexes. This chapter is given to relating some of them.

One of Northampton's earliest manufacturers Sir Phillip Manfield, a true disciple of St Crispin, was noted for his benevolence. He was a governor of Northampton and Modern Technical School and President of the Freehold Society he was a treasurer of the Hospital Week Fund, Vice Chairman of the Nursing Institute and Labourers' Society. One of his largest enterprises was the building of the Unitarian church in Kettering Road. Probably one of the greatest gifts to the town by a shoe manufacturer came also from the Manfield family. After a world tour in 1920 his son James Manfield and his successor as Managing Director of M.P. Manfield Limited made an announcement that was destined to perpetuate his memory and the name of Manfield within the Borough. He decided to offer his home, Weston Favell House, free of charge to Northampton Crippled Children's Committee for use as a hospital. The members of the committee were overwhelmed by this magnificent gesture; they readily accepted and it was turned into a children's orthopaedic hospital. A letter dated 17th July 1924 from the Crippled Children's Committee said: "It is the agreed opinion of the committee that the gift contains the possibilities of unlimited development and there is in the near future, the opportunity provided of converting the mansion into a first class Children's Orthopaedic

Hospital which will be able to give scientific medical treatment not only to children of this town and county but also ultimately to children from the whole of the Midland Counties".

The generosity of James Manfield became a challenge and a stimulus to both town and county and the response gladdened his heart. Manfield died on 9th July 1925 and an obituary in the Northampton Independent of two days later noted: "he absorbed most of life's finest qualities, when he became mayor he gave a £1,000 to be spent on the poor of the town, and a similar sum yearly for a benefit fund for his employees. When he heard how the physique of poor school children at Bradford had been improved by the philanthropic provision of Free Meals he said in a gracious way, "I shall be pleased to provide two meals a day for 110 children for three months". Amidst the comfort and culture of his own home life he was ever mindful of others less fortunate. As chairman of the Borough Improvements Committee he paid a visit to the slum areas of Northampton. The squalor, poverty and suffering he witnessed had sunk into his soul and he made a vow that if he could be blessed with health and strength he would sweep away these pestilential places breeding dirt, disease and moral danger. He was largely responsible for municipalising the tramways and extending the Borough boundaries'.

Harry Manfield, brother of James and one time chairman of M P Manfield and Company Limited, who died a year earlier than James left as his permanent memorial the village institute at Pitsford which was fully equipped at a cost of over £1,000. His home had been at the Grange Pitsford for many years. It was in 1899 that he succeeded his father as Treasurer of Northampton Hospital and threw himself heart and soul into the Hospital Week Movement. He became chairman of the board of management and was a distinguished freemason. Whilst he was hospital treasurer the first cheque presented to the hospital for the Hospital Week Movement was £750; later it was as much as £5,500. Harry Manfield was a man of high Christian character and the love of God and man who was prompted to do such public spirited and charitable work.

Over the years there have been recorded munificent gifts to the Northampton General Hospital, many from local shoe manufacturers. In 1918 George Thomas Hawkins donated £3000 to help build a pathological laboratory. The building of this new department began on the 31st December 1918 and was completed and opened on 1st April 1920. The entire cost of £655,717 was eventually defrayed by Hawkins.

During 1922 Sir James Crockett who was then Chairman of the House Committee of the General Hospital gave £200 to convert a floor of the old part of the hospital into a lecture room for nurses. He had already given £1000 in 1921 to endow a bed in memory of his son Leonard Clifton Crockett who was killed at Thiepval in the First World War. Sir James took a deep interest in the running of the hospital dependent as it was in those days on voluntary contributions. He was a public spirited man who also figured prominently in Northampton public life. He held it wrong for any man to take action in business without first considering its effect on the community. He also held the view that it was the duty of all who could do so to give a certain amount of their wealth and time to public service. In both these beliefs he was an outstanding example and carried out his ideals to the letter and in practice. In 1924 he gave £5000 towards an isolation block at the hospital; incorporating a small theatre this opened in 1925. The extension became known as the Crockett block and in 1926 Sir James gave another £1000 to endow a bed in memory of his wife. A further gift of £1000 at a later date provided the nucleus for a fund for the purpose of building an Ear, Nose and Throat department together with new operating theatres. Then in 1932 at his expense balconies were finally added to the Crockett wards. These gifts do not complete the list for which he was responsible.

Another well known figure in Northampton was Thomas Singlehurst J.P. a shoe manufacturer who first started work as an errand boy to Messrs Brice and Sons, well known drapers whose shop was at the top of the Drapery adjoining Bradshaw Street. Singlehurst left to enter the shoe trade under Joseph Gibbs and he became so proficient in the art of manufacture that in 1886 he entered into partnership with Thomas Gulliver. Although the original partnership was dissolved in 1890 we know that Singlehurst conducted a successful business and was a progressive employer until he retired in 1929. Moreover he was a bountiful benefactor who did much to soften the sufferings of others. After a long illness he suffered the affliction of total blindness following a period of failing eyesight. This trouble stimulated his sympathy with similar sufferers to such a generous degree that in 1923 he presented to Northampton General Hospital at great cost, said to be over £10,000, a fine ophthalmic department which was named after him. Prior to this he had endowed a bed in the Manfield Orthopaedic Hospital and a ward with twelve beds at Creaton Sanatorium (later Creaton Hospital which was closed in 1984). He also subscribed £500 to the Bethany Homestead and provided maintenance grants of £10 per year for nine boys to remain at the Northampton Town and County Grammar School until they were sixteen. An ardent Methodist and treasurer of Grove Road (now Queensgrove Methodist Church) he gave generous gifts to the Methodist cause and other charitable movements. He was a prominent Liberal and an alderman of the Borough of Northampton and was appointed a magistrate in 1930. It was Thomas Singlehurst who gave money to purchase the site on which Park Avenue Methodist Church was eventually built. A president of Northampton Sunday School Union Thomas Singlehurst was also a life long abstainer and served the Temperance Cause in the principal offices of Northants and Bucks Band of Hope Union. He died in 1941 but will be long remembered for his charitable works in the Borough.

It has been said of William Arnold, who was a struggling shoe manufacturer in the 1880's, that he was tortured with business worries and religious doubts when he walked into Grove Road Chapel Northampton. It proved to be the turning point in his life. The Rev George Parkin was preaching and the stranger was inspired by his words and his subsequent warm welcome to join the Methodist Church. As a member of the church he became, like his friend and colleague Thomas Singlehurst, a great benefactor. From that very moment there had come a wonderful turn in the tide of his fortunes. Arnold was a generous benefactor to the Primitive Methodist cause offering to give £3000 for a new chapel in memory of his late wife Elizabeth; this was subsequently increased by his family to £5000. The new church was eventually erected in 1924 on a site given by Thomas Singlehurst at the corner of Abington Avenue and Park Avenue North becoming known as Park Avenue Methodist Church.

The Northampton General Hospital was a recipient of another splendid gift on 30th July 1929 when Mrs J G Sears, widow of the late John George Sears, donated a sum of £3000 for the purchase of radium and a further £2000 for the endowment of two beds in the named of Mrs C Sears.

Probably one of the finest and most notable gifts was that of William Barratt J.P. who gave to the hospital and town the maternity home which bears his name. It was in 1934 that he first gave the sum of £20,000 towards building a maternity wing to the hospital. Both Mr and Mrs Barratt had been most concerned that there had hitherto been little opportunities for working class mothers to enter a nursing home to have their babies. This in the later days of affluence inspired the gift and erection of a maternity and gynaecological hospital which has proved to have few equals. Eventually Barratt announced that he wished to bear the sole cost of building the new maternity wing. The new hospital was opened on 4th July 1936 by her Royal Highness Princess Alice Countess of Athlone. Planned at first to care for thirty-two patients with a flat for the sister in charge it was to expand even further. In due course the Barratt Home, as it became known locally, became recognised as a training school for pupil midwives. The whole concept of the Barratt Home and the care and training it provided for both mothers and nurses implanted in the heart of the donor and his wife and unshakable spirit of self service. Later on Mr and Mrs Barratt gave an additional sum of money to build the present gynaecological block which was fully equipped at a cost of £20,000. This new wing came into operation in 1938. It was said that the founder and his wife never fully disclosed the total cost of their benevolence. It may have been more than £60,000. There is little doubt that the home has proved to be a great blessing to the town and immediate district. The munificent gift to Northamptons Hospital triumphantly fulfilled the prediction of the late Doctor Salisbury that it would materially help to reduce the mortality rate of mothers and infants. The Barratts took a keen personal interest in the home from its inception and reflected the same sympathetic concern for the welfare of the two thousand employees working in the Barratt model factory in Kingsthorpe Road. It was a gift that would be remembered for years to come and has been used by many generations of Northampton mothers.

The Barratt Maternity Home.

Support for the hospital, too, came from shoe operatives through their union. During the early part of the First World War the Allied War Fund came into existence as a result of the efforts of Councillor James Gribble J.P. Jimmy Gribble, as he was affectionately known, was the fiery trade unionist, Labour councillor and an organiser for the boot and shoe union. During the four years of the existence of this fund £40,000 was received in subscriptions of which some £17,322 was allocated to local charitable institutions. The great success of this fund led those associated with it to established the Northampton Hospital and Convalescent Home Fund in 1919. Gribble was the chairman of the Maternity and Children's Committees and was responsible for the changeover and continued success for the fund. The fund was maintained principally by the regular weekly subscriptions from the town's workforce who had deductions made from their wage packets. In July 1925, however, Gribble's failing health forced his retirement from the union. He left the town to take over the proprietorship of the White Friars Hotel, Westhill, Hastings where he stayed for two years before returning to Northampton. He died from a cerebral haemorrhage in Northampton General Hospital on 14th August 1934 at the age of 66 years. The hospital fund continued over the years and the Gribble Ward at the hospital is named after him. With the introduction of the National Health Service the fund which James Gribble had set up took a new form and became the Hospital Guild.

Sir Henry Randall was another local shoe manufacturer who was noted for his benevolence. During 1919 he donated a sum of £5,000. to a local charity known as the John and Ann Camps Charity of which he was a trustee. The gift was intended to provide an annuity to lift from despair to happiness those who required help; Randall thought that this charity had done more good than any other in Northampton during that period. The fund of which the Mayor of the Borough, Councillor F Kilby was chairman was henceforth known as the Sir Henry and Lady Randall Annuity Fund. Randall was also known to be associated with many other local charities including the poor children's Christmas Dinner Fund and the St John's Convalescent Homes.

The *Northampton Independent* often disclosed news of such public spirited gifts and on 5th June 1926 there appeared a tribute to yet another shoe factory employer, W T Sears who had "contributed in no small measure to the welfare of a vast body of Northampton workers, and incidentally to the prosperity of the Boroughs Staple Trade - His expert knowledge and sound judgement has been responsible for remarkable development of retail branches his vast business calls have not however prevented Mr Sears from playing a worthy part in public life. As county councillor for the village of Weston Favell the village had good cause to appreciate his generosity when he presented their community with a Cricket Ground. Under his chairmanship the hospital sports were revived in 1923 and a magnificent sum of £1,700 raised for the General Hospital. It was a record surpassing previous years".

The Lewis brothers were prominent shoe manufacturers in the town and took a full and active part in the affairs of the borough. Almost every good cause had Edward Lewis as a good friend whether its watchword was temperance, education, liberty, benevolence, thrift or religion. To the Northampton General Hospital, the Bethany Homestead and especially the Congregational cause Edward Lewis was a generous donor. He was the mainspring of great causes which he served with a spirit far beyond his strength in later years. When Harry Manfield died Lewis succeeded him as honourary treasurer of the Hospital Week Fund and took an active part in the administration of the Hospital. The greatest gift for which the Lewis

Brothers will be remembered was the gift in 1921 of twenty-three acre Dallington park to the Borough. This lovely park will ever remain as a memorial to the public spirited philanthropy of Edward Lewis and T D Lewis who gave it with the proviso that it should be used as a park for the benefit of residents of the town.

One of the county's most known and distinguished philanthropists was John White the Higham Ferrers shoe manufacturer. He was a very generous person who gave much of his wealth away. Among his known gifts he was responsible for restoring the Chantry Chapel in 1936 and he built a bandstand in the local park. His unique gift during the Second World War was a donation of £5000 for the purchase of a Spitfire fighter aircraft; it was named the "Impregnable" after one of his famous brands of footwear. The aircraft had a very successful flying career with a Polish Squadron. White also arranged for a donation of 100,000 pairs of shoes to the Red Cross in Switzerland. At his retirement in 1962 it was said that he had become a millionaire but it was also said that he had given most of his wealth away to local causes dear to his heart.

During 1968 Dennis George Webb a former managing director of the Northampton firm of George Webb and Sons Limited and his family set up a charitable trust known as the Dennis George Webb Charitable Trust. The trustees make grants to general charitable causes with a preference to health and medicine, children and youth organisations and educational and religious purposes. Mr Webb was for many years a National Vice President of the Boys Brigade and local president of the movement. He was Elder Emeritus of Doddridge and Commercial Street United Reformed Church.

To the men and women mentioned in this chapter we the citizens of Northamptonshire today must owe a debt of gratitude. Today we may have our sponsored walks, marathons and favourite ways of appealing for the support of our friends for charitable causes that are dear to our hearts. As we do so let us not forget but always remember the vast numbers of shoe workers who silently gave their time and energies for raising money for such charitable causes as the hospital by means of the 'cycle parade' (carnival), hospital sports, or by the factory levy.

I am reminded of some words written by Professor Henry Drummond author of that great devotional classic "The Greatest Thing In the World" published in 1893: "Holiness is an infinite compassion for others. Greatness is to take the common things of life and walk truly among them. Happiness is a great love and much serving."

We must be equally glad that this spirit of giving, serving, and compassion for others has been handed down from generation to generation. Happy that such love and thoughtfulness still lives on in Northampton and County in whatever form it now takes. It is surely a tribute to the memory of the many philanthropists and Samaritans in the shoe trade of yesteryear whose concern for their fellow men was their first priority.

A little self denial is a mighty good tonic, Feel for others...in your pockets".

Chapter 26

A Band of Brothers

Few people are aware that the boot and shoe trade can claim to have applied Trade Union methods more than three centuries before trade unionism became an established fact in this country. Colonel L'Estrange Malone, the member of parliament for the Borough of Northampton during the early thirties made this disclosure when he published an interesting survey of the boot and shoe industry in The Social Democrat. He stated that "Operatives in the Boot and Shoe Trade, can claim to be pioneers in trade unionism for records stated that in 1538 the Bishop of Ely reported to Cromwell that twenty one journey-men shoemakers of Wisbech, had assembled on a hill in order to insist upon an advance in their wages threatening that there shall none come into our town to serve, for that wages within a twelve month and a day. But we will have a harme or legge of Hym except they will take an Othe as we have Doon!"

When trade unions began to spring up in the latter half of the Victorian era they insisted that a man's home should not be his workshop and during the introduction of machinery in factories there were many disputes between workforce and managements. The agitations of operatives culminated in the great lockout of 1887 which lasted six weeks. The employers had insisted on an ultimatum of seven proposals which were known as "the seven commandments". These disciples of Saint Crispin were very determined to see things through and some manufacturers appealed to operatives to leave their union but their request met with little success. There were, however, some respected men amongst the manufacturers who tried to look at things from the workers point of view.

One employer, Simon Collier, whose factory was in Harlestone Road, St James bought an ox which he had slaughtered. The beast was shared out amongst his workers thrown idle by the lockout, and parcels of grocery, bread and potatoes were added for good measure. Not all employers were sympathetic and after the lockout they began installing lasting machines. To everyone's surprise the machines were accepted, thus paving the way for a final settlement of the long dispute in 1895 after a conference at the Board of Trade in London. Even today no shoe centre in the country has more cordial relations between employer and employee than in Northamptonshire. This foundation of good relationships made it possible for local industry to advance by leaps and bounds. The progress made was one of the great industrial achievements of the century. It is a story of and and endurance courage and adventure at a time when Non-conformity was strong in Northampton and county. There was evidence that the Non-conformist churches throughout Northamptonshire claimed the support of a vast number of shoemakers, both manufacturers and trade unionists. It seemed that they brought to their deliberations the same kind of understanding they achieved within their churches and the dynamism used in an exacting business and their kindred societies.

Founded on the 2nd February 1874 the Boot and Shoe Operatives Union has a great history. It was registered under the Friendly Societies Act on 24th December 1885 and has continued to play an important role in the industry in both the county town and the whole of Northamptonshire ever since.

It was on October 14th 1873 that a Mr T Smith carried a resolution at a special meeting for the Stafford Branch of Rivetters and Finishers authorising the calling of a special delegate conference of representatives of all towns that were directly interested in the new methods of shoe manufacture. The idea of the meeting being to discuss grievances that had arisen. There was a big response to the calling of the conference at Stafford. It assembled on 29th December 1873 and the Northampton delegates were W C France and R McMillan. At the end of the deliberations it was decided to withdraw from the old Cordwainers Society and form a completely new organisation. The title agreed upon was the National Amalgamated Union of Boot and Shoe Rivetters and Finishers. This rather ambiguous title was subsequently altered in 1890 to the National Union of Boot and Shoe Operatives. An immediate effort was made to recruit clickers and pressmen. In this instance lasting and finishing was placed in the number one branch and the clickers and pressmen in the number two branch in both Leicester and Northamptonshire.

After this new union was launched there was some very bitter feelings of antagonism between the old and new members but with a determination to succeed the officials stood their ground. Alderman T Smith J P was appointed as first general secretary and H Horsfall the first general president. The early stages of the union's existence were full of anxiety for its leaders and there was little support and sympathy from the larger and more powerful organisations. In the first year of the movement its ability to protect its members was often put to the test with severe and frequent disputes and conflicts with the employers. Success or failure frequently hung in the balance but the union's pioneers had faith in their cause. They were men of courage patience and hope fighting for ideas in which they believed. With patience and sincerity their efforts on behalf of their members were ultimately rewarded with success. Hours of work were reduced, wages improved, and strikes diminished. As a result the union's relationships with employers improved as the membership of the union also increased.

On 27th April 1874 there were thirty-five branches with a total membership of 4,204 and in February 1974, a hundred years later, it was 76,100. By 1894 lasters and finishers were earning twenty-eight shillings for a 54 hour week. The best clickers also earned the same amount and in 1896 this rate was fixed at twenty-six shillings. In 1909 a completely new wage scale was introduced giving men of 20 years of age at least thirty shillings a week. Boys or girls of 14 years of age earned four and sixpence a week which rose a year later to thirteen shillings for girls and eighteen shillings for boys of 17. This wage increased by three annual increments to adult wages at 21 years of age. Girl closers earned thirteen shillings at 18 years of age and this rose to the adult wage of sixteen or seventeen shillings at 21 years. The pre 1914 wages were twenty-eight shillings. In 1939 £4.00 for adult men and two pounds ten shillings for adult women for a 48 hour week and with annual three weeks holiday including statutory days was the norm. There were no holidays with pay but some firms maintained a holiday fund to which the company contributed a percentage to the workers contributions.

During the 1914-18 war over 25,000 members of the union left the factories of Northamptonshire for the battlefields in Europe and 2,574 of these members were killed. The union played an active part at home during the world conflict. In addition to the daily work of making army boots for the war office money was raised for various funds for the troops and in March 1916 the union presented a motor ambulance to the British Red Cross for carrying wounded soldiers in France. Throughout this difficult period the union maintained its hold upon its membership, many of whom were women workers who had taken men's places in the factories.

The union has had from its inception a long list of distinguished general secretaries who not only gave unstintinglgy of their time to the Trade Union Movement but also played a very important part in public life. Many of them served their towns and cities as councillors and aldermen, some were magistrates whilst others entered Parliament. The union's first general secretary was Aldermen Thomas Smith, OBE, JP from Stafford (1874-1878). The first head office was established in Leicester, that city having at that time the largest branch. It followed that the next three secretaries were citizens of Leicester: George Sedgewick J.P.(September 1878-October 1886); William Inskip JP (November 1886-April 1889); W B Hornidge JP (August 1899-September 1908) when Edward L Poulton of Northampton took over. A similar pattern followed in the election of the general president.

The first National President was H Horsfall, the earliest presidents remaining in office for twelve months. The first full time president was W B Hornidge JP who was appointed in August 1893 and served until August 1899 when he became General Secretary. He was followed in the presidential chair by Charles Freak TC from October 1899 to July 1910 when T F Richards was appointed. All these men were fulltime presidents and were from Leicester. One of the earliest honours to be accorded to a member of the union was in November 1906 when Alderman E L Poulton was elected as the first working man to be Mayor of Northampton. This was no mean achievement for he had commenced work at the early age of nine as a "knot tier" in a boot factory. At the age of ten he became a "sprigging boy" eventually becoming a "tapper" (laster) in the shoe trade. He was actively engaged in municipal life for many years. He received the OBE in 1917 for national services and in 1924 he collaborated with T F Richards the then General President to write the first fifty years of history of the union.

Another early official of the union who had a distinguished career in local politics and who gave much of his spare time to the local Labour Party cause was James Gribble. Born in Northampton at 25 Bailiff Street in 1868 he was the son of James and Eleanor Gribble. His father was a machine closer in the shoe trade and at one time a publican. Young James Gribble received a formal education at Spring Lane School and Vernon Terrace School in Northampton. Here he only attained a basic education but by studying at the Northampton Adult School whilst in his teens he vastly improved his general standard of education. He started work as an outdoor finisher before the age of twelve for Turner Brothers and Hyde of Northampton. He was a short stocky man with a generous disposition. Although an activist of the Left he commanded the loyalty and respect of all who knew him. Gribble also served for seven and a half years in the regular army, enlisting in 1885 and returning to his old trade in January 1893. After becoming a union official he was quick to enter into local politics as a Labour candidate and first became a town councillor in 1903. As the trade union organiser he was very efficient and was well respected both in the community and in the factories and for his untiring work on the Town Council. He was appointed a Justice of the Peace in 1923. In 1905, during the great Raunds Strike, (recalled in another chapter)"Jimmy" Gribble, in an effort to get a settlement of the bitter dispute, led the men to a march to the Houses of Parliament in London. This resulted in an eventual settlement and the nickname "General Gribble". In his history of the boot and shoe union Alan Fox describes Gribble as "one of the most attractive and heart warming personalities in union history. A man with a long, vigorous and turbulent career in the Labour Movement during which he was to earn a reputation as a generous unswerving friend, persistent, vigorous and ready to sacrifice his own interests without hesitation or regret".

Whilst it would be difficult to single out any one person, from such a devoted band of officials of the union there were following Edward Poulton's election a number of members of the Northampton Branches who like Poulton and Gribble were Northamptonians born and bred; men who started work in shoe factories at very early ages. They became involved in trade union work, eventually giving up their employment to serve their fellow workers as organisers, secretaries or presidents. Stalwarts like Sir George Chester CBE, who was elected as General Secretary on Poulton's retirement in 1930. He was born at Loddington near Kettering on 16th January 1886. He had only a very elementary school education but he attended Workers Educational Classes and furthered his education in technical schools. He became an officer of Kettering Number One branch in 1915 and was appointed Chairman of Kettering Urban District Council in 1926 and also a magistrate. He was a man who was very keen on Further Education and sought to establish this for shoe trade workers. He immediately bought a new vision to the union and having been a boot and shoe operative from 1899-1915 he understood its many problems. He was awarded the CBE in 1944 and later he was knighted in 1948 to become Sir George Chester CBE, FRHS, FBSI. Outside his union work Sir George was a keen gardener and botanist and was secretary of Kettering and District Naturalists Society from 1908-1930. He also became a director of the Bank of England. Sir George Chester died in 1949 aged 63, leaving a notable impression on the boot and shoe trade, his union, and the general public during his nineteen years as union General Secretary.

A union official who worked very closely with Sir George Chester and was elected to office in the same year was W R Townley who became General President in 1930. "Bill", as he was known to union colleagues, also began his working life in the shoe factory as a handfinisher to the trade. Townley joined the Northampton Number One Branch of the Union at the age of fifteen. He was elected Vice President of the Branch in 1913 and President in 1917. Townley and Chester were together responsible for much of the union's progress in the years preceding the Second World War. Townley served on Northampton Town Council both as a councillor and an alderman. He pushed himself to the limit as a full time official, disregarding health and leisure in an effort to improve the lot of his members. As General President he dedicated his efforts to peaceful relationships between employers and workers. Ill health prevented him from public acknowledgement of his work as he was unable to accept the mayoralty of the Borough in 1949.

Chester's successor as General Secretary was Sir Lionel Poole JP, FBSI who was appointed in 1949. He was also born in the county on 28th October 1894 and had only an elementary education plus attendance at Workers Educational Classes. He was first employed as an office boy but later began working in the clicking room of a local factory. He took up union work after service in the First World War and was for over forty years a union official. He was the first full time president of the Wellingborough Branch becoming a full time official in 1919. Lionel Poole was appointed a national organiser in 1922 and became Assistant General Secretary in 1943. He became a member of the Board of Trade Advisory Committee and Industrial Estates Management Committee in 1960 having previously served as Chairman of the National Council for Recruitment and Training from 1957-1959. A fellow of the British

Boot and Shoe Institute and its Vice President in 1956 he was appointed a part time member of the board of BOAC from 1960-1964. In addition Lionel Poole was a member of the following bodies: British Productivity Council, Industrial Training Council, National Production Advisory Council on Industry, Board of Governors of Loughborough College of Technology, and Governor of the National Leather Sellers College. A life-long Methodist he was very active in church work. He was appointed a magistrate in 1949 and was also a member of the Urban District Council. He retired in October 1959 and was knighted for his services in 1966, and died in 1967.

Townley was succeeded as general president by Leonard Smith who was born of humble origins in the Northamptonshire village of Ringstead, the son of an army shoemaker. "Len" was cradled, reared and spent the whole of his working life in shoemaking. He joined Northampton Number One Branch in 1899 having became an active trade unionist in early life. In 1918 Smith was elected Vice President of his Branch and during this time served on Long Buckby Parish Council. In 1919 he was elected to Northampton Town Council and was for over forty years engaged in the political and industrial life of the Borough.
He was appointed a National Organiser of the Union in 1923 at a time when there was much unemployment and short-time working. He was much loved and respected, possessing a great sense of humour, a skilled negotiator and yet a stormy petrel in the sea of political orthodoxy. He became General President of the Union in 1938 and was elected Chief Citizen of the Borough on May 26th 1949 during his retirement. He was the third union official to be appointed mayor of the town.

When Smith retired from the presidency of the Union in 1944 the office went to James Crawford CBE of Kilmarnock.In 1957 Sydney Robinson, a native of Wellingborough and born there in 1905, became President. He,too, had left school at an early ge to work in the factory. He became president of the Wellingborough Branch in May 1940 later becoming a National Organizer and Assistant General Secretary before becoming General President. Robinson served as President from April 1957 to August 1970 and was succeeded by Herbert Comerford until November 1980 when R B Stevenson was appointed. When Sir Lionel Poole retired as General Secretary he was in turn succeeded by R Gregson (November 1959-October 1968), T A Moore (November 1968-March 1973), W G T Jones (September 1973-April 1976), S F Clapham (May 1976-July 1983) and in 1983 G C Stewart.

Returning for a moment to my recollections of local figures Alderman Arthur W (Toby) Lyne OBE was yet another official who first joined the union in 1904. A member of the Northampton Number Two Branch he became Vice President in 1919. In 1924 he was appointed a magistrate and gave to the town many years of public service. Lyne was Mayor of the Borough in 1938. Here also was a union official who was typical for the self sacrificing spirit and human sympathy with which he devoted himself during his many years of public service. Besides his work on the town council as President of the union's largest branch he helped materially to preserve peace in the industry and promote the prosperity and progress of Northampton.

It is interesting to note that for some eighteen years the headquarters of the Number Two Branch of which Alderman Lyne was President was in Robert Street. It was in 1930 that the union acquired from the Charity Commissioners the old Saint Crispin's Church building situated at the top of Robert Street and the junction of Earl Street. This building was the only

Northampton church dedicated to the Patron Saint of shoemakers. It was first built as a mission church to the Holy Sepulchre during the Vicarage of Canon Thornton in 1883. The church was dedicated the following year by the Bishop of Peterborough but was never consecrated. The church was used mainly for Parochial purposes and was leased at one time to the Salvation army. When ownership passed to the Boot and Shoe Union in 1930 it became the headquarters of the Number Two Branch and remained so until the branch amalgamated with the Number One Branch in Overstone Road in 1943. Demolished in 1991 the building was replaced by a block of flats known as Saint Crispin's House.

Other Northamptonians who came into prominence were: A J Dobbs who was born in Bozeat and joined the Union in 1902 but left the area for Leeds in 1909 eventually serving the union as one of the its first members of parliament. In later years there was Malcolm Nash who had been employed by the firm of Jonathan Robinson and who became President of the Northampton Number One Branch in 1938 later becoming Joint President of the united branches in 1948. Nash, who was a magistrate, served as President until 1952. He was not only well skilled as a union negotiator but was devoted to his work for the union and the welfare of its membership. He was a prominent local Congregationalist and a leader of the Doddridge Young Mens Bible Class. He was a fluent speaker and also a prominent local preacher who was much respected for his Christian ideals.

Following in Nash's footsteps the mantle of branch president fell upon J Gordon who was succeeded in turn by Herbert (Bert) Comerford, who served the branch until his appointment as the union's General President on 31st August 1970. He was succeeded by George Browett, G Yule, and later Ron Hart and P A Robinson. These men were all shoemakers, Saint Crispin's Men, who served both the industry and the union during some of the most important years of its existence. For those who were in office up to the Second World War and the post war era there were times of prosperity and times of decline but they came smiling through. The result has been that the union though depleted has continued to serve its members and preserve a cordiality in its relationships with others and with the manufacturers association.

On the 1st July 1918 Ernest Bordoli, a member of staff at the Union Central Office in Leicester, was elected as confidential clerk. He was a competent shorthand writer holding the certificate of the Royal Society of Arts for Office Management and also held and associate degree of the Faculty of Insurance. He moved with the union to new headquarters at 34 Guildford Street, London WC1, in 1919 where he served as a respected member of staff with a thorough knowledge of the work appertaining to a Boot and Shoe Union until 1929. Bordoli will be remembered as an ardent publicist who was also an author of a number of publications dealing with the boot and shoe trade. Eventually he was chosen for the post of secretary of Northampton Town Boot Manufacturers Association in 1929 and served them diligently until his death in 1940.

The credit of becoming the union's first MP went to T F Richards who became a member of Parliament for West Wolverhampton in January 1906. He continued in Parliament until 1910 when he became General President of the Union. There had been one previous attempt in 1893 to secure a Labour MP in Northampton when Alderman William J Inskip was the candidate, but he was forced to retire from the contest through ill health. The union campaigned strongly for the Labour cause. In December 1918 W R Smith JP was elected to

Parliament for Wellingborough but failed to secure re-election in 1922. In that year John Buckle was elected MP for Eccles, Alfred Hill MP for Leicester West and Walter Smith as MP for Norwich. Although no union candidates stood locally after 1922 union officials and members were to have a share in the campaign to elect Northamptons first Labour MP, Margaret Bondfield, who became a member of the Cabinet under the Prime Minister Ramsay MacDonald. She was followed by Colonel Cecil L'Estrange Malone and later by R T Paget (now Lord Paget). In the Labour landslide victory of 1945 the boot and shoe union secured four Labour MPs in other constituencies. Alderman A W Lyne JP, was returned for Burton on Trent, Humphrey C Attewell for Market Harborough, Arthur C Allebone for Bosworth and A J Dobbs for Smethwick. In 1950 Arthur Allen became Parliamentary Secretary to Sir Stafford Cripps and Hugh Gaitskell. All of these men were prominent union officials who were dedicated to the Labour cause. It was not until 1979 that another attempt was made to secure a Labour MP for the union. This was when Graham Mason a Union Branch official was the unsuccessful candidate.

During the Second World War many hundreds of union members left their workbenches to serve in the armed forces. All were kept in membership during the war years and on their return to the factories the union had the problem of helping to secure their re-instatement and the gradual cessation of "green labour". New officials came and the union went on to accept the new challenges with as much determination and vigour as their forebears. It was a difficult path to follow and a high standard to keep up. During the late fifties, the Union commissioned Alan Fox, Research Fellow of Nuffield College, Oxford to write a full and comprehensive history of the union over its eighty years of existence from its beginning in 1874-1957. This was published in 1958 and is a most detailed history of its fluctuations and fortunes. The union's
present headquarters are located at the Grange, Earls Barton where they have been since October 1940 when the Bedford Square offices in London were rendered unsuitable by bomb damage.

With the closure of many boot factories in the late sixties and the imminent possibility of others resulting in a depletion of membership the amalgamation of allied trades was sought. In May 1971 the National Union of Boot and Shoe Operatives assumed a new identity. A union embracing the following trades was established: the National Union of Glovers and Leatherworkers, Amalgamated Society of Leatherworkers, and National Union of Leather Workers and Allied Trades. The new union became the National Union of the Footwear, Leather and Allied Trades. (NUFLAT) It was the end of an era.

The Boot and Shoe union reached its century in 1974 but it was ten years later on December 6th 1984 that its members in Northamptonshire were to receive its greatest accolade. About 3,000 members of NUFLAT were given the Freedom of the Borough of Northampton at a special ceremony at the Guildhall. It was one of the first trade unions in Britain to receive such an honour which was in recognition of the union's long contribution to the life of the town. The official scroll, which was presented to the Union Branch President Ronald Hart JP, read: "The Freedom Award is to perpetuate the close bonds of friendship and mutual respect which exists between the Borough and the Union". Presenting the award, Councillor Cyril Benton, Leader of the Borough Council, declared it a tribute to the part the footwear industry had played in the prosperity of Northampton, its responsible representation of its members and the very good example set to other unions. In responding Hart presented the Borough

Council with a plaque showing a cobbler at his last, a unique symbol of the trade.

When Hart retired from office in June 1986 he had been president of the local branch of the Union for twenty years. He began work in the shoe factory of Oakeshott and Finnemore and before he became a full time union official he was employed as a clicker at Church's factory. He was a former "Desert Rat" in Montgomery's Eighth Army. The biggest disappointment and greatest problem that he had to face in his period of office was the beginning of the decline of the industry; in 1970 problems began with the flood of cheap imported footwear from behind the Iron Curtain and Third World Countries. During his period of leadership of the local branch of the union he saw the union's membership in the town wither away from 45,000 to 3,500 members as factories closed and members were made redundant. The number of factories were simultaneously reduced from around forty to just eight. In a new industrial era when the boot and shoe industry fights for survival and in an age which is dominated by computer technology and the micro chip the shoe workers union is still very much part of the citadel where the trade began.

Sir George Chester.

W. R. Townsley.

P Pinder.

Humphrey C. Attewell.

Lionel Poole.

S. A. Robinson.

E. L. Poulston.

T. F. Richards.

156

A. W. (Toby) Lyne.

Len Smith.

J Crawford.

Ernest Bordoli.

"People Seldom attempt to sit on a man who stands up for himself".

Chapter 27

The Decision Makers

The establishment of a boot and shoe union for the benefit of all factory workers was quickly followed by a decision to form what some have since regarded as a "union" for manufacturers. It was on 19th December 1878, just five years after the formation of the operative's union, that Moses Philip Manfield (Later Sir Philip) decided to call a meeting of nineteen other manufacturers in Northampton with a view to forming an association for the mutual protection of boot manufacturers.

The result of this meeting was that a decision was taken to launch an association which was first known as the Northampton Boot, Shoe and Leather Trades "Creditors" Association of wholesale dealers. This ambiguous title was like the Shoe Union's title later shortened to a more pronounceable form when it became Northampton Town Boot Manufacturers Association. The first meeting of the new association held on 30th January 1879 elected Moses Philip Manfield as its first president and appointed John Adin as its first secretary. The office of secretary was at first a part time position and Adin held the position for fourteen years. The first known list of members records the names of Frederick Bostock, Church and Company, Simon Collier, Crick and Company, Hornby and West, Manfield and Sons, John Marlow, Edmund Pollard, Henry E Randall, J Robinson and G M Tebbutt. The name of Alfred Allinson appeared on the 1880 list of members. During that period there were a number of skirmishes in various factories with operatives who were displeased in some ways with their working conditions. Both representatives of the manufacturers and the operatives met and decided to form a board of arbitration. At the first meeting prices for various operations were fixed but the manufacturers considered that they were in need of greater protection and in 1884 James Crockett suggested that every member of the association enter into a bond of £100 for "mutual protection and support". The bond was signed by every member and renewed annually.

The second president of the Association was Henry Wooding JP who succeeded Philip Manfield in 1886 and served for five years until 1893. William Hickson was the next president and he held office for eleven years until 1904. It fell to Hickson's lot to steer the manufacturers through the Great Strike of 1895. C F Lea was elected as the first full time secretary and remained in office until 1929 a total of thirty six years. In August 1892 the association together with the Boot and Shoe Union held a joint conference in Leicester. Wooding was one of the representatives elected by the Northampton Association. It was quite an important meeting for the trade because the following decisions were taken. 1) A uniform meal hour, 2) A fifty hour week. 3) Minimum weekly wage for Northampton clickers to be twenty-five shillings, and after March 1893 twenty-six. 4) Minimum wage rate for Pressmen in Northampton of twenty-two shillings. Northampton can rightly claim to have set the first uniform rate of wages in the industry.

The next event of importance took place on 1st July 1893 when the Northampton employers reached an agreement to increase the minimum wage of shoe operatives to twenty-eight shillings per week. There then followed a period of unrest in the industry which culminated in a strike which began in March 1895 and lasted for six weeks. The strike inevitably brought hardship to the workers and their families; there was a great deal of poverty and acute suffering in both Northampton and district. As a consequence of this upheaval in the industry Terms of Settlement were agreed beginning the start of a cordial relationship between employer and employee. Since that time there has not been a serious dispute or general strike in the industry either in Northampton or elsewhere.

Following the eleven year term of office of William Hickson, Walter Beale was elected president and served for three years retiring from office in 1907. He was followed by the distinguished manufacturer Sir James Crockett who was president for two years until 1909. John H Marlow was the next shoe manufacturer to occupy the presidential chair. It was during his first term of office that the first town clicking statement was prepared. Also the original articles for the Association which were first drafted in 1879 were re-considered and eventually cancelled. In their place new rules and regulation were instituted and these, with minor amendments or additions, were in operations for more than thirty years. Under the new constitution a summary of the chief objects of the association were: "To promote the general interests of the Boot and Shoe Manufacturers of Northampton Town by combination and united action on the part of the members. To render aid and defence to members in case of disputes with their workpeople and to effect the settlement of disputes by Arbitration".

In 1912 Edward Lewis JP became the Association President until 1913 when John George Sears was elected. However, during the period of the Great War 1914-18 the chief office was held by Albert E Marlow who served the Association as president for seven years retiring from office in 1920. During a period when member firms generally rendered great service to their country by producing 23,000,000 pairs of footwear for both the British and Allied armies it was said that much was undoubtedly due to the inspiring leadership of A E Marlow whose efforts on behalf of Northampton and its trade were indefatigable.

After the end of the war in 1919 a revision of piecework statements was called for and much of this work was thrown upon the officers of the association. In connection with this period credit must be given to the work of Henry C Oakeshott and H Edwards who were responsible for much of the drafts. The completion of the work was continued during the Presidency of Albert E Tebbutt who occupied the office from 1920-1924. A record was created by John H Marlow, a past president, who returned to office for a second time from 1924-1926. Following him H Edwards became president from 1926-1927. During the jubilee of the Association the president was A H Hollister JP who was in the presidential chair during 1927 and 1928. Like all his predecessors Hollister, who was the Managing Director of F Cook Limited of Long Buckby, did much to further the work of the Association before he retired from office in 1931. During his term of office the General Purposes Committee re-organised the work of the Association.

In 1931 C G B Allinson was elected president and during his year of office he was presented to their Royal Highness the Duke and Duchess of York (later King George VI and Queen Elizabeth) when they both visited the town in November 1932 to open the new College of Technology (now Nene College) in St Georges Avenue. During their visit Allinson presented them with a number of pairs of locally made footwear. After thirty six years of faithful service G F Lea retired from the Secretaryship in April 1929. In recognition of his long and devoted service the members of the Association presented him with an illuminated address, a cheque and a life pension.

The new secretary was Ernest Bordoli BSc, who was to be Secretary for the next eleven years until his untimely death at the age of forty nine in August 1940 robbed the shoe trade of one of its most outstanding personalities. A native of Leicester Bordoli began his working career on the staff of the Leicester Evening Mail. While still in his teens he joined the headquarters staff of the National Union of Boot and Shoe Operatives later becoming confidential clerk to the union's General Secretary Edward L Poulton OBE. His post with the union had afforded him a very valuable insight into the problems of the shoe trade. Under his guidance the Manufacturers Association set itself a forward policy making a special effort to regain some of Northampton's export trade. Many tariff barriers were overcome and the town's production became known by the slogan "quality first". All efforts were directed in maintaining Northampton's pre-eminence in the overseas markets. On behalf of the industry Bordoli carried on an almost continuous crusade to prove to all that Northampton was truly the home of the best shoemaking in the world.

He was the author of much shoe trade literature and various books on the industry. His ability as an organiser won him merited recognition as an outstanding ambassador for the industry. Soon after his appointment in 1929 as secretary of the Association he was appointed organising secretary of the Northampton Festival Week, Shoe Trades Exhibition held on 26th May 1930. His infectious enthusiasm and organising genius helped to raise a sum of £8,000 at the Exhibition which was donated to charity. Accordingly the sum was divided between the Northampton General Hospital, Manfield Hospital, the Queens Institute of District Nursing and the Northamptonshire Nursing Association. Bordoli's great sympathy with the work of Northampton General Hospital led Lord Hesketh to invite him to become Chairman of the Northampton Council which had been set up to raise a sum of £45,000 as the Borough's part towards a hospital appeal. When the new nurses home was being built Ernest was invited along with the Duchess of Gloucester to lay one of the foundation stones. His wide interest in publicising Northamptonshire footwear caused him to set up a special publicity department. In this connection he was responsible for writing a script for a film "Smart Footwear" which was shown in cinemas throughout the country. Although his activities in the trade absorbed most of his time and energy he had a great many other interests of a voluntary character including membership of Northampton Rotary Club and Northampton Round Table. He owned a private collection of boots and shoes from the earliest times to more modern times and he was often called upon for his services as an arbitrator during disputes in other trades.

As the Association entered into its second half century of existence it was recognised as the duty of every member to maintain the foothold in the industry and the esteem with which Northampton Shoe Manufacturers and their products were held. In turn most of the leading manufacturers became presidents of the Association some serving on two occasions. From 1933 when William Barratt accepted office, the following names appear in the associations records: 1934 S J Davis, 1935 D R Church, 1936 W Parker, 1937 Percy C Jones, 1938-1939 J H C Newton, 1940-1941 L H Church, 1942-1943 A C Tebbutt, 1944-1945 H G White, 1946-1947 F E Webb, 1948-1949 J D Houison-Crauford 1950 E S Percy, 1951-1952 K C Finnemore, and 1953 Philip J Branch. It was Norman Barraclough who succeeded Ernest Bordoli as Secretary of the Association serving until 1960 when G D Franklin took office; in 1977 the local association was disbanded and a new county association was formed.

The manufacturers for some generations had gathered a volume of experience that could not be matched elsewhere. When Moses Philip Manfield formed the first association in 1879 little did he realise he was launching an organisation that would last nearly a century and would also see other similar associations being established in Northamptonshire. It had long been the ideal of a few manufacturers in the industry to form a county federation. The first idea was an alliance embracing 80-90% of all the county boot manufacturers. This was eventually abandoned but during 1916 a committee was set up consisting of T Almond, E Barker, A W Minney, J W Coles, C W Clarke, F Sharwood, John Shortland, W Charles Cattell, C W Horell, F Wright, L Austin, F W Page, John Adams, F T Riley and A H Bryan (who was elected president). This federation embraced some 160-170 manufacturing firms employing over 22,000 workers in the county.

No records appear to be available which tell us how long this association lasted but we do know that over the course of time this developed into several different associations. As the number of factories closing down increased the manufacturers, like the operatives' union, saw the need for streamlining their operations. With this in mind a new association came into being in 1977. In this year five local associations (Northampton, Kettering and District, Desborough and Rothwell, Raunds and District, Rushden and District), amalgamated to form the Northamptonshire Footwear Manufacturers Association with its headquarters at Satra House, Rockingham Road, Kettering. Although over the last decade Northamptonshire has witnessed the reduction in the number of shoe factories and the introduction of other industries the county is still leading the world in shoe manufacture. More than 70% of all footwear produced in the country is Northamptonshire made. The footwear Manufacturers Association ever mindful of the recession which hit the staple industry continues to maintain a forward approach of co-operation and not confrontation with its many operatives who are still unique in their craftsmanship.

Chapter 28

Changing Fashions and Fortunes

"It is considered by those who have a knowledge of the intricacies of the manufacturing of all types of wearing apparel that none call for more technical knowledge, skilled workmanship and attention to detail than the craft of the modern shoemaker". These challenging words appeared int the George Webb Factory Bulletin in February 1954. The article went on to say that "in the first place, no other article of clothing covers such a wide range of materials available for use". Leather is available in scores of different textures, tannages, substances and colours. Then there is the unlimited field of fabrics whilst the inventive genius of man is continually providing alternatives for the traditional materials which have held the field in the past. Visitors to a modern shoe factory for the first time are completely staggered at the large number of different types of machines used in our industry and by the varied processed needed in manufacture. Shoe making is a very complicated and interesting job and calls for continuous and diligent thought on the part of all engage in it. There is certainly great satisfaction and pride of craftsmanship in turning out good shoes".

The shoemakers of Northamptonshire have always been conscious of the changing fashions in the trade and have sought to improve their fortunes by using the great skills for their hundreds of operatives to produce the finest fashions in everyday footwear. In 1910 most men wore boots and Northampton was famous for mens Derby boots made to lace up. A button-up boot for women became popular followed in 1922 with the high-legged lace boot. "How many girls would care to lace up 22 large holes before going to business today"? commented the Northampton Independent on 10th May 1935. In 1917 a standard boot was made. The Great War of 1914-18 had far reaching effects on the industry when Northampton factories turned out 23 million pairs of boots for the allied armies ranging from airman's boots, Russian boots, French, Italian, Serbian, and British army boots.

The importance of these wartime orders certainly created further trade as was told in an article in Northampton Independent during 1919 under the title "Buyer of a million pairs of boots"! The report continued: "A bombshell burst on the boot and shoe trade the other day when it announced that a million pairs of boots preferably those produced in Northamptonshire were required by a private purchaser of high standing. Sch an enormous order has never been placed by a private speculator and the trade is agog with excitement. Visions have arisen of the possibility of them being wanted for another war but happily such is not the case. The buyer is a Mr Fleetwood Jones of the Anglo American Corporation Limited and the importance of the order may be gauged by the fact that it is worth over a million pounds. If as seems very possible the bulk of the order is placed here the spending of a million pounds must have a very stimulating effect of the staple industry with cumulative advantage to other local trade. Mr Fleetwood Jones, head of the Leather and Boot Department of the Anglo American Corporation Limited is a keen business man and has preferred not to disclose the name of his customers for boots but said that they were required for the American civilian trade. Since the war he has already done a big trade with America by placing 600,000 pairs of boots and 800,000 feet of leather from this country. The boots he now requires are the famous B5 army pattern which he describes as the best in the world. 'I do not want Foreign Boots', he is reported to have said, 'for they cannot compare with

Northampton's productions. There is no doubt in my mind that Northamptonshire turns out the best boots in the world'".

The year 1931 saw the "Sahara" type sandal whilst in 1935 sandals came in all types. Shoe fashions for women changed with the length of the skirt and the shorter dresses meant smarter footwear. Following the First World War the industry was, however, in a state of chaos and turmoil and recovery was very slow. After 1926 the manufacturers became hopeful of some improvement. The weekly returns of unemployment figures showed decreases and there was a steadiness in the leather market. Their great hope was to maintain and justify Northamptonshire's great reputation and to this end they began to encourage technical education and research. These new developments were promoted with a view to constantly improving craftsmanship.

Many of the Northampton manufacturers turned their attention to the production of high class ladies footwear. Northampton created the popular demand for reptile skin shoes, such as crocodile, lizard and python, different suedes and coloured footwear for women. Men's footwear turned to lightness, flexibility and style. Shoe designing machinery, too, played an important part in manufacture, there now being machines available to do practically every operation mechanically.

The post First World War era has often been referred to as the "Roaring Twenties" yet as far as Northampton's staple trade was concerned it was one of perpetual gloom. Despite new styles and fashions being introduced the economic climate of the country is in the later twenties and early thirties found the working classes suffering a great deal of unemployment, hardship and even poverty. There just wasn't the money in the paypackets to create a boom in trade. It was probably with this in mind that steps were taken by the Borough Council to organise a Northampton Festival and Trades Exhibition. The date for which the festival was planned to take place from 26th May to 31st May 1930 when HRH Duke of York (later King George VI)as special guest of honour. An opening ceremony was planned for each day with a distinguished guest for each occasions as follows:-

Monday 26th May,   The Rt Hon J H Thomas MP
Tuesday 27th May, HRH The Duke of York
Wednesday 28th May,The Rt Hon William Graham MP
Thursday 29th May, The Rt Hon Lord Burghley
Friday 30th May,   Sir Edward Renton KBE
Saturday 31st May, Colonel Cecil L'Estrange Malone MP

There was a carnival each day, a pageant, concerts, dancing and side shows. The whole event was held in Abington Park. On Sunday 1st June there was a special festival service in All Saints church with singing by the Northampton Ruri-Decanal Choral Association under the directorship of R Richardson Jones FRCO. The highlight of the festival was the royal visit on the Tuesday when the Duke of York opened the festival exhibition. To mark the occasion gifts of shoes were presented to his Royal Highness on behalf of the town's industry. The presentations included two pairs of Dainty Toe shoes for Princess Elizabeth. The gift was accompanied by a letter which read:

Sir

On behalf of the Northampton Town Boot Manufacturers Association and in accordance with our promise herewith you will find, one pair of riding boots and one pair of golf shoes which your Royal Highness has graciously offered to accept; together with three pairs of shoes which are being presented by the Association to Her Royal Highness the Duchess of York, who has graciously consented to accept same.

We trust that your visit to Northampton will live long in your memory and that the shoes will ever be a reminder to your Royal Highness, that Northampton is the home of the best shoemaking in the world.

Signed. A H Hollister - President
Ernest Bordoli - Secretary

Northamptons Festival Week was a triumphant success and an indelible credit to all who had been connected with its organisation. In the words of the Rt Hon J H Thomas MP, who opened the festival exhibition on the first day:

"She does not intend to hoist the white flag in this period of temporary industrial depression. But what is still more important Northampton is determined to keep the flag of optimism, energy, enterprise and progress flying not for one week but for all time. Within our homes, our businesses, our public institutions we must apply ourselves with re-doubled diligence in adopting and adapting any and every means of increasing their efficiency. Above all we must resist the incursion of panic stricken depression. Great Britain is not going to the dogs. Northampton is not receding into a slough of commercial despondency. Things are difficult for a time but there is a way into a sunshine of renewed prosperity as brilliant as that which has graced this week's epic event".

The success of the festival and its exhibitions did indeed foster a new spirit of endeavour and progress within the staple trade and to some extent those prophetic words of J H Thomas echoed around the industry. There was some measure of renewed prosperity but sadly it was to be short-lived. There was unrest in Europe and before another decade was over war clouds were fast gathering over the European Continent and it seemed that another world conflict would be inevitable. The subsequent upheaval in 1939 meant that the lives of every man, woman and child in the county was to be affected. The boot and shoe trade Northamptonshire was affected immediately for the second time in a quarter of a century. As men and later women were conscripted into the armed forces so the workforces for Northamptonshire shoe factories were rapidly depleted. The call went out to retired workers too old for war service to return to the factories and women were required to be trained to replace the men worked the factory machines. This new labour force was most known as "Green Labour" and many served the industry throughout the long war years some staying on in the factories having become used to and skilled in the trade. There is no record of a factory having to close because of loss of skilled labour and factories quickly adapted to supporting the war effort by making army boots and shoes. As in the first world war factories turned out thousands of pairs of army boots to equip the British and Allied armies and together with Munitions this gave full employment to the people of Northamptonshire.

With the end of the war in 1945 Northampton began to look forward to future prosperity and the return of their menfolk and womenfolk who had been serving in the armed forces or in war time industries. It was,however, to be an extended time of austerity and rationing. With the return of skilled workers in the shoe factories the Northamptonshire manufacturers began to revert to making many different styles of footwear, or specialising in ladies' or men's shoes. Salesmen travelled far and wide and there was a concerted effort to revive the export side of the industry. In the fifties a more interesting variety of materials began to be used in manufacture. Throughout the years materials used in the footwear industry had included fabrics, thread, metal, fibreboard, and rubber besides the most important material of all, leather. The reasons for leather's pre-eminence are easily explained. Although it is a by-product of the meat industry it is normally in good supply at reasonable prices. It is also available in all substances, colours and finishes. It is easily cut, joined, moulded and decorated. Moreover it has the property of allowing water vapour and air to pass through it, so ventilating the shoe even though the leather may be almost waterproof.

The shoe industry is the greatest user of all the leather produced. The sources and varieties at this time were many; pigskin from Yugoslavia and Brazil, snake from India and Africa, crocodile from Ethiopia and America and kangaroo from Australia. It was however the domestic animal cattle, goats and sheep that provided the majority of skins. The smaller skins and hides were suitably tanned for the uppers whilst the heavier hides provided the stouter and more rigid sole leather.

It was in the period following the second world war when the industrial chemist began perfecting certain specialised plastics such as Corfam and micro-cellular rubber so that with every guarantee of satisfaction they could be used with confidence in shoe production. Some of these new materials enabled manufacturers to make a lighter and even daintier footwear. One of the most modern styles of this kind of footwear was produced in the Webb factories. It was a shoe with a micro-cellular sole and they were popularly known as "Boundabouts", a style which carried par excellence the advantages of suppleness and lightness in weight.

Leather is still widely used and a pair of shoes with a leather upper and a leather sole is probably the best and most expensive pair of shoes that can be bought today. Over the years since 1945 various other materials have been introduced into shoemaking which have proved just as durable and popular. The introduction of these also provided the industry with the opportunity to produce many new styles of footwear. The discovery of powerful new adhesives led to the abandonment of traditional sewing techniques. Whilst the old methods were not entirely discarded these new methods of production and the new types of machinery they brought meant the production of many new types of footwear. One of the most revolutionary of these styles which soon became popular was the appearance of the moulded or vulcanised shoe. Each of these new methods in turn saved many operations hitherto performed by skilled operatives. Some of these old operations became obsolete and therefore resulted in labour problems in a similar way as was the case many years before when machinery was first introduced.

It was during the early sixties that there began to dawn a new age in shoemaking because of the increase in the use of semi-automatic and automatic machines in footwear production. The insistent call for the quicker delivery of footwear had been answered by the technical advances in production. Not the least of these was the introduction of automatic and semi-automatic machines as distinct from those which assisted the operator to perform his job. In most factory operations such a Rough Rounding in the Roughstuff and Preparation Department or Edge Trimming in the Finishing Department the skill of the operator was paramount. It was his eyes and hands that determined whether the shoe he was holding was given character or was simply ruined. When the automatic and semi-automatic machines were introduced a different kind of skill was required to handle the more complicated mechanism. But once the button controlling the machine was pressed or the lever depressed then the machines itself took over and completed the operation. The introduction of these new methods of shoemaking raised the old question of man or machine and challenged attitudes of mind towards automation.

One of the first ventures into automation in the shoe trade was the introduction of precision injection moulding in the early sixties. This was a machine installed in the Making Room for bottoming conventionally lasted footwear. By this method soles could be moulded without difficulty and in any substance from heavyweights down to six iron. Definition was good and no finishing necessary. The process was simple; the operator merely loaded shoes into the machine, initiated the moulding cycle and then removed the finished shoe from the machines removing the injection sprue and a small cut off tab. The injection moulding machine consisted of a horizontal rotating ring carrying twelve moulded boxes (six pairs), the plasticiser-injection unit being mounted in the centre. The PVC moulding compound was simply tipped into a floor-mounted hopper and then automatically metered into a plasticiser barrel. The plastic was delivered at the injection nozzle at the right temperature and viscosity for injection the machine automatically filling each mould. When the mould became full injection stopped. This particular process is still is use today and many shoes being sold in the shops are of the vulcanised variety.

Following these developments the number of automatic sewing machines in the Closing Room increased considerably. For instance, the Singer Sewing Machine Company developed a single basic type of automatic machine designated 269 W Class which was able to sew literally any pattern of stitching within certain size limitations. The only skill required by the operator was to reposition the work under the clamp facilitated by the use of positioning guides. Once the treadle was depressed the complete sewing cycle became automatic including the trimming of the thread ends. This custom built machine was capable of sewing leather at a speed of about 1,400 stitches per minute. The sewing machine firm of Pfaff also devoted much time and research to automate many upper sewing machines. What a long way sewing machines have come since Elias Howe introduced his early machine in 1852.

Such is the penalty of progress as at the time in which I am writing we have entered upon the second industrial revolution with its highly mechanised and computerised machinery; like the first Industrial Revolution the age of the micro-chip has led not to a period of more leisure time for the workers but increased unemployment. We can but hope that time itself will as in the past find a solution to these very acute problems. Meanwhile I am reminded of some words of wisdom spoken many years ago in that well known cinema screen documentary of the forties: "Time Marches On"

"As Lousy as things are now, tomorrow, they will be somebody's good old days".

Chapter 29

Days of Decline, Years of Expansion

Henry Francis Lyte author of the well known hymn Abide With Me that is sung on so many national and famous occasions wrote: "Change and decay in all around I see". The world is ever changing: some things remain, others give way to new. Old buildings are sometimes preserved as historical monuments, others are replaced by more modern edifices. Old industries give way to modern ones and life goes on. What provides happy memories for some are just eyesores to others.

In 1964 Northampton was earmarked for expansion and four years later was designated a new town. A Development Corporation was set up and a great deal of expansion took place particularly on the eastern extremities of the town and later to the south, until in 1981 a population of 150,000 was reached. An attempt was made to attract new industry to replace much of the ailing boot and shoe industry which had begun to fall into decline mainly because of cheap imports from various places around the world. There were other factors too.

It was thought by some shoe manufacturers that much of the trouble began when certain big financiers sought to get a grip on the industry and sell some of the factories to property developers. Shoes were bought from foreign outlets where cheap labour was employed and British shoe shops were flooded with footwear that was inferior to that made in Northamptonshire, but it found a ready market because of lower prices. Instances of the making of cheap foreign footwear were reported where the use of child labour could be found in the back street of foreign cities engaged in shoe production. In every high street today there are shoe retailers and stores whose stock is made up with imports from foreign factories. The trade has made representations to Parliament to curb imports from time to time to no avail. It is a sad story, but some Northamptonshire factories have survived and there is no doubt that the shoes produced in them are still the finest in the world.

Whilst the staple trade began its decline so many new developments were taking place in Northamptonshire towns. Daventry became an "overspill" town for the city of Birmingham; Kettering saw re-development of its town centre some of which was replaced by the Newborough Centre, and Wellingborough besides building industrial estates erected the modern Arndale Centre shopping precinct. In Northampton the whole of the central area was entirely rebuilt. During 1960 the old Peacock Hotel on the Market Square was demolished and replaced by a shopping arcade only to be removed in 1986 for a further re-development; Peacock Place opened in 1988. During 1962 the Beaumont House and Claremont tower blocks of flats appeared in the old Castle Street and Harding Street area, part of the earliest town centre. In 1964 the old fountain which had stood on the Market Square for ninety nine years was considered unsafe and removed. The seventies saw a tremendous growth and expansion; the old Emporium Arcade, Newland, Princes Street with its Baptist Church and Masonic Hall all disappeared to make way for a new indoor shopping centre. This was the now popular Grovesnor Centre and was opened in 1975.

As vast new estates sprang up on the Eastern District huge industrial estates attracted industries to both town and county. There also came an era of rapid inflation and soaring prices and high wage claims from workers who felt that they could not cope. Many of the older inhabitants of the county towns regretted the disappearance of some of the old streets and buildings which were steeped in history. There was, for instance, a public outcry when the old Peacock Hotel was removed for apart from the building being an ancient hostelry many remember the old balcony where many former famous politicians delivered their addresses to Northampton shoeworkers and others at election times. The ancient Welsh House on the Market Square was re-built and preserved. The beautiful Notre Dame Convent building and chapel were demolished by property developers in 1979. Among the many boot factories to disappear was the old Campbell and Hyde factory on Campbell Square.

Although it was considered to be almost impossible for many of the great names in shoe manufacture to be eliminated from the industrial scene in Northamptonshire, especially the factories established for more than a half or even a complete century, the cold wind of economic recession cut keenly through their ranks. The first large factory closure in Northampton was probably that of Padmore and Barnes which closed in 1956. This was followed by the well known firm of C and E Lewis which closed in September 1965. Their Progressive factory was empty for some years and was eventually demolished and replaced by modern flats. The closure of Lewis's was quickly followed by Sears and Company (the True-form Boot Company) which closed in September 1968. The factory of W Barratt and Company closed in 1971 along with the Stead and Simpson factory at Daventry which ceased production in the same year. These closures were followed by the famous Kettering firm of Timpson and Company in 1972.

There were others caught up in the disintegration of the industry during the years of decline all leading firms in Northamptonshire including A and W Arnold, Arnold Bros, John Branch Bective and Philip Branch of Northampton, the Co-operative factories in Northampton and Rushden, John Cave of Rushden, E G Gravestock of Kettering, C W Horrell of Rushden, the Hutton Shoe Company, Mounts Factory Company, the Norvic Companies of John Marlow and Oakeshott and Finnemore, Strickland and Tebbutt Taylor of Northampton and more recently the well known firm of George Webb and Sons of Northampton which closed in 1982.

During the last decade every shoe factory closure has not only robbed the county of one of its long standing livelihoods it has deprived the nation of the manufacture of quality footwear and contributed to the rising tide of unemployment. Amongst these are young people no longer able to follow in their father's footsteps by becoming shoe craftsmen but unable to find any kind suitable employment. This must remain one of the most tragic situations in the history of the county of Northamptonshire and even the whole country.

Arthur Adcock wrote that the shoe industry produced performers and great thinkers more than any other. In English history there have been many able men who were in their early lives apprenticed to shoe makers: George Fox the founder of the Society of Friends, Samuel Bradbury the Methodist leader, Thomas Hardy the radical politician, William Carey the orientalist and missionary, Samuel Drew the meta-physician, Robert Bloomfield the rural poet, John Pounds the founder of the Ragged Schools, Robert Morrison the great missionary to China, and many more. Such men started in humble surroundings and it may well be more than a coincidence that being trained in shoemaking engendered in their lives a quality of workmanship that enabled them to seek to enrich the lives of others.

The majority of leading manufacturers were all members of the Nonconforist churches and brought up in a Christian tradition. Each possessed a quality of concern and compassion for others which spilled over into other spheres of life; many were magistrates, politicians, councillors, youth leaders, local preachers, and served bodies such as the St John Ambulance Brigade, the Red Cross and the police. Men like James Manfield, James Gribble, Sir James Crockett, George Thomas Hawkins and William Barratt have left a lasting contribution to the life of society. The memorial to William Bradford, one of the Pilgrim Fathers, is inscribed: "What our fathers with so much difficulty secured, do not basely relinquish". In a similar sense we should not lightly dismiss the lives, workmanship and dedicated years of public service given by the "St Crispin's Men" (and women) of old.

Whilst we may look back with pride upon the record of those who founded and the operatives who manned the great shoe factories of Northamptonshire let us look forward with faith. The shoe industry has survived through five royal reigns and throughout the long years of our present monarch. Remembering those who have given so much to establish what is known as the industrial heritage of our county and to those who may follow we might heed the words of Henry Wadsworth Longfellow:

"Lives of great men all remind us
We can make our lives sublime
and departing leave behind us
Footprints in the sands of time".

The derelict factory of John & G.H.Roe, Freeschool Street, Northampton.
A symbol of a declined industry.

Some Notable Dates in the History of the Shoe Trade

1833 New Factory Act forbids work of more than 12 hours a day.

1837 Queen Victoria's reign begins.

1847 Hours of work for young people reduced.

1852 Home Sewing Machine invented.

1853 Improved sewing machine of Elias Howe and Isaac Singer introduced.

1853 Normal working day of 10.5 hours established by law.

1853-1856 Crimea War - Large army boot orders executed by the trade.

1856 Howe and Singer sewing machines adapted for leather and upper closing.

1859 Thomas Sewing Machine exhibited at Milton Hall, Newland.

1865 The Blake Sole Sewer invented by Lyman R Blake.

1872 Charles Goodyear welted machines introduced.

1874 2nd February - National Union of Boot and Shoe Operatives founded.

1878 Factory and workshops consolidation act, passed by Parliament.

1879 30th January - Northampton Town Boot Manufacturers Association founded.

1887 Workers Strike, culmination in Great Lockout.

1894 Abolition of all outdoor work except closing.

1898 Machinery fully in operation in most factories.

1899 British United Shoe Machinery Co. Ltd formed, machines available on rental basis.

1901 King Edward Seventh's reign begins.

1905 8th May Raunds strikers march to Houses of Parliament, London.

1907 26th January. General Strike of shoe workers to secure higher wages.

1909 New agreement known as supplementary terms of settlement agreed giving hours of work as 52.5 a week and graduated wages scales 18-21 men's aged defined as 19 years.

1910 King George Fifths reign begins.

1913 3rd December. State visit of King George and Queen Mary to Northampton.

1914 New agreement introduces to piece work and recognises right of all workers to belong to a union and a "closed shop" is established.

1914 5th August. First World War begins; shoe workers called to colours and shoe factories produce millions of pairs of army boots.

1918 Armistice signed, Victory celebrations in town and county.

1919 February, new national agreement fixes minimum wage for men at 56 shillings at age of 23 for women over 20 in closing, stock or shoe rooms 30 shillings. Hours reduced to 48 hours a week.

1921 Gift of Dallington Park to Northampton by Lewis Brothers.

1924 17th July Northampton Crippled Childrens Committee announce gift of Weston Favell House (Manfield Hospital) by James Manfield.

1926 May. The General Strike boot and shoe industry adopts half time working in support of miners and others involved.

1927 Visit of Edward Prince of Wales. (Later King Edward the Eighth and Duke of Windsor) to Northampton.

1930 26th May. Northampton Festival and Footwear Exhibition begins.

1930 27th May. Visit of H.R.H the Duke and H.R.H the Duchess of York. (Later King George Sixth and Queen Elizabeth) to the festival.

1935 New agreement signed reducing working hours to 46 per week and a new minimum wage rate for females of 36 shillings per week.

1936   4th July. Barratt Maternity Home (gift of Mr and Mrs W Barratt) opened.

1938   New agreement signed between manufacturers and union granting a 45 hour week with basic mens rate of 58 shillings and women 37 shillings per week.

1939   3rd September. Outbreak of Second World War. Shoe factories again lose workers to the armed forces. Remaining shoe workers execute large orders for military footwear.

1945   War ends, peace signed, workers begin to return to factories

1948   South African Government impose ban on imported footwear.

1952   Queen Elizabeth the Second's reign begins.

1960   Onwards - semi automatic and automatic machines including precisions injection moulding machines introduced.

1965   Visit of queen and prince phillip to Church and Company Limited.

1984   6th December. Freedom of the borough conferred on national Union of Footwear and Leather trades, members (formerly NUBSO) at Northampton.

1987   7th May - Queen Elizabeth the Queen Mother visits Earls Barton to open the modern shoe factory of A Barker and Sons Limited.

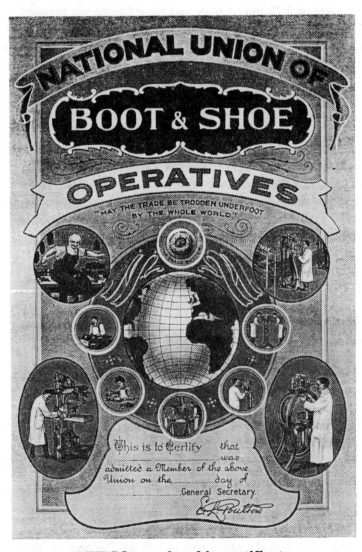

NUBSO membership certificate.

Bibliography

The following books, brochures, periodicals, and manuscripts were referred to when researching the information needed for this book. Certain dates, extracts and references may have been used in the compilation of this history and are gratefully acknowledged.

Books

A History of the National Union of Boot and Shoe Operatives - fifty years - T Richards and E W Poulton.
A History of the National Union of Boot and Shoe Operatives 1874 - 1954 - Alan Fox.
A History of Northampton General Hospital 1743 - 1948 - F F Waddy   *British Shoe and Leather Trades Biographical Directory 1912-1916.*
Cradle of the Shoe Industry - Ernest Bordoli
Footwear down the ages - Ernest Bordoli
From a British Industry 1908 - Manfield and Sons Ltd
How our working people live - 1869
Kelly's Directories of the Leather Trades 1893, 1896, 1922, 1933, 1940
Life in Old Northampton - John Stafford
Life and Struggles of Successful People - Amalgamated Press 1902
Northampton Boots and Shoe Industry 1800-1914 - W C Griffin
Recollections of Wellingborough - Caleb Archer
Recollections of William Arnold - James H Saxton
Romance of Barratts
Shoes - June Swann
The Northampton Shoe - Arthur Adcock
The Northampton Shoemaker - Richard Rowe

Brochures

A century of shoemaking (Manfield and Sons Ltd) - E W Burnham
A centenary brochure 1879-1979 - Crockett and Jones Ltd
A Hundred Years in the Boot and Shoe Trade (Stead and Simpson) 1834-1934
Keep Believing - John White
A Norvic Century 1846-1946 - F W Wheldon
Northampton Town Guide
William Timpson, A Century of Service - D J Timpson

Periodicals and Newspapers

British Boot and Shoe Trades Journal 1898, 1905
British Boot and Shoe Institute Journal, 1957 - Gotch of Kettering - Roy Church
Northampton Town Boot and Shoe Manufacturers Association 1879-1954
Northampton Chronicle and Echo - Past issues
Northampton Independent - Past issues
Shoe and Leather News 1927 and 1955

Other Sources: (leaflets, typescripts etc)

Out and about in Northamptonshire - Northampton Leisure Services and Christine Johnson.
Barker and Sons Limited - A History.
Church and Company Limited - A History.
Shoemaking in Long Buckby - A History.
Earls Barton Shoemakers - A History.

Northampton and County Shoe Manufacturers
Mentioned in the Text

Abbott and Bird
Allen and Caswell
Allinsons
A and W Arnold
Arnold Brothers
Avalon Footwear
W Barratt and Company
Arthur Barker and Sons
H. J. Bateman
Walter Beale (Unicorn Boot Co)
Harry J. Bigga
George Bishop (Sewer)
Thomas Bostock (Lotus Ltd)
Bozeat Boot Company
W. Botterill (Botterill Sports)
John Branch
James Branch
Brevitt Shoe Company
British Shoe Company (H. E. Rose)
British Shoe Corporation
William Brookes
H. E. Browett
Bryan and Son
E. R. Bush and Company
Isaac Campbell
John Cave
Joseph Cheyney
Church and Company
Robert Coggins
Frederick Cooke
Simon Collier
Co-Operative Manufacturing Society
Cove and West
Crockett and Jones
H Dawson Samuel and Carter Davis
Denton and Company
John Drage
Thomas Dunkley
Charles East
Eaton and Company
Ekins, Son, and Percival
Frank Eyre
John and Thomas Eyre
Finedon Boot Company
Flack and Durrant
Roland Fisher

Glover Brothers
Gola Footwear (Botterill Sports)
Thomas Gotch
E. C. Gravestock
Edward Green
George Green
C. E. Gubbins (Joseph Gibbs)
G. T. Hawkins
Haines and Cann
William Hickson
Hornby and West
C. W. Horrell and Company
Alfred and Joseph Howe
Albert Hulett
Hutton Shoe Company
Latimer and Crick
Albert Letts
C and E Lewis
Loake Brothers
Lotus Ltd (F. W. Bostock)
M. P. Manfield
A. E. Marlow
T. C. Mann and Sons Limited
W. T. Mark
John Marlow
Marriott and Company
Mounts Factory Company
Munn and Felton
Muscatt and Company
Norvic Shoe Company
Nurish Pallett and Company
Arthur Nutt
Oakshott and Finnemore
Padmore and Barnes
F. W. Panther
Charles Parker
Parker and Company (Long Buckby)
Parker and Tearle (Mounts Factory Co)
A. W. Partridge
T and C Partridge
Perkins and Bird
F. J. Pitts
S Pollard and Son
H. E. Randall

Read, Myall and Read (J. W. Read)
Rice and Company
B. J. Riley
Jonathan Robinson
John Rogers
J. G. Sears (True Form)
George Sellwood and Company
H. Sharman and Son
Harry Shaw (Sewer)
John Shortland (Wearra)
G. W. and R. Shelton
Singlehurst and Gulliver
William Saunders (American Boot Co)
Charles Smith (Top Boots)
W. B. Stevens and Company
John Spencer
Stead and Simpson
W. F. Strickland
Sudborough Brothers
George Swann
Tebbutt and Hall Brothers
G. M. Tebbutt (Tebbutt Taylor)
William Timpson and Company
B Toone and Company
Technic Boot Company
R. E. Tricker
C. F. Tompkins and Son
Unicorn Boot Company (Walter Beale)
Stephen Walker (Walgrave)
Ward and Sheffield
Wearra Shoes (J Shortland)
George Webb and Sons
Henry Wooding
White Brothers (Earls Barton)
Frank Wright and Sons
H. Wright and Sons
George York and Son

INDEX OF SURNAMES OF SHOEMAKERS AND OTHER PERSONAGES (EXCEPT ROYAL VISITORS) MENTIONED IN THE TEXT OF THIS BOOK

Bostock Louisa
Bostock Neville
Bostock Thomas
Booth General William
Botterill W
Bounds Thomas W
Bradlaugh Charles
Branch John
Branch Phillip
Brown Doctor Harold J.
Brightman Mr
Brookes William
Brooks W. J.
Browett George
Browning R. A. M.
Brunel Marc Isombard
Buckle John
Bullock Norman
Burghley Rt. Hon. Lord
Bush E. R.
Butlin John Thomas
Bryan A. H.
Bryan J

Cahill Martin
Campbell Isaac
Carey William
Carnegie Andrew
Carpenter Miss
Caswell Herbert William
Cattell George
Cattell W Charles
Cave John
Cheaney John
Chester Sir George C.B.E
Chichelle Henry
Church Alfred
Church D. R.
Church J. G.
Church L. H.
Church Thomas Dudley
Church Thomas
Church William
Clifton H.
Clifton Samuel
Clore Sir Charles
Cobb James
Coggins Robert

Coleman Cecil
Coles J. W.
Collier J. V
Collier Simon
Collier Simon Jnr
Collier Alderman William
Cook Frederick
Clarke C. W.
Clapham S. F.
Cooper Reverend J. J.
Comerford Herbert
Cordeux Mr
Cove John
Crawford James C.B.E.
Cripps Sir Stafford
Crockett Ann
Crockett Harry
Crockett James
Crockett Sir James Henry
Crockett Leonard Clifton
Cox Eileen
Cox George
Cox Harold
Cox Jean
Cox William
Cunnington B. W.
Cheyney Arthur.

Davis Carter
Davis C. G.
Davis P. S.
Davis Richard
Davis Samuel
Davis Sydney J.
Dayton Ambrose
Dayton Joe
Dickens John
Dodson J.G.
Drage C
Drage F
Drage John
Drage William Chambers
Dunkley Abel
Dunkley Charles
Dunkley F
Dunkley Thomas
Dobbs A. J.
Drew Samuel

East Charles
East Frederick
East Walter C
Eaton Frank
Eaton Harry
Edwards H
Edwards Jean (nee Cox)
Ekins Edward
Ekins John
Ekins Robert
Elliott George
Eyre John
Eyre Thomas

Fairhurst Bob
Farey J. K. L.
Farey Oliver J
Fawcett Richard
Finnemore K. C.
Finnemore Walter
Fisher Roland
Fitzwilliam Lord
Flint Alfred
Fox Alan
Fox George
Franklin G. D
France W. C.
Freak Charles

Gaitskell Hugh
Gascoigne John
Gee H. Simpson
Gibbs Joseph
Glover William J. T.
Goffe Peter
Gotch David Frederick
Gotch Thomas
Graham Rt. Hon. William M.P.
Gravestock A. W.
Gravestock E. C.
Gravestock E. C. Jnr
Green Edward
Green George
Green S.M.
Gregson R.
Gribble James (Jimmy)
Griggs R.
Groocott T.

Gubbins C.E.
Gulliver James
Gunn Mr

Hagar B
Halestrap Albert H.
Hall W.
Hall J.P
Hamel Gustav
Hardy Thomas
Hart Ronald
Hawkins George Thomas
Hawkins William
Hawthorne Ewart T.
Haynes Edward
Haynes Frank
Hickson G.
Hickson Tom A.
Hickson William
Hickson William Jnr.
Hill Alfred
Hill James
Hollister A.H.
Horrell Charles
Horrell W.M.C.
Hornidge W.B.
Horsfall H.
Houison-Crauford J.D.
Howe Alfred
Howe John York
Howes Geoffrey
Hulett Albert
Hulls Rev. Canon

Iliffe S. W
Inskip William

Jackson A
Jenkinson Patrick
Jenner-Jobson W
Johnson H
Jones Charles
Jones Frank
Jones G. H.
Jones Gilbert
Jones J. A. Eyton
Jones Fleetwood
Jones Jonathan

Jones Richard
Jones Percy C.
Jones W. G. T.
Joseph P

King Betty
King C. J.
Knight E
Kitchener Lord
Kucek Karel

Laidler Rev.
Langley John
Latimer Mr
Lea C. F.
Lee Thomas
Lees Abrahams
Lewis Charles
Lewis Charles W.
Lewis Edward
Lewis Edward Jnr
Lewis George
Lewis H. G.
Lewis James T.
Lewis T. D.
Lightwood A
Loake C. M
Loake E. W
Loake John
Loake T
Loake W. F.
Lyne Arthur W. O.B.E

Malone Colonel Cecil M.P.
Manfield Ellen
Manfield Harry
Manfield James
Manfield Moses Philip
Mann Thomas C
Mann Thomas C Jnr
Mann William
Mark W. T.
Marlow Albert E
Marlow John H.
Marlow Rev J. H.
Marris Mr
Marshman W. F.
Mayes G. A.

McMillan R
Miller Bert
Miller Owen
Miller William
Minney A. W.
Moore T. A.
Morrison Robert
Morton H
Mott W. H.
Mursell Thomas A.

Nash Malcolm
Newton J. H. C.
Nichols Arthur
Noakes F. J.
Noakes Geoffrey
Norton George
Nutt Arthur

Oakshott Henry
Osborne George

Padmore George
Page T. W.
Pagett R. T. Lord
Pancoust Sylvia
Panter F.W.
Parker Charles
Parker Owen J
Parker W
Parkin Rev. George
Partridge A. W.
Partridge Cyril
Partridge Owen
Partridge Tom
Pateman Dorothy
Pateman Frank
Pateman Thomas
Pearson John
Perceval Spencer M.P.
Percival Harry
Pendleton Thomas
Perry E. S.
Pettit C.
Pickett Rev. Henry J.
Pitt William
Pitts Alfred
Pitts F. J.

Plowright George
Pollard A. E.
Pollard E.
Pollard F. W.
Poole Sir Lionel
Poulton Edward L. O.B.E.
Pounds John
Priest Mr.

Quinn C. A.

Randall Sir Henry
Read John Thomas
Read William
Reeves W. Harvey
Renton Sir Edward M.P.
Rice Ernest
Rice George
Richards Sir Albert
Richards C.
Richards T. F.
Riley Benjamin
Riley F. T.
Robinson Jonathan
Robinson J. P.
Robinson Sidney
Rodhouse A. E.
Rodhouse C.
Roe G. H.
Roe John
Rogers Elijah
Rogers George
Rogers John
Rouse John B.
Rudlen Robert
Rutter W. Ralph

Salisbury Doctor
Saunders William
Sears John George
Sears Mrs J. G.
Sears William T.
Sedgewick George
Sellwood George
Shackleton Sir Ernest
Sharman H. P.
Sharman Joseph
Sharwood F.

Shaw Harry
Sheffield Daniel
Shelton G. W.
Shelton R. S.
Shortland John
Shorltand William
Singer Isaac M.
Singlehurst Arthur
Singlehurst Thomas
Simpson Edward
Simpson F.
Simpson William
Simpson Willis
Smith Herbert E.
Smith Leonard
Smith W. R.
Smith Alderman T. O.B.E.
Smith Walter
Sparrow J. C.
Spencer The Earl
Spencer Charles
Spencer John
Spiers William J.
Spooner James
Stead Edmund
Stevens W. B.
Stevenson R. B.
Stewart J. C.
Stirling Dora (nee Webb)
Stirling James
Strickland Sidney
Strickland W. F.
Sudborough John
Sudborough E. H. S.
Sudborough H. J. S.
Swann George
Swann Mr
Swann Mrs
Swift Richard

Taylor Dennis
Tearle A. D.
Tebbutt Albert E.
Tebbutt A. C.
Tebbut Alfred
Tebbutt G. M.
Tebbutt T. T.
Tebbutt Alderman Thomas

Thornton Canon
Thomas Rt. Hon. J. H. M.P.
Thomas Mr
Timpson Alan G.
Timpson Anthony
Timpson David J
Timpson H. Y.
Timpson Noel Mursell
Timpson William
Timpson William Henry Farey
Toone B.
Townley Rev. George
Townley William R.
Tricker R. E.
Turner W. H.
Tysoe Leonard

Walker J
Walker John
Walker Josiah
Walker Pratt
Walker Stephen
Walker Thomas
Ward Joseph Griffin
Webb Dennis G.
Webb Dora (Mrs Stirling)
Webb Frank E.
Webb George
West B. E.
Westley Joseph
Whitby Harold H.
White Alfred
White Arthur
White Don
White Rev. Edwin
White Sir Ernest
White Ernest
White Frank
White Fred
White Godfrey
White Harold
White H. G.
White John
White Keith
White Percy
White Walter
Whitney Henry
Willis Mr

Witton Sidney L.
Wolfson Isaac
Wooding Gladstone
Wooding Henry
Wright E. M.
Wright E. V.
Wright Frank
Wright George
Wright Harry
Wright H. P.
Wykes Raymond

York George
Yule George

SHOEMAKERS AND THE MAYORALTY OF NORTHAMPTON

As far back as the 17th century shoemakers were known to have played an important role in the civic life of the town and the following shoemakers occupied the office of chief citizen.

Thomas Gutteridge was Mayor twice, John Herbert once and the Thomas Pendleton once. During the 19th and 20th centuries many other names allied to the shoe trade are recorded as tenants of this high office and these are as follows:-

1845	John Groom
1847	Joseph Wykes
1848	Joseph Wykes
1849	Francis Parker
1850	Francis Parker
1871	Henry Marshall
1872	William Jones
1873	Richard Turner
1876	George Turner
1877	Thomas Tebbutt
1880	Robert Derby
1882	William Coulson
1883	Moses Philip Manfield
1891	Edwin Bridgewater
1893	Henry Edward Randall
1896	Henry Edward Randall
1903	Edward Lewis
1904	Albert Ernest Marlow
1905	James Manfield
1906	Edward L Poulton OBE
1923	Thomas Davies Lewis
1934	Albert Burrows
1938	Arthur W Lyne OBE
1944	Sydney Strickland
1947	Sydney Strickland
1949	Leonard Smith
1955	Walter Lewis
1961	Kathleen Maud Gibbs
1965	Donald Wilson
1973	Evelyn E. Fitzhugh
1975	John Gardner
1992	Frank Tero

ACKNOWLEDGEMENTS

Mrs Anderson, Northamptonshire Footwear Manufacturers Association
Mr Roy Ashby JP.
Mr William Barker, Managing Director A Barker and Sons Ltd, Earls Barton
Church and Company Ltd, Northampton
Crockett and Jones Ltd, Northampton
Northampton Chronicle and Echo
Rev. Malcolm Deacon
Mrs Stephanie Deacon
Mrs Mary Eason (for assistance with typing the original manuscript)
Mr J K L Farey former Technical Director, George Webb and Sons Ltd, Northampton
Edward Green & Co Ltd
Mr J Hadley, Glebe Graphics, Wilby, Northants
Northampton Independent (Independent Image)
Northamptonshire Libraries especially Marion Arnold and the staff of the local room.
Northamptonshire Leisure Services and Christine Johnstone
Northamptonshire Record Office especially Mr P I King former Chief Archivist
National Union of Footwear and Leather Trades, Mr E Mallon Assistant General Officer
Mr I Bayes and Mr Graham Mason, Northamptonshire Branch NUFLAT Northamptonshire Branch.
Mr Roy Plowman,(former Personel Manager, Church and Company)
Mr John Rawlings
The late Miss Phylis Rawlings (Crockett & Jones Ltd)
Mr Ben Ringrose formerly of Lotus Ltd, Northampton
Mr Derek Simpson
Mr George Streather
Miss June Swann OBE, former Keeper of the Shoe Collection, Northampton Museum.
The late Mr Dennis Webb and the late Mr Frank E Webb former joint Managing Directors,(George Webb and Sons Ltd, Northampton).
Northampton Arts Development and Stephanie Record and Ruth Lewis.

Acknowledgements for financial help:

A.Barker & Sons Ltd, Elaine Barratt Trust, Mrs M. Barker, Mr J. Chaplin (former Managing Director of Headlam group plc), the Eason family, R. Griggs & Co Ltd, National Union of Footwear, Leather and Allied Trades, The Oliver Group plc, Mr J. Tilley and the Dennis George Webb Charitable Trust.

Acknowledgements for photographs and other illustrations:

The author, Beedle & Cooper, Northamptonshire Libraries, Northamptonshire Newsparers Ltd., John Roan, Mrs J. Sykes, Mrs J. Webb, A Barker & Sons Ltd, National Union of Footwear, Leather and Allied Trades (formerly NUBSO) and Mr Charles Ward. Cover design and photography, Charles Ward Photography, Earls Barton.

About the Author

Albert V Eason was born the son of a shoemaker and was educated in Northampton. He comes from a family of shoemakers who have been associated with the trade in Northampton in various factories.

His own association with the industry began when at the age of fifteen he became an employee of W Barratt and Company Limited of Kingsthorpe Road, Northampton and was in their employ for some seventeen years.

In 1939 he was one of the first employees of the Company to be called for military service. He served first with the Northamptonshire regiment and was later seconded to the Royal Army Medical Corps with which he served in North Africa and Italy for nearly four years. On demobilisation in 1946 he rejoined the firm of W Barratt and Company Limited as a factory operative.

A keen youth worker he has over the years taken a prominent part in the affairs of the Northampton Battalion of the Boys' Brigade, serving them as a Company Captain, Publicity Officer, Extension Officer and a convenor of the Special Projects Committee set up in 1963 to raise funds for the provision of a new BB Training Centre. In 1947 he was elected to represent the Battalion on the Executive Committee of the West Midland and Later South Midland Districts, serving for more than thirty years.

He is the Author of "Remember Now Thy Creator" a history of the Boys Brigade in and around Northampton which was published in 1983 and is at present a Battalion Honourary vice president.

A former member of the National Union Boot and Shoe Operatives he was in later years a member and Branch officer of the Clerical Union APEX and is a life member of that union.

Mr Eason still lives in Northampton and is now retired. He is a member of the Doddridge and Commercial Street, United Reformed Church, Castle Hill, Northampton.